JUST WHAT
I ALWAYS
WANTED!

JUST WHAT I ALWAYS WANTED!

UNWRAPPING THE WORLD'S MOST CURIOUS PRESENTS

ROBIN LAURANCE

Quercus

For
Aileen

CONTENTS

Gold, Frankincense and Pressure Cookers

The history of present-giving goes back a long way – and long before gold, frankincense and myrrh were brought, as legend has it, by three wise men to celebrate a birth in Bethlehem 2000 years ago. The exchange of presents had by then already become a social custom satisfying our desire to give, testing the obligation to receive and prompting the need to reciprocate. As such, this exchange of gifts has become one of the rituals we use in the building and sustaining of relationships, invoking such virtues as love, kindness, compassion, honour, respect, generosity and gratitude, and triggering a whole raft of emotions, from surprise, joy and pride to embarrassment and disappointment. And, as any psychologist or anthropologist will tell you, it is often the giver rather than the receiver who gains – or loses – most from the exchange.

Birthday presents followed later. The giving of presents on the anniversary of a birth required first an understanding of the passing of time. When people took notice of nature's repeated patterns – the seasons and the cycles of the moon – they were at the same time registering the passing of time. But it was not until the cycle of the sun through 365¼ days that a year was first measured. It was the Egyptians who were first to come up with a calendar. This was modified by Julius Caesar to become the Julian calendar, and then modified again in 1582 by Rome on the orders of Pope Gregory XIII, who gave his name to the Gregorian calendar that we use today.

But the ability to measure the passing of a year did not immediately bring with it the celebration of a birth. And it is only comparatively recently that the registration of a birth (as opposed to baptism) has become an accepted custom, and in most countries a legal requirement. There are communities today who still don't bother to do either, and for whom the giving of birthday presents is anathema.

For the rest of us, the giving of birthday presents has become an essential part of the way we show love, honour and respect as we celebrate the birthdays of friends, relatives and those to whom we feel connected in some way or another. This book unwraps the stories behind some of the most unusual birthday presents that have changed hands during the last 300 years or so.

For those who believe it is merely 'the thought that counts', the variety and imagination reflected in the material gifts recorded in these pages will come as a revelation, and possibly even as a source of some shame. From beautiful, remote islands to black pigs, the presents range from the sublime to the ridiculous – although the well-known recipient of the black pig would say her gift was anything but ridiculous. In value there are gifts worth a few dollars and gifts worth millions of pounds and even more millions of dollars. (Researchers in America suggest that men are more price-conscious about gifts, while with women it is the emotional significance that counts.) And while for some the price tag clearly matters a lot, for the majority these presents are genuine tokens of love given with a genuine desire to please – in one way or another – even if altruism is sometimes lost in self-interest.

But whatever lies behind the giving of presents, the majority are intended to bring pleasure, and in this they succeed – most of the time. Some of these set out to do so in the most macabre of ways. A court in the United States heard how a particularly nasty murder was perpetrated as a birthday present; and more than one recent assassination was carried out on the birthday of the man who stood most to gain from the victim's demise. And a birthday present delivered to Scotland Yard very nearly killed a former commissioner of London's Metropolitan Police (*see pages* 246–247).

Not that the intention to please always succeeds. A woman in Australia died under her present, and a policeman in the United States died on his. A well-intentioned wife could not possibly have imagined that a present for her husband would end in their divorce, nor could a pilot have imagined that flying lessons would land his innocent son-in-law in jail.

Heads of state, needless to say, do rather well on their birthdays, and it was thoughtful of one police force to give their king a satellite navigation device for his car. The Queen of Thailand seemed delighted with her railway cast-offs, and the Queen of England was delighted with Susan. And birthdays exposed the gentler side of Yasser Arafat. But it has been the communist dictators who have milked their birthdays as they built about themselves a cult of personality. Kim Jong Il of North Korea – like his father Kim Il Sung before him – has received so many presents over the years he has built a palace to put them all in; Stalin's 70th birthday resulted in one of the most extraordinary exhibitions ever mounted in the Russian capital; and a present for Robert Mugabe's 81st birthday was a piece of sycophantic nonsense that beggars belief.

Birthday presents have triggered careers, caused international incidents, warmed a Hollywood penis, and benefited the nation. Britain's former prime minister Sir John Major, the singer Madonna and Osama bin Laden became unlikely bedfellows when they received the same birthday present. Walt Disney's imagination entertained generations, but when it came to presents his imagination always failed him. And sensible motherly pragmatism produced a rather mundane pressure cooker for the artist Sophie Calle. On the whole though, imagination has seen no bounds: a constipated snake, a portrait in marzipan and another on a grain of rice, new breasts, railway carriages and double-decker buses, a fairground carousel, aeroplanes and a wisdom tooth dipped in gold have all been given as birthday tokens of love or respect.

The 17th-century French dramatist Pierre Corneille wrote *Le Menteur* (*The Liar*) in 1643. There is a line in the play that claims the manner of giving is worth more than the gift. Read on and decide for yourself.

Robin Laurance
Oxford, 2008

'... there are 364 days when you might get un-birthday presents... and only ONE for birthday presents, you know,' said Humpty Dumpty to Alice.

Lewis Carroll, *Through the Looking-Glass*

1 Idi Amin / E.M. Forster / Lorenzo de' Medici / J. Edgar Hoover	**2** David Bailey	**3** Wilhelm Pieck
8 Junichiro Koizumi	**9** Richard Nixon	**10** Frank Sinatra Junior
15 Aristotle Onassis	**16** Clement Greenberg	**17** Alva Smith
22 Claire Rayner	**23** Sergei Eisenstein	**24** Neil Diamond
29 Anton Chekhov	**30** Dick Cheney	**31** Queen Beatrix

1

2

4 Jacob Grimm	**5** Shah Jehan	**6** Reverend Sun Myung Moon	**7** Gerald Durrell
11 L'Esperance quintuplets	**12** Sir William McAlpine	**13** Linda Tripp	**14** Louise Jilek-Aall
18 Peter Roget	**19** Sir Simon Rattle	**20** Diana Walker	**21** Jack Nicklaus
25 Virginia Woolf	**26** Jacqueline du Pré	**27** Kaiser Wilhelm II	**28** Alan Alda
1 Clark Gable	**2** Libby Purves	**3** Norman Rockwell	**4** Charles Lindbergh

Numbers on a plate

If you were born on 1 January you saw the New Year in with Idi
Amin, E.M. Forster, Lorenzo de' Medici, J. Edgar Hoover and a lot
of car number plates. New Year's Day 1904 saw the beginning of
compulsory registration for motor vehicles in England and Wales.
Decades later number plates were no longer just a legal requirement
but had become collectors' items. In July 2006 the number 'M 1', first
used on a 1903 Darracq, was sold at auction for a record £331,500.
(The number 'VIP 1', created for Pope John Paul II's Popemobile on
his tour of Ireland in 1979, had previously been sold for a mere
£46,500. The buyer was Roman Abramovich, the Russian oligarch
and owner of Chelsea Football Club.) The successful bidder who
secured 'M 1' over the phone asked Bonham's the auctioneers not to
reveal his name. But he did tell them that he had bought the number
as a birthday present for his son – who was six.

Sex and old eggs

Born in London's East End in 1938, the son of a tailor's cutter, the
photographer David Bailey left school at 15, did his National Service
with the RAF in the Far East, and got his first job in photography as a
dogsbody in a London studio. It was Picasso, he says, who made him
want to take pictures. By the time he was 22 he was working
for *Vogue*, and with fellow photographers Terence Donovan
and Brian Duffy he did much to create the spirit of the

JAN

FEB

MAR

APR

MAY

JUN

AUG

SEPT

OCT

NOV

DEC

Swinging Sixties with fashion shots that were as much about sex as they were the cut of the cloth. Having been brought up among the austerities of wartime London – and with a birthday so close to Christmas – as a boy Bailey missed out on birthday presents. His wife Catherine has been making it up to him since – with a succession of old eggs. But these aren't just any old eggs – they are fossilized dinosaur eggs.

3 JANUARY

Marxist balls

Wilhelm Pieck, the founder of the Communist Party of Germany and the president of East Germany from 1949 to 1960, was born on this day in 1876. During his time in exile in the Soviet Union in the 1930s, Comrade Pieck – a carpenter by trade – received for his 60th birthday two presents from unimpeachably proletarian sources: the First State Ball-Bearing Works gave him some ball bearings, mounted in a fancy presentation piece, while workers at the Second State Clock Factory in Moscow gave him a clock. Then, when the Second World War was over, and he became leader of the German Communist Party in the Soviet zone of occupation, he received a particularly unusual birthday present from Mexico. The party's cell in exile there sent him a sombrero, beautifully cast in metal.

4 JANUARY

Grimm tales

4 January was the birthday of Jacob, the elder of the brothers Grimm, who was born in Hanau in 1785. Wilhelm came a little over a year later. Brought up by an aunt who lived in Cassel, then ruled by Jerome

Bonaparte, the brothers spent years together researching and collecting folk stories (Jacob worked for Jerome as his private librarian). By 1812, as Jerome's brother Napoleon was beating a wintry retreat from Moscow, they had found enough of them to publish *Children's and Household Tales*, the collection which became known as *Grimm's Fairy Tales*. The stories included 'Cinderella', 'Hansel and Gretel', 'Rapunzel', 'Rumpelstiltskin', 'Snow White' and 'Little Red Riding Hood'. These stories have so often been given to children as birthday presents that the brothers deserve star billing here.

5 JANUARY

Frugal Mughal

Born during the night of 5 January 1592, the Mughal emperor Shah Jehan, the man who built the Taj Mahal as a tomb for his wife Mumtaz, was quick to learn the ruthless ways of his predecessors. He came to power after murdering his two elder bothers, their two sons and two male cousins. He very probably carried on an incestuous relationship with his favourite daughter Jahanara, seduced the wives of all his generals, and when he moved his court from Agra and built the Red Fort at Delhi had several criminals decapitated so he could incorporate their heads in the Fort's foundations. Might such extreme behaviour have been caused by over-indulgence in alcohol? Emphatically not. Shah Jehan experienced his first taste of wine – a birthday present from his father – at the ripe old age of 24. He appears to have remained a reluctant drinker: before setting out on his second Deccan campaign in 1655, he poured the entire contents of the imperial wine cellar into the River Chambal.

Shah Jehan shares a birthday with the American actress Diane Keaton, who was born in Los Angeles in 1946. Her one-time boyfriend, actor Warren Beatty, once bought her a pair of handcuffs for her birthday. He somewhat tantalizingly told *Vanity Fair* that 'there would be as much chance of Diane Keaton being into that kind of stuff as there would be of her becoming interested in skydiving'.

6 JANUARY

Diplomatic moonlighting

The Reverend Sun Myung Moon – who went on to establish the
Unification Church and made himself extremely rich in the process
– was born on this day in 1920, in what is now North Korea. In 1982
he famously matched and then married 2,075 'Moonie' couples on
the same day. According to the US Defense Intelligence Agency, the
proceeds of a land sale in Pennsylvania organized by Moon were
given to North Korea's Kim Jong Il as a birthday present. In return,
Kim's birthday gift for Moon was some very rare wild ginseng.

7 JANUARY

Animal crackers

The naturalist Gerald Durrell was born on this day in 1925 in India.
As recounted in his comic masterpiece, *My Family and Other Animals*, he
was brought up by his mother and elder siblings (including the novelist
Lawrence) in somewhat wild fashion on the island of Corfu. On one
birthday, young Gerald was to be presented with a donkey, but before
he could receive it, it defecated on the hall floor. It was then wrapped
in coloured paper and led upstairs to Gerald's room. Here it ran amok,
causing untold chaos – much to the birthday boy's delight.

8 JANUARY

Grace and favour

Junichiro Koizumi, Japan's reforming prime minister from 2001 to
2006, shares a birthday with rock legend Elvis Presley. Born in 1942,
seven years after Elvis, Koizumi is one of the 'King's' most ardent
fans. In 2006, on his last official visit to the United States, President
Bush accompanied Koizumi on a tour of Graceland, the Presley
home in Memphis, and then, as an un-birthday present, gave him a
refurbished 1950s jukebox – ready loaded with Elvis songs.

Tricky Dickie

On its website the Californian city of Yorba Linda boasts that its success in preventing crimes before they happen is one of the reasons it continues to be one of the safest communities in Orange County. It's the kind of city with folk you can trust. Richard Milhous Nixon was born in Yorba Linda. On 9 January 1913. Gonzo journalist Hunter S. Thompson described the disgraced president as '… a man with no soul, no inner convictions, with the integrity of a hyena and the style of a poison toad …' But his wife Pat loved him. For his 48th birthday in 1961 she gave him a rather special chair. Covered in rich leather, and with a deep seat and an ottoman for the feet, this luxurious item of furniture followed the Nixons in and out of various homes, and in and out of the White House. While in office, Nixon kept it in the Lincoln Sitting Room, on the second floor, and wrote some of his most important speeches stretched out in it.

Junior goes missing

Being born to a high-flying celebrity can be a hindrance. Some children break through the competition barrier and avoid the inevitable comparisons; others don't stand a chance. Frank Sinatra Junior didn't stand a chance. Within days of his birth in New Jersey on 10 January 1944, his father stormed out of Frank Jr's christening service when the officiating priest objected to Frank Sr's choice of his Jewish mentor Manie Sacks as godfather. The only occasion when Junior stumbled into the limelight was when he was kidnapped during the evening of 8 December 1963. Barry Keenan and Joseph Amsler, small-time amateur criminals in their twenties, bundled the 19-year-old away at gunpoint from the motel at Harrah's Casino on Lake Tahoe, drove him blindfolded through a snowstorm to the outskirts of Los Angeles and, with a third gang member helping them out, demanded a ransom of $240,000. Sinatra produced the cash, the FBI recorded the notes and an agent made the drop – filmed by undercover colleagues. John Irwin, the third member of the gang, released Frank Jr on a quiet stretch of highway and then made the fatal mistake of bragging about the escapade to his brother. His brother made a phone call and the game was up. The next day, 12 December, was Frank Sr's 48th birthday. He arranged an impromptu birthday party at the Sands Casino in Las Vegas, telling his friends not to bother about presents. 'Getting Frankie back,' he told them, 'is the best birthday present I could ever have.'

Five alive!

Born in quick succession on this day in 1988 at the William Beaumont Hospital in Michigan were Alexandria, Danielle, Erica, Raymond and Veronica L'Esperance, the first quintuplets in the United States conceived outside the womb. Their parents, Michelle and Raymond L'Esperance, already had three sons from previous marriages, but had been unable to have children together. Coming up with appropriate birthday presents for quins isn't easy, but here are five suggestions: five gold rings; five nights in a five-star hotel; Chanel No 5 (for the girls); a shopping spree on Fifth Avenue; or perhaps T-shirts with five designer holes in them.

12 JANUARY
All the fun of the fair

The construction tycoon Sir William McAlpine, whose younger brother is a former treasurer of the Conservative Party, was born at the Dorchester Hotel in London's Park Lane on 12 January 1936. The hotel had been bought by the family business in 1929, and remained in their hands until 1976. McAlpines don't retire, but these days Sir William finds more time to indulge his love of railways. He keeps a number of trains at home, and used the railway station he erected in the grounds of his country estate for the blessing after his marriage to his second wife, Judy. It was she who decided to move away from trains for his 70th birthday in 2006, for which she bought him a magnificent old-fashioned fairground roundabout. Originally driven by steam, but now running on electricity, the roundabout boasts a 65-key organ, and the horses, made of wood and beautifully decorated, gallop three abreast. It must be exhausting having all these toys to play with. But Sir William and his wife have a special way of relaxing after a hard day. 'Towards bedtime,' he told the *Sunday Times* magazine, 'we often flop in the bath together with a glass of champagne.' Of course, Sir William is only testing Archimedes' principle.

13 JANUARY
Conversation piece

This was the day in 1998 that Linda Tripp, wearing a wire carefully secreted by the FBI, met a friend at the Ritz Carlton hotel in Pentagon City. It was in late August of 1997 that Ms Tripp began taping her telephone conversations with Monica Lewinsky while Lewinsky was working in the Clinton White House – work that eventually brought Lewinsky to her knees and Clinton to the edge of impeachment. Although 24 years her senior, Tripp had become the young intern's confidante, and in one call, in November 1997, Monica tells Tripp that she had tried to find her a birthday present at a New York flea market. Lewinsky was later to tell the Washington Grand Jury, 'I hate Linda Tripp.'

14 JANUARY

Healing and conceiving

Dr Albert Schweitzer was a man of extraordinary talents. In addition to being a physician, he was also a theologian, an organist and a noted musicologist – he produced an authoritative biography of J.S. Bach. The hospital he established in 1913 in the jungle village of Lambaréné in the French colony of Gabon became a place of care and healing where a congenial atmosphere prevailed between blacks and whites, patients and staff. Birthdays were special occasions. One young doctor, Louise Jilek-Aall, a Norwegian, whose birthday fell on 14 January, remembers hers well. Songs introduced by Schweitzer were sung outside her room as she woke. Gifts were heaped around her place at breakfast – a carved chess board from Eric the carpenter, a new stethoscope and tribal wood carvings from the medical staff, personal gifts from the nurses, and a copy of Dr Schweitzer's book with a personal dedication from the author. Mothers of sick children brought their own offerings – a bowl of rice, a cooked banana. And in a quiet moment Gustave, her African helper, put a small object in her hand, closed her fingers around it, whispered something she did not understand and wished her good luck. When she opened her closed fist she found in it a tiny carved figure of a pregnant woman.

UNWELCOME GIFTS

- A PILE OF MANURE (21 JANUARY)
- A PLASTER-OF-PARIS PUG DOG (29 JANUARY)
- DOG POO (17 FEBRUARY)
- A SMELLY SINGING GORILLA (4 APRIL)
- A LIE DETECTOR (6 MAY)
- A DEAD RAT (25 JUNE)
- A LADDER FOR A 90-YEAR-OLD (28 JULY)
- A DOLL IN A COFFIN (9 AUGUST)
- HAVING ONE'S WIFE STABBED TO DEATH BY ONE'S GIRLFRIEND (20 OCTOBER)
- POISONED CHOCOLATES (9 NOVEMBER)
- BEING HANDCUFFED TO ONE'S CHAIR WHILE A POLICEWOMAN TAKES OFF HER CLOTHES IN FRONT OF ONE, SINGING THE WHILE (24 NOVEMBER)

A diplomat is a man who always remembers a woman's birthday but never remembers her age

The Greek shipping tycoon Aristotle Onassis was born on this January day in 1906. Given that he was the original 'man who has everything' he cannot have been an easy person to find a present for, particularly if one's pockets weren't that deep. He himself had no such difficulties. In 1968 he dumped his long-term mistress, the world-famous opera singer Maria Callas, to marry Jacqueline Kennedy, the widow of the assassinated US president; a year later, Ari marked Jackie's 40th birthday by giving her a 40-carat diamond. Some might say that to give a lady a present that reminds her of her age is something of a faux pas – especially if you have just traded in an older woman for a newer model.

The art of giving

The son of Polish Jews, Clement Greenberg, born on this day in 1909, was one of the most influential American art critics of the 20th century. He championed the abstract expressionists of the New York School and described Jackson Pollock as the greatest painter of his generation – much to the chagrin of Pollock's contemporary, Willem de Kooning. Pollock repaid Greenberg's friendship and support with a present for his 42nd birthday in 1951, an ink drawing that hung in the bathroom of Greenberg's apartment on Central Park West. Cheekily, in his dedication the artist had added the name Helen at the edge of the drawing. Helen Frankenthaler, herself an artist of considerable merit, had fallen in love with Greenberg the year before. But feelings were not entirely mutual, and in 1956 Greenberg married the writer Janice Van Horne. (They divorced after 21 years and then re-married 12 years later, by which time Greenberg was 80.)

17 JANUARY

She ain't got no satisfaction

Alva Smith was born to high-society cotton growers in Mobile, Alabama on this day in 1853. Staying within her privileged class she married, at 22, the railroad and steamship tycoon William Vanderbilt. For her 39th birthday he built her what the inhabitants of fashionable Newport on Rhode Island call 'a cottage'. This neo-classical mansion was built almost entirely of marble at a cost of $11 million. Not the most grateful of women, Mrs Vanderbilt divorced her husband three years after her 'cottage' was finished, and married Oliver Hazard Belmont, a wealthy socialite who lived in a castle.

18 JANUARY

Alternative presents

Peter Roget, compiler of the thesaurus that bears his name, was born on this day in 1779. Roget was a doctor who indulged his passion for language in his spare time. He began compiling his dictionary of synonyms when he retired at 60 and saw the first edition published in 1852 when he was 73. So thanks to Dr Roget your next birthday present could be described as an anniversary gift or a handsel or a fairing or a celebration of one's natal day or …

19 JANUARY

What second movement?

Sir Simon Rattle, born on this day in 1955, was one of many gifted musicians born in Liverpool. He won the competition for conductors at the Royal Academy of Music, rose to prominence conducting the City of Birmingham Symphony Orchestra, and is now principal conductor with the Berlin Philharmonic, a post he won on the vote of the orchestra's members. Rattle has spent time as guest conductor with all the leading orchestras in the United States, and it was the American composer John Adams who wrote *Lollapalooza* for him as a 40th birthday present. It was a rather extravagant present requiring a piccolo, two flutes, two oboes, an English horn, two clarinets, bass clarinet, three bassoons, contrabassoon, four horns, three trumpets, two tenor trombones, bass trombone, tuba, timpani, four percussionists, piano and strings. The title comes from early 20th-century American slang word meaning something special. The piece lasts for all of six minutes.

20 JANUARY

Smile please, Mr President

Diana Walker's birthday coincides with the day American presidents are inaugurated, and as part of her birthday treat when she was young her parents would take her into Washington for the inauguration parade. She grew up, she says, in a city where politics is the dominant industry. Her interest in photography began as a hobby, then one thing led to another and she ended up as a White House staffer photographing presidents Ford, Carter, Reagan, Bush Sr and Clinton.

Dirty tricks

It might have been a joke, and the two men were close friends, but having five tons of manure dropped on your front lawn would not be most people's idea of a great birthday present. 21 January is golfer Jack Nicklaus's birthday. He was born in 1940, and to celebrate the event his friend John Montgomery – with whom he

shared a taste for practical jokes – had the manure delivered. What must have tested the friendship further was the payback the following evening when Nicklaus shovelled the manure into the back of Mrs Montgomery's newly upholstered Cadillac.

The agony and the ecstasy

As Britain's most enduring agony aunt, Claire Rayner – born on this day in 1931 – has ministered to tabloid readers on every subject from masturbation to mastectomies. Yet she too has suffered agonies, both physical and emotional, at many stages of her life – not least of all as a child. Brought up by parents she describes as 'horrible', she can recall only one present she received from them: a leftover stuffed snowman. Her most treasured birthday present, she said, was her daughter Amanda, who was due on her mother's birthday but arrived early on the Twelfth Day of Christmas.

A posthumous present

They say it's the thought that counts, but it is rather nice to get your hands on the actual goodies. The Soviet film-maker Sergei Eisenstein had no such luck. Born on 23 January 1898, he made his name internationally with *Battleship Potemkin*, released in 1925. Silent and in black-and-white, it used the editing techniques for which Eisenstein became famous. Two years later, in 1927, he was commissioned by the Soviet government to make *October* (known also as *Ten Days That Shook The World*), commissioned to celebrate the tenth anniversary of the Russian Revolution. Eisenstein, who died of a brain haemorrhage in 1948, shortly after his 50th birthday, missed out on a present that the American film historian Jay Leda had long been preparing for him. The planned gift was a book compiled by Leda himself, based on documents by the novelist Herman Melville, author of *Moby Dick* and *Billy Budd*. But before Leda could finish it, Eisenstein was in his grave.

A present with strings attached

The son of Polish-Russian parents, Neil Diamond was born on this winter's day in 1941. He was brought up in the Bronx, and went to Erasmus Hall High School, where he sung in the choir with Barbra Streisand. He won a fencing scholarship to New York University and was on course to study medicine when he decided to follow a career in music instead. His parents gave him a guitar for his 16th birthday, Pete Seeger gave him inspiration, and by 2002 he was ranked third behind Streisand and Elton John in the list of the world's most successful singers. He said once that he found it easier to sing 'I love you' than to say it. Yet he was only married twice. He paid his second wife Marcia Murphy a reported $150 million in a divorce settlement after 26 years of marriage. If that sounds a lot, compare it with the $1.7 billion Rupert Murdoch paid his wife Anna after their 32 years of marriage.

Reading the tea leaves

Virginia Woolf's 33rd birthday in 1915 fell on a bright and frosty winter's day. Presents from her husband Leonard included a green purse, a first edition of Walter Scott's *The Abbot* and a treat at Buzzard's Tea Rooms in Oxford Street. (They were to see a film at the Picture Palace, but after waiting for an hour and a half for the film to start, gave up.) During tea they made the decision to invest in a printing press, although they put off buying it for a couple of years because of Virginia's depression. Their Hogarth Press was eventually founded in 1917 and was to publish, amongst others, Katherine Mansfield, T.S. Eliot, Robert Graves and E.M. Forster, not to mention translations of Freud. And all thanks to a birthday tea.

A mother's ambition

Jacqueline du Pré was born in Oxford on this day in 1945. On the morning of her fifth birthday her mother Iris crept into her room with a three-quarter size cello. It was the instrument that got her started. Eleven years later, in 1961, an unknown admirer gave her an exceptionally fine Stradivarius cello on which, in 1962, she performed the Elgar cello concerto in public for the first time (at the Royal Festival Hall). Three years later she recorded the same concerto under the baton of Sir John Barbirolli. The recording, one of the most popular in the classical discography, not only established du Pré's place amongst the world's finest cellists, but also made her name synonymous with Elgar's elegiac masterpiece. She died of multiple sclerosis at the age of 42, leaving behind a wealth of sublime recordings and a multitude of fans crying for more.

The love that moved mountains

Queen Victoria's first grandson – who was to become Kaiser Wilhelm II, the last German emperor – was born on this day in Berlin in 1859. In a moment of wild generosity Victoria gave him Mount Kilimanjaro as a birthday present after he complained that she had two African mountains (Kilimanjaro and Mount Kenya) while he did not have any. (Less romantic historians wary of perpetrating myths say the transfer of Kili had more to do with carefully constructed treaties than with hastily arranged birthday presents.) The mountain was known as Kaiser Wilhelm Spitz while it was within the borders of German East Africa, only regaining its original name when the territory reverted to British rule after the Treaty of Versailles in 1919.

Pasta and M.A.S.H.

Alan Alda is the son of a Tony Award-winning actor and a one-time beauty queen. Best known for his role as Hawkeye Pierce in the television series *M.A.S.H.* (his was the only character to appear in every episode) and later for playing opposite Leonardo DiCaprio in *The Aviator*, Alda was described by the *Boston Globe* as 'the quintessential Honorary Woman: a feminist icon'. His photographer wife Arlene reaffirmed those credentials by sending him to a Tuscan cooking school for his 50th birthday in 1986. It was apparently a great success, and Alda showed off by producing a Florentine pasta dish on the *Martha Stewart Show*.

Unwanted four-legged friend: doesn't do walks

Anton Chekhov, the son of a grocer in Taganrog, a port on the Sea of Azov in southern Russia, was born on this day in 1860. Although he had a love of the theatre from childhood, Chekhov chose a career in medicine, qualifying as a doctor in 1884. He wrote only in his spare time to help support his family, and continued to practise medicine for the rest of his life: 'Medicine is my lawful wife,' he once said, 'but literature is my mistress.' With his mistress he produced a succession of masterpieces, including *The Seagull*, *Uncle Vanya*, *The Three Sisters* and *The Cherry Orchard*, all of which have gained a permanent place in theatre repertoires the world over. Fame brought the dramatist a constant flow of visitors – friends and strangers alike – and although these visits irritated him he was always welcoming and courteous. One such visitor was a female admirer who brought a huge pug dog made of plaster of Paris as a birthday present for Chekhov. The dog apparently sported a most disagreeable expression, which Chekhov complained put fear into him. Nevertheless it was placed prominently on a landing near the dining room lest his admirer, on any subsequent visit, gain any notion that her birthday gift was not appreciated.

30 JANUARY

War room

Dick Cheney, George W. Bush's vice president, was born in 1941 in Lincoln, Nebraska. His association with the White House began when he became the youngest ever chief of staff under President Gerald Ford. He reached 60 in 2001 soon after he and George W. had been sworn in. (Given Cheney's poor health record – he suffered his first heart attack at the age of 37 – reaching 60 was an achievement in itself.) The new VP was treated to a birthday celebration in his West Wing reception room, and during lunch his daughters Elizabeth and Mary gave him the present they had conceived and spent many hours researching – a map showing the battles fought by his great-grandfather, a commander in the 21st Ohio Infantry, during the American Civil War. It hangs in Cheney's office, where thoughts of more present battles hang thick in the air.

31 JANUARY

Ruling the waves

Queen Beatrix of the Netherlands was born on this day in 1938. Her 18th birthday present from the Dutch people was a 50-foot Dutch barge called *De Groene Draeck* ('The Green Dragon'). Named after the flagship of the 17th-century Dutch admiral Piet Hein, it is a beautiful craft and is still used by the royal family today.

1 Clark Gable	2 Libby Purves	3 Norman Rockwell
8 John Ruskin	9 Mia Farrow	10 Joyce Grenfell
15 Marge Simpson	16 Kim Jong Il	17 Ma Wan-ching
22 Steve Orwin	23 George Frideric Handel	24 Michel Legrand
29 Gioachino Rossini	1 Frédéric Chopin	2 Mikhail Gorbachev

4 Charles Lindbergh	**5** Charlotte Rampling	**6** Eva Braun	**7** Anna Ivanovna
11 Thomas Edison	**12** Charles Darwin	**13** Robbie Williams	**14** Jack Benny / Stelios Haji-Ioannou
18 Bobby Robson	**19** Ukraine	**20** Gordon Brown	**21** Robert Mugabe
25 Tea Leoni / Manfred Petri	**26** Fanny Craddock	**27** Lotte Lehmann	**28** Peter Stothard
3 Alexander Graham Bell	**4** Patrick Moore	**5** Momofuku Ando	**6** David Gilmour

A question of manhood

The marriage is over. He is going out through the door and she pleads, 'Where shall I go? What shall I do?' Cue the most enduring line in sackfuls of Hollywood screenplays. Adding the word 'frankly' to the original line in Margaret Mitchell's Pulitzer prize-winning novel, Rhett Butler (Clark Gable) gives Scarlett O'Hara (Vivien Leigh) the final put-down as *Gone with the Wind* draws to a close. Gable, the son of an oil-well driller, was born on the first of the second of the first in Cadiz, Ohio. He was married in real life for the third time to actress Carole Lombard. It was she who gave him a hand-knitted penis warmer for his birthday. If an outburst from Lombard about Gable's performance in bed had any truth in it, it would not have taken her long to knit it.

Black, sexy, and only a red ribbon round her neck

Libby Purves, one of the outstanding journalists of her generation, was born in London on 2 February in 1950. A diplomat's daughter, she grew up all over the place but managed to get back to Britain to read English at Oxford, after which she found a job with the BBC. While still in her twenties she became the first female presenter on Radio 4's agenda-setting *Today* programme, and now presents *Midweek* and *The Learning Curve* as well as writing a column for *The Times*. 'I once got a pig,' she told the author. 'Her name was Alice and she was a pedigree Large Black. With a red ribbon round her neck. My husband says he was advised that women like something expensive, black and sexy …'

Breaking Home Ties

The painter and illustrator Norman Rockwell was born a New
Yorker on this day in 1894. During a prolific life he was commissioned
to paint the portraits of four presidents – Eisenhower, Kennedy,
Johnson and Nixon – but was probably best known for his illustrations
on the covers of the *Saturday Evening Post*. He did 321 of these during
his career, among them a moving piece called *Breaking Home Ties*,
which appeared on the cover of the 25 September edition of the
magazine in 1954. The picture shows a father and son sitting side by
side, the young man looking bright and hopeful, the father looking
thoughtful and dejected. The original was bought some years later by
a friend and fellow artist, Don Trachte Sr, as a joint birthday present
for himself and his wife. But the marriage unravelled and the
painting – along with others – became the subject of a dispute. In
the end, Trachte kept the Rockwell and his wife had the rest. *Breaking
Home Ties* was a popular
painting and was constantly
on loan to museums and
galleries at home and abroad.
But from time to time
questions about the picture's
authenticity began to emerge,
and when Trachte died in
2005 his son Don Jr began to
ask questions. He discovered
to his embarrassment that his
father had been a master
copier, not only making an
extraordinarily good copy of
the Rockwell but of a number
of other paintings too. Trachte
Sr had fooled a lot of the people
a lot of the time.

*The original version of Norman
Rockwell's painting* Breaking
Home Ties *behind the secret panel
where Don Trachte Sr had hidden it.*

An ocean becomes a pond

Charles Lindbergh, the pioneering aviator who made the first solo crossing of the Atlantic in 1927, was born on 4 February 1902. His *Spirit of St Louis*, the single-engine plane in which he made his historic flight from New York to Paris, had pride of place at the National Air and Space Museum in Washington when it was opened in 1976 by President Gerald Ford. The museum, said Ford, was 'a perfect birthday present for the nation' – which that year celebrated its bicentennial. Lindbergh's plane took just two months to build, and made the crossing in 33½ hours on 451 gallons of fuel. Lindbergh took with him five sandwiches and very little else; the USA acknowledged his bravery by awarding him the Medal of Honor, the nation's highest military decoration.

How to make bosoms, bums and legs erotic

Charlotte Rampling was born in Sturmer, Essex on this day in 1945. She has turned sixty and still oozes eroticism because she knows about the combination of mind and body. 'A need to devour, punish, humiliate or surrender seems to be a primal part of human nature,' she said once, 'and it is certainly a big part of sex.' Her most memorable film roles cast her as a victim of concentration camps, first in Visconti's *The Damned* and then in *The Night Porter* opposite Dirk Bogarde, who plays her former guard, and with whom she has a sadomasochistic relationship. Hardly surprising then that before long she was taking her clothes off for the photographer who said he had no interest in the inner life of his sitters, 'just their bosoms, bums and legs', and whose career was set in motion with the present of a camera on his 12th birthday. Helmut Newton was born in Berlin in the Roaring Twenties. His father made buttons and would have liked

Helmut to join the business. But the present of the camera stimulated somewhat more creative ideas, and Helmut soon discovered that the only buttons that interested him were those that he could undo to reveal curves of feminine flesh. The curves were to become the subject of his life's work. Rampling saw Newton as a film director who shot stills: 'Still photography is like being brought to a climax,' she said, 'then you stop and start again.'

Dogs from dear Adolf

Born on this day in 1912, Eva Braun was the second daughter of a school teacher. She became an assistant to the Nazi Party's official photographer and met Hitler in 1929. Six years later she wrote in her diary on her birthday: 'The truth is I have rather large ideas about the importance to be attached to this day: if I had a dog I would not not feel so lonely, but I suppose that is asking for too much.' It seems possible that Hitler gave her two Scottish terriers as a result, but it is equally possible that she bought the dogs herself, telling people they were a gift from 'dear Adolf'. She called them Negus and Stasi.

Ice maiden

Anna Ivanovna became empress of Russia in 1730 on the death of Peter II. Born in Moscow on 7 February 1693, Anna grew into an unattractive woman whose lack of physical charms was not

Gifs of intriguing accessories

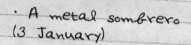

- A metal sombrero (3 January)

- A pair of handcuffs (5 January)

- A hand-knitted penis warmer (1 February)

- Vibrators (15 March)

- Red braces from an unknown female admirer (22 May)

- A fur-lined jockstrap (25 August)

- A male escort (5 September)

- A pair of silk knickers with diamanté buttons up the back (3 September)

- A copy of the Kama Sutra (17 October)

compensated for by much of an intellect. She was married off to the Duke of Courland who died – fortuitously some would say – a couple of months later. She restored the secret police and used it to get rid of people who crossed her, and left the running of the country to a German called von Biron while she played cards and went hunting. (Loaded rifles were left in all the rooms of her palace so she could take a pot shot at anything she spied from the window.) During the last winter of her life she had an ice palace built and, in keeping with her disdain for the old nobility, forced the ageing Prince Galitzine to marry an unattractive court entertainer and then spend their wedding night in the freezing palace. But she did continue the programme of westernization set in motion by Peter I ('the Great'), and she promoted and encouraged the arts. In fact it was as a birthday present to her in 1736 that an Italian company performed the first opera in Russia. And there were further birthday performances in subsequent years by new troupes from Italy who made it to St Petersburg.

8 FEBRUARY

Collectors' pieces

John Ruskin met J.M.W. Turner soon after he, Ruskin, graduated from Oxford, and although he was just 21 to Turner's 65, he made it his mission in life to rescue this great painter from what he saw as obscurity. Ruskin was born on this day in 1819 and educated at home before going up to Oxford. He first became interested in Turner's work when he was 13, acquiring *The Slave Ship* as a birthday gift from his father, a wealthy wine merchant. Over time he amassed a considerable collection of Turner's work, including a picture of the pier at Margate where Turner lived. Ruskin died in 1900, and in 1911 *Margate Pier* found its way to America where it was given to Franklin D. Roosevelt as a birthday present when he was a young man. It travelled from the governor's office in New York to the White House, and from Washington found its way back to England and into the private collection of Dorothy Scharf, a spinster whose two-bedroom flat in what used to be a council block in St John's Wood housed paintings by Constable and Gainsborough as well as Turner. She left the collection, thought to be worth around £5 million, in her will to a very grateful Courtauld Institute in London.

9 FEBRUARY

Growing up

Maria de Lourdes Villiers-Farrow, better known as Mia Farrow, was born on this day in 1945. The actress begins her memoir *What Falls Away* with the words: 'I was 9 when my childhood ended.' What she lost in childhood she made up for in early adulthood. She was 17 when she starred in *Peyton Place*, the soap that launched a thousand soppy soaps; 18 when she dined out on butterfly wings with Salvador Dalí (then 59); and 19 when she met Frank Sinatra, whom she married two years later. For her 19th birthday Dalí gave her a glass jug, inside which a rat and a lizard were fighting. Her mother shrieked 'Get it out of here' and her brother dutifully threw it out of the window into Central Park. Later they realized that a jug painted by Dalí was going to be worth a small fortune and they went out looking for it – but they never found it.

10 FEBRUARY

Guess who's coming to lunch

Joyce Grenfell did not approve of birthday celebrations. 'I really do not like birthdays and wish I could forget mine,' she wrote to her friend Virginia Graham. And she considered it the kindest of presents when, on the approach to her 62nd birthday in 1972, the chief executive of *The Times*, Marmaduke Hussey, intervened to ensure her name did NOT appear in the paper's birthdays list. There was probably not the same degree of appreciation on her tenth birthday, when her mother invited Ivor Novello and Noël Coward to

lunch and Coward gave Joyce a copy of *Five Children and It*,
E. Nesbit's story about a sand fairy called Psammead.

11 FEBRUARY

A very inventful life

Thomas Edison left us much to be grateful for. Born in 1847 in
Milan (the one in Ohio), he left us with a means of seeing in the
dark, of recording and listening to music, and of recording and
watching moving pictures. Edison did not invent electric light but he
did find a way of using it effectively and efficiently through his long-
lasting electric light bulb. He also produced the phonograph, the
forerunner of the gramophone; the essentials of the microphone
used in the Bell telephone, and one of the first cine cameras. It seems
Edison's extraordinary mind gave him a taste for younger women.
He was 24 when he married his first wife, Mary, who was just 16.
Mary died in 1884 and two years later he married his second wife,
Mina, when he was 39 and she was only 19. Mina knew that the way
to a man's heart was through his work and built him a small office at
his laboratories in Florida for his birthday in 1929, the year Edison
celebrated in the company of President Hoover and Henry Ford.

*Birthday boy:
Thomas Edison
(second from right)
celebrates his 82nd
birthday with (left
to right) Herbert
Hoover, Henry
Ford and Harvey
Firestone.*

The world of science
pays homage

Charles Darwin, the son of a doctor, was born on this day in 1809 at Shrewsbury in Shropshire. For his 68th birthday in 1877 he was given an album of photographs – photography was still then in its infancy – to which no fewer than 154 eminent scientists had contributed their portraits. The present was the brainchild of the eminent German biologist Emil Rade. It was, said Darwin, by far the greatest honour he had ever received.

Sex god

The singer Robbie Williams – who has matured from teen squeeze to housewife's delight – was born in Stoke-on-Trent, a city formerly known largely for its pots. When the one-time boy-band member turned 30, BBC Stoke and Staffordshire opened a website for fans to post their birthday messages. The result was an outpouring of highly charged (if barely literate) female passion. One such message must suffice here. 'I'd love to give you the best birthday present ever,' wrote Michelle (39), 'which would be me mmmm yesss, 300 Orgasms a day Lady.' Michelle rounds off her delicately phrased salutation thus: 'im Rich with Love for you, id make you so so happy inside with my warmth'. It is possible, of course, that Michelle was merely inviting Robbie round for a cosy chat and a nice cup of tea.

14 FEBRUARY

Fly me to the moon – charges and taxes included

American comedian Jack Benny was born on Valentine's Day in 1894. For his 80th birthday Frank Sinatra gave him two copies of 'Life Begins at Forty'. Today is also the birthday of the entrepreneur Stelios Haji-Ioannou, who was born in Athens in 1967. He founded easyJet in 1995 and with Tony Ryan's Ryanair pioneered the boom in cheap flights that revolutionized European travel in the 1990s. His father had given him a Porsche 928 as an 18th birthday present, a car he sold when he launched easyJet because, according to the magazine *Der Spiegel*, he did not want people saying 'Stelios does everything on the cheap at work, and in private lives in the lap of luxury.'

15 FEBRUARY

The Simpsons: episode something or other

Amongst his many sins, Homer – Homer Simpson that is – forgets birthdays. On one of the rare occasions when he did remember Marge's birthday he bought her a bowling ball that had his name on it. He knew she wouldn't use it because she never went bowling – and therefore, Homer calculated, she would likely let him keep it. Simpsons scholars are not absolutely sure that Marge has her birthday on 15 February. However, in one episode set in May she talks about emeralds being her birth stone if she had been born three months earlier. So that puts her birthday in February – and the middle of the month seems a good average.

Presents fit for a Kim

The North Korean leader Kim Jong Il, born on this day in 1942, is known to the rest of the world as a corrupt and paranoid tyrant, but to his local media he is Renaissance Man: not only is he (they say) a great statesman, but also a skilled pilot, a creator of operas, and an unsurpassed sportsman – who, on his first outing on a golf course, reportedly managed 11 holes-in-one. But golf isn't Kim's only sporting interest. Madeleine Albright, Bill Clinton's secretary of state, did her diplomatic homework, and discovered the Korean was also a basketball enthusiast; so for his birthday she gave him a ball, signed by Michael Jordan. Not to be outdone, CNN's Ted Turner presented Kim with a paperweight decorated with his company's logo. Topping that was an alleged $3 million from Sun Myung Moon, leader of the Unification Church, a donation the Pentagon's Defense Intelligence Agency described as a birthday present destined to lighten the North Korean's weapons bill. Official biographies claim that Kim's birth took place on top of Baekdu mountain, and was heralded by a double rainbow and the appearance of a new star. He took over from his father Kim Il Sung in 1994 and has run the Hermit Kingdom relying heavily on the cult of his own personality and the least possible respect for human rights. Kim has a profound fear of flying and travels to China and Russia by train. According to a BBC report, a Russian emissary who travelled with him on one occasion recalled how live lobsters were airlifted to the train on a daily basis and eaten by Kim with silver chopsticks, which he believed would detect poison – although it's difficult to see why anyone would want to poison a decent, open, peace-loving, golfing phenomenon like Kim.

17 FEBRUARY

Crap story

Ma Wan-ching and Liu Chia-pei worked in the same factory in Taichung, in the centre of Taiwan. But they didn't get on, as Taiwan's *Apple Daily* newspaper reported in 2007. That year, on her birthday – which falls on 17 February – Ma received a parcel by special delivery. Unwrapping the parcel Ma found a shoe box, and inside the box was a plastic bag containing a bowl, a pair of chopsticks and some dog excrement. There was a note that said, 'This is my gift for your 28th birthday. I will keep greeting you this way from time to time. You just wait.'

The police traced the package to a convenience store near Liu's home in the north of the country, where CCTV cameras had caught her sending the package. Liu was indicted on a charge of intimidation.

18 FEBRUARY

Celebrating with the winnings

Bobby Robson is the son of a coal miner who took the young lad on long Saturday hikes to watch Newcastle United play football. But it was at Fulham rather than Newcastle that Robson began his playing career. Born in 1933, he won his first England cap in 1957 against France. He scored twice during that game, the first time within a minute of kick-off. On his 70th birthday, as coach of Newcastle United, he was in Germany to see his side achieve a comfortable 3–1 win over Bayer Leverkusen in the 2002–3 Champions League. 'This was the only birthday present I really wanted,' he said. He probably said something similar on his 54th birthday when his England side beat Spain 4–2 in Madrid.

A generous Mr Khrushchev

The West must have been in the grip of acute Cold War nerves during the 1950s and 1960s not to notice Khrushchev giving the Ukraine a birthday present. And not any old birthday present. He gave them the Crimea, which had previously been part of the Russian Soviet Federative Socialist Republic. It was, he said at the time, to mark the anniversary on 19 February 1954 of 300 years of Russian–Ukrainian friendship.

Preaching to the converted

Gordon Brown, Britain's prime minister, born on 20 February in 1951, rather presumptuously gave Pope Benedict XVI a book of sermons during a visit to Rome in 2007. It is not recorded whether in return the Pope gave Brown some prompts for prime minister's question time. In Brown's defence the sermons were not his, but those of his father, the Rev. Dr John Ebenezer Brown, who had been the minister of St Brycedale Church in Kirkcaldy, a small coastal town on Scotland's Firth of Forth. The book of sermons was put together by Mr Brown and his two brothers as a present for their father on his 80th birthday.

An African disgrace

Robert Mugabe, president of Zimbabwe, was born on this day in 1924. On his 81st birthday in 2005 Zimbabwe's Open University made him a present of an honorary doctorate in agriculture. The university said it was honouring Mugabe for his 'outstanding contribution to the land-reform programme'.

22 FEBRUARY

A sting in the tale

The animals he loved and sometimes taunted for his millions of fans got him in the end. Steve Irwin, the Australian naturalist and television presenter born this day in 1962, was fatally attacked by a stingray that whipped its venomous tail into his chest. Irwin made his name as a crocodile

hunter, first catching them and then making television films with them. His parents were also both naturalists, and by way of introducing their son to their world, in 1968 they gave him a 12-foot scrub python for his sixth birthday.

23 FEBRUARY

Lofty ambitions

Although George Frideric Handel was born on this day in Germany in 1685, he spent most of his adult life in England. His musical talents were evident at an early age but were discouraged by his barber-surgeon father, who wanted him to study law. His mother, however, was more supportive of her son's musical ambitions, and so too was his Aunt Anna. She even gave him a spinet for his seventh birthday, which his mother and Anna secreted in the attic out of Handel Sr's earshot. Nevertheless Handel obeyed his father's wishes and went to Halle University to study law. When his father died a year later, Handel switched immediately to music and took a job as organist at the city's cathedral. He was on his way.

Le grand geste

This was the day Apple co-founder Steve Jobs was born in 1955. Bettino Craxi was born on the same day in 1934, Lleyton Hewitt in 1981 and William Grimm, Jacob's brother, in 1786. And it was the day Michel Legrand was born in Paris in 1932. The pianist and composer, who penned some 200 movie and TV scores, wrote the music for films by Jean-Luc Godard, Claude Lelouch and Robert Altman, but it was his haunting 'The Windmills of Your Mind' – written for Norman Jewison's 1968 film *The Thomas Crown Affair* – which won the Academy Award for best song. Legrand made recordings with many of the great vocalists of his generation, including Sinatra, Ella Fitzgerald, Neil Diamond, Diana Ross and more recently the Dutch singer Laura Fygi. So impressed was he with Fygi's interpretations of his songs that he wrote 'Rachel' as a birthday present for her daughter. The song appears on a 1997 album Legrand and Fygi made together.

Water music

It was the birthday present everyone dreams of while singing in the bath – or, in Tea Leoni's case, in the shower. The American actress had hankered after a singing career, but hadn't the voice to match her aspirations. However, she does have a thoughtful husband – David Duchovny (star of *The X Files* and *Californication*) – who rented a recording studio as her 33rd birthday present. What's more, he hired ten musicians and supplied them with the sheet music of the songs he had heard his wife singing while she soaped herself behind the frosted glass.

This was also the day in 1955 that Manfred Petri was born. You can be forgiven for not having heard of Manfred Petri. Not many people have. Or they hadn't until he took out a newspaper advertisement on his 50th birthday. Costing 6000 euros, it was no mean present he was giving himself. And the ad? It was a thank you to America. A whole-page, star-spangled thank you on the day George W. Bush arrived for his 2005 visit to Germany. Petri wanted to express his belief in German–American friendship and to shame those who did not share it. But nobody told him that Mr Bush has somebody to read the papers for him.

26 FEBRUARY

First of the celebrity chefs

Fanny Cradock was the first of the TV celebrity cooks. Not as pretty as Nigella nor as vocal as Gordon Ramsay – but it was Fanny, dressed in a series of ball gowns, who, in the 1950s, first made the performance more important than the cooking, spicing it all up with bitter comments tossed in her husky voice at her assistant, Johnnie Cradock, the man everybody thought was her husband (although they didn't get round to marrying until 1977, long after her TV career had come to an end). Much of her early life is clouded in uncertainty, but she claimed to have been given to her grandmother as a birthday present when she was one year old. Later in life, she claimed it was her grandmother, with whom she lived in genteel poverty until she was ten, who had taught her everything she knew about food. As she got older, Miss Cradock's behaviour became increasingly idiosyncratic, leading her into a number of contretemps with the general public and the law, usually in relation to her erratic driving habits. She once called a police constable who asked her to move her Rolls Royce, which she'd stopped in the middle of the road to chat to a friend, a 'uniformed delinquent'.

Love's cruel tricks

The soprano Lotte Lehmann was born on this day in 1888 at
Perleberg, between Hamburg and Berlin. She herself became a
birthday present with an extraordinary and unfortunate outcome.
Otto Krause was a successful insurance man married to a very
wealthy woman. Otto loved opera and Lehmann was his favourite
singer. So as a special birthday present Frau Krause hired Lotte to
sing for her husband. By the most cruel of twists, Otto fell in love
with his birthday present and she with him. For four years his wife
refused to divorce him, only giving in after providing Viennese
society with years of deliciously scandalous gossip.

A birthday at Number Ten

Peter Stothard, editor of *The Times* for ten years, was born on this
day in 1951. He himself became a rather unusual gift for Tony Blair,
who celebrated his half century on 6 May 2003. 'This is your 50th
birthday present, prime minister,' announced Alastair Campbell,
introducing him to Stothard in Number Ten Downing Street. The
two men eyed each other up and shook hands. Stothard was to
shadow the British prime minister for the crucial 30 days that led up
to and into the Iraq War, later producing an intimate and sometimes
humorous account of life inside Number Ten. Campbell chose well:
Stothard is too nice a man to take advantage.

The Barber of Seville, and other less well-known pieces

Opera lovers leap to celebrate the birth in Pesaro, on Italy's Adriatic coast, of Gioachino Rossini on this day in 1792. His father played the horn and inspected slaughterhouses, his mother sang and baked bread, and the young Rossini was also left for a while in the care of a Bolognese butcher. So the odds were only even that he would follow a career in music rather than food. But music it was, and by the age of 18 he had written his first opera – a one-act comedy called *La Cambiale di Matrimonio* (*The Bill of Marriage*, 1810). *The Barber of Seville* (1816) took him just over a fortnight to write and had a rough ride on its first night. But it subsequently won international acclaim, with Verdi calling it 'the most marvellous comic opera in existence'. In 1855 Rossini settled in Paris, where his home became a kind of cultural meeting place. In 1862 Arthur Sullivan and his friend Charles Dickens paid the 70-year-old maestro a visit. Rossini had recently written a series of compositions for piano and voice that he called his *Sins of Old Age*, but the jolly piece Sullivan and Dickens heard as they were ushered in was unfamiliar to both of them. 'It is a piece for my dog's birthday,' Rossini told them, and assured them, should they think otherwise, that he wrote a new piece for the animal's birthday every year.

1 Frédéric Chopin	2 Mikhail Gorbachev	3 Alexander Graham Bell
8 Gyles Brandreth	9 Vyacheslav Molotov	10 Osama bin Laden
15 Eva Longoria / Philip Green	16 Daniel Patrick Moynihan	17 Captain Lawrence Oates
22 Reese Witherspoon	23 Joan Crawford / Prince Felix Yusupov	24 William Morris
29 John Major / William Walton	30 Vincent van Gogh	31 John Rogers

4	5	6	7
Patrick Moore	Momofuku Ando	David Gilmour	Sir Henry 'Chips' Channon
11	**12**	**13**	**14**
Sir Henry Tate	The farmer's wife	Bethany Robinson	Albert Einstein
18	**19**	**20**	**21**
Queen Latifah	Hans Küng	Spike Lee	Ayrton Senna
25	**26**	**27**	**28**
Elton John	Paul Hiller	Mstislav Rostropovich	Neil Kinnock
1	**2**	**3**	**4**
Otto von Bismarck	Camille Paglia	Dr Hans Pinckernelle	Robert Downey Jr

If music be the food of love ...

The great Polish composer Frédéric Chopin was born in a village some 35 miles from Warsaw on this day in 1810. At least the Chopin family maintained this was Frédéric's birthday – his certificate of baptism records his birthday as 22 February. He was six when he was introduced to his first piano teacher, a mildly eccentric 61-year-old Bohemian musician called Adalbert Zywny. The two got on well, and the young Chopin gave his first public performance just one year later, and was still only 11 when he wrote his Polonaise in A flat major as a birthday present for his revered tutor. Romanticism filled much of Chopin's music, yet romance was largely absent from his personal life. (Contemporaries believed he was simply not interested in sex.) However, he did have relationships with several Polish women and was even secretly engaged to one in 1836. Some years later he moved to Paris where he met the novelist and feminist Aurore Dudevant at a party thrown by Liszt's mistress, Marie d'Agoult. Dudevant, better known by her nom de plume George Sand, was at first ambivalent towards Chopin, but in the end the two spent ten tempestuous years together before splitting up, leaving the composer broken-hearted. But he remained in the hearts of the Polish people, who honoured their favourite son by re-naming their capital's airport Frédéric Chopin International, following the example of the musically inspired authorities in Louisiana, who re-named their airport Louis Armstrong New Orleans International, and the similarly inspired Liverpudlians who named their local airport Liverpool John Lennon Airport.

A man to do business with

Today marks the birthday of Mikhail Gorbachev. Born in 1931, the son of peasant farmers, he was brought up during Stalin's darker days and drove a combine harvester on a state farm before going to law school and joining the Communist Party. Having reached the number one position in the Party, he embarked on a series of profound reforms, and it was his policies of *glasnost* and *perestroika* that signalled the end of European communism and with it the end of the Cold War. He was, Margaret Thatcher famously said, a man she could do business with. His relations with politicians at home fared less well, and he fell out badly with Boris Yeltsin, a soured relationship that was again exposed when tapes of telephone calls to President Putin's chief of staff, Alexander Voloshin, came to light. The tapes, leaked to Russia's *Stringer* magazine, included one call in which Voloshin, who previously worked for Yeltsin, told his secretary to tone down birthday greetings about to go out from the Kremlin to Mr Gorbachev. 'Take out the words "good health and wellbeing",' Voloshin commanded.

3 MARCH

An ill wind

His father and grandfather were elocutionists and yet by a cruel irony both his mother and his wife were deaf. However, as a result of trying to communicate with the two most important women in his life Alexander Graham Bell came to invent the telephone. Born in Edinburgh in 1847 but later a naturalized American, Bell learned on his 29th birthday in 1876 that his patent application was to be granted by the US authorities. The news, Bell was to say some years later, came as a kind of birthday gift.

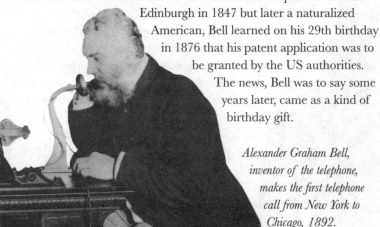

Alexander Graham Bell, inventor of the telephone, makes the first telephone call from New York to Chicago, 1892.

Stars in his eyes

Patrick Moore, the amateur astronomer who lit up the sky at night for television viewers with his breathless schoolboy enthusiasm and his trademark monocle, was born a Pisces on 4 March 1923. As a birthday present for Sir Patrick and for all other Pisceans how about a jar of Iranian Almas beluga caviar at £1750 for a mere 250 grams? Or maybe some Bluefin tuna at $100 per portion? Failing that, one could fall back on a pair of 'Kiss me I'm a Pisces' boxer shorts at $15.99.

Healthy eating

Momofuku Ando was born in Taiwan on 5 March in 1910. Fast-food addicts – particularly those health-inclined addicts who resist burgers and chips – have a lot to thank Mr Ando for. He it was who, after moving in his early twenties to Japan, invented the instant noodle. Thirteen years later he went even further and produced the instant Cup Noodle. You can see them now, those hundreds of thousands of Japanese salarymen chained to their desks tucking into fast, satisfying cups full of instant nourishment. Not to mention the millions of capitalist-inclined Chinese trying desperately hard to catch them up. One poll in Japan voted the instant noodle the country's best invention of the 20th century. For many Asian cultures, long noodles symbolize long life and are commonly a feature of birthday celebrations. Fresh noodles are even left at family graves, which seems a little odd unless they are deemed to secure a long afterlife. And if all of this seems unlikely, hasten ye to the Museum of the Instant Noodle at Ikeda not far from Osaka. It opened in 1999 and doubtless has a long life ahead of it.

The spirit of Hendrix

David Gilmour got his big break when Pink Floyd lead guitarist Syd Barrett – whose drug-induced behaviour on stage was making life difficult for the rest of the band – was left behind one night early in 1968 when the band was on its way to a gig at Southampton University. Born in Cambridge on 6 March 1946 to parents who were both teachers, Gilmour's career encompassed singing and song writing as well playing the guitar. On his 60th birthday his second wife Polly gave him the cross-stitched leather guitar strap once used by the rock guitarist's rock guitarist – Jimi Hendrix.

It's in the post

Most people would regard a late-arriving birthday gift as evidence either of forgetfulness on the part of the donor or the final disintegration of the Royal Mail. But for Sir Henry 'Chips' Channon the present in question brought a poignant reminder of a death in the family. An American-born socialite, later a British Conservative politician, Channon was born on this day in 1897, and would become better known for his diaries than for his achievements as a Member of Parliament. He married the brewing heiress Lady Honor Guinness, but later had affairs with a number of male lovers, including the dramatist Terence Rattigan. (Rattigan dedicated *The Winslow Boy* to Channon's son Paul, who would later serve in Mrs Thatcher's cabinet in the 1980s.) In his diaries – the published parts of which are heavily expurgated – Channon refers at one point to a birthday present from his mother. He appears to have received a package of food, including chocolate, a couple of weeks after his 45th birthday in 1942. The present came as something as a surprise to him because his mother had died the year before. 'I was touched and saddened as I ate her chocolate,' he wrote in his diary that day.

UNLIKELY GIFTS AND GIVERS

- Monica Lewinsky knitted Sir Ian McKellan a woolly scarf (25 May)
- Yasser Arafat presented Benjamin Netanyahu with a bunch of flowers (24 August)
- Queen Victoria gave Prince Albert an erotic painting (26 August)
- Conservative leader David Cameron received a bottle of Ann Summers Love Oil from his constituency party (9 October)

In contrast:

- Churchill refused to send Stanley Baldwin a present or even good wishes (3 August)
- The Australian premier John Howard pointedly ignored the birthday of his finance minister Peter Costello (14 August)

8 MARCH

Tom Stoppard and tales of relativity

Sir Hans Sloane founded the British Museum, Sir Henry Cole created what is now the Victoria and Albert Museum, and Gyles Brandreth established the Teddy Bear Museum. Mr Brandreth, born on 8 March 1948, has turned his hand to all sorts of things. He was Conservative MP for Chester for ten years. He has written scripts for and presented radio and television shows, and written books about John Gielgud, Charles and Camilla, and the Queen and Prince Philip. He is an ace board-game player, excelling at both Monopoly and Scrabble. He and his wife Michele have been together since 1973 and have fallen into the rather strange habit of giving each other presents on their own birthdays. So Michele gets a present on Gyles's birthday, and vice versa. Michele was born on 14 March, the same day as Albert Einstein, and so it was that Gyles gave her a poem by the playwright Tom Stoppard. It ran like this:

Einstein born
Quite unprepared
For E to equal
MC squared

9 MARCH

A Molotov cocktail of resentment and abuse

It has come to a sorry state of affairs when a man has to ask his boss to let him have his wife back as a birthday present. Vyacheslav Molotov, born on 9 March 1890, was for many years Joseph Stalin's right-hand man. But the closeness of the two men did not prevent Molotov's wife Polina becoming a victim of one of Stalin's anti-Jewish campaigns.

At the Kremlin, Polina had become friendly with Stalin's second wife Nadezhda Alliluyeva. The marriage was on the rocks and it was Polina who was comforting Nadezhda the night she finally committed suicide in 1932. But Stalin was suspicious and for many years resented the woman who had been close to his wife. Eventually, in 1948, he arranged for the Politburo to vote on having her arrested on a trumped-up charge of treason. Molotov himself abstained from voting, but failed to speak in his wife's defence. Polina was exiled, years passed, and Stalin died. His funeral happened to fall on Molotov's birthday in 1953, and as he and Khrushchev were leaving the mausoleum, Khrushchev wished him happy birthday and asked him what he would like as a present. 'Give me back Polina,' Molotov said. Khrushchev passed on the request to the ghastly Lavrenti Beria, still then head of the secret police, the NKVD. Beria ordered her release, but only after interrogating her under torture for a week. By the end of the year Beria himself had been purged and shot.

1 0 M A R C H

The world's most wanted

Muhammed Awad bin Laden ran a construction company that had done very nicely thank you, owing largely to his connections with the Saudi royal family. His wealth enabled him to marry 22 women, and to father more than 50 offspring. The bin Ladens were living in

Riyadh when young Osama – the only son of his father's tenth wife – was born on 10 March 1957. The boy was given a good education, but by his early twenties he had become involved in radical politics, and went to Afghanistan to join the *mujahideen*, who were fighting to rid the country of the Soviet occupiers. After the Soviet withdrawal in 1989, bin Laden began to turn his sights towards what he regarded as the infidel West. After some years in Sudan, bin Laden returned to Afghanistan in 1996. The following year, at his base in the east of the country, he celebrated his 40th birthday. His followers marked the occasion by presenting him with a white stallion, and, despite a bad back, he spent the day charging around the camp. It must have been an imposing spectacle: bin Laden is a giant of a man, the FBI estimating his height at between 6 ft 4 in and 6 ft 6 in. With his cloak flying out behind him, he might have been taken for the fourth horseman of the Apocalypse: 'And I looked, and behold a pale horse: and his name that sat on him was Death …'

1 1 M A R C H

Birthday greetings for a sugar daddy

This should be an inspiration to all of us who throw up our hands in desperation when faced with finding a present for an 80-year-old father or grandfather. In 1899 the children, grandchildren and great grandchildren of Sir Henry Tate produced a magnificent illuminated address in water colours and ink on vellum. It contained a birthday greeting, 47 signatures, a miniature portrait of Sir Henry and miniature illustrations of both the Tate Gallery – which he had endowed – and Park Hill, the family mansion in south London. Sir Henry was born in Lancashire on 11 March 1819, the eleventh child of a clergyman. He left school at 13, became a grocer's assistant, and by the age of 20 had bought his own shop. The shops multiplied and he soon had enough money to take control of a sugar-refining business in which he had become a partner. What finally made his fortune was his purchase of a system that produced sugar in lumps. The businesses of Henry Tate and Abram Lyle merged in 1921. (Lyle's golden syrup, first tinned in 1885, still retains its original packaging design. The syrup itself lasts pretty well too. When a tin taken by Scott on his ill-fated expedition to the South Pole in 1910 was opened in 1956 the syrup was still good enough to eat.)

Disaster in the outback

There are birthday presents that have led to disaster, none more so than the one given to a farmer's wife in the Australian outback in 2007. Her love of exotic animals prompted her family to give her a young camel for her 60th birthday. They had considered a llama and an alpaca, but they were too expensive, so they settled for the camel. It seems the ten-month-old animal, which was still being bottle fed, knocked her off her feet, lay on top of her and then exhibited what local police described as mating behaviour, killing her in the process. Her husband found her body on their farm about 400 miles west of the Queensland capital Brisbane.

Milking it for all it's worth

Bethany Robinson was envious if not jealous. Her mother was a strong advocate of breastfeeding, and was still giving Bethany's younger sister Elizah her daily feed when she was eight years old. Bethany, who had not been breastfed since she was five, felt she was missing out. So with her ninth birthday just around the corner on 13 March, she asked her mother if she could have breast milk as a birthday present. 'I was delighted if a little taken aback,' said Mrs Veronika Robinson, who lives with her family in rural Cumbria. 'My girls were brought up to think it was perfectly natural to ask for a breast in a shop. That was bad enough when they were toddlers, but now they are big girls people get freaked out by it.'

Beyond relativity

Theoretical physicist and Nobel prize-winner Albert Einstein was born on this day in 1879 in Ulm, Germany. For his fourth birthday, which he spent ill in bed, his father gave him a compass. He still had it when, for his 50th birthday, friends gave him a specially designed Bermudan-rigged sailing boat, constructed largely in mahogany and complete with a small two-stroke auxiliary engine. He loved it but did not have many years to enjoy it, because in 1933 it was confiscated by the Nazis and sold on to a dentist.

Orgasms all over Hollywood

Actress Eva Longoria , star of the TV series *Desperate Housewives*, was born in Texas on this day in 1975. She gives her female friends vibrators as birthday presents. An orgasm, she told *Rolling Stone* magazine, is the best gift anyone could have.

Today is also the birthday of retailing magnate Philip Green, born in Croydon, south London in 1952. For his 50th birthday his wife gave him a gold personalized Monopoly set that featured all his retail outlets. Nice idea for the man who has everything – well, Topshop, Burton, Dorothy Perkins, Miss Selfridge and British Home Stores is nearly everything in the rag trade.

A question of paternity

Daniel Patrick Moynihan was the man whom Hilary Rodham Clinton succeeded as senator for the state of New York. He had been a senior White House staffer working in four consecutive administrations from Kennedy to Gerald Ford, and then US ambassador to the United Nations, before entering the Senate in 1977. On his 71st birthday on 16 March 1998 he was surprised to receive a message from Vice President Al Gore (the man now in charge of global cooling) congratulating him on the birth of twins. It seems someone in Gore's office had gone through the happy-events database on the computer and double-clicked the wrong message and sent it to the right man, or vice versa. Press another wrong computer button in the White House and there would not be much of the globe left to cool. As it turned out, Moynihan said he'd never had a birthday present that made him laugh so much.

A present sacrifice

In 1911 an expedition led by Captain Robert Falcon Scott landed in Antarctica and set off to beat the Norwegian Roald Amundsen to the South Pole. By the end of the year, seven men had turned back, leaving Scott and four companions to make the final arduous journey to the Pole. One member of the party, Petty Officer Edgar Evans, suffered a serious injury shortly before they arrived at the Pole on 18 January 1912, only to find Amundsen had beaten them to it by a month. As they began the return journey, Evans's condition deteriorated rapidly, and he died on 17 February. By now Captain Lawrence Oates (*below, top left*) was suffering from frostbitten feet, making progress for the party painfully slow. They were desperately short of provisions, and Oates knew his frostbitten feet would hold his comrades back from reaching the next food dump. He told the others: 'I'm just going outside, and may be some time.' He never returned. It was 17 March 1912, his 32nd birthday. His sacrificial birthday present for his colleagues was in vain. They struggled on for a few more miles before another blizzard set in. They were trapped in their tent, only 11 miles from their destination, and one by one they succumbed to cold and starvation.

18 MARCH

A fatal gift

It was one of the cruellest twists of fate imaginable. Queen Latifah, the New Jersey rapper born on this day in 1970 to a school teacher mother and policeman father, gave her older brother, Lance Jr, a motorbike for his birthday. It was while riding this bike in 1992 that Lance was fatally injured in an accident. Latifah still wears the key to the motorcycle around her neck.

19 MARCH

Lucky Friday

Hans Küng, the Swiss-born Catholic theologian and president of the World Ethos Foundation, was born on this day in 1928. When he met the then UN secretary general, Kofi Annan, in Berlin, he slipped him a note asking him to give a lecture at his university at Tübingen in southwest Germany as a 75th birthday present. The secretary general agreed and delivered his present – a lecture on Global Ethics – on a Friday in December of 2003. Küng had done some homework. He knew that Kofi meant 'born on a Friday'; delivering this birthday present on a Friday was, he told his guest, particularly auspicious for his university.

20 MARCH

Happy Birthday, Spike

When Spike Lee, the Hollywood director (*Do the Right Thing, 4 Little Girls* and *When the Levees Broke*) reached 50 he rather hoped the day would pass without too much fuss. But in the evening he couldn't resist indulging his love of basketball, and went to watch the New York Knicks play the Dallas Mavericks. To his horror and embarrassment, at the end of the first quarter they splashed birthday wishes all over the scoreboards.

Early rider

Birthday presents have a habit of forging careers. Ayrton Senna was born on 21 March 1960 in São Paulo. By the age of eight he was driving the family car, and for his tenth birthday his father gave him a 100 cc go-kart. He was too young to race it, so he spent the next three years practising at a local kart track. At 13 he won the first race he entered, and went on to become South American go-karting champion. He began his Formula One career in 1984, becoming world champion for the first time in 1988. He won the championship again in 1990 and 1991. He died in 1994 at the age of 34 when he crashed into a concrete wall at 192 mph during the San Marino Grand Prix. 'Winning is like a drug,' he once told journalists. 'I cannot justify in any circumstances coming second or third.'

The coming of age of a southern belle

Award-winning actress Reese Witherspoon was born in New Orleans on this spring day in 1976. Her father was a surgeon and her mother a nurse and college professor. At her 21st birthday party she met Ryan Phillippe and uttered the widely reported words, 'I think you are my birthday present.' It seems he was: the couple were married on a plantation in South Carolina just two years later.

Loos talk

Joan Crawford, one of the early Hollywood stars who was seen and then heard and seen, was born in San Antonio, Texas at some point between 1904 and 1908. There was no birth certificate and no records for births in San Antonio before 1908, and Ms Crawford liked to maintain that that was the year of her birth. Late in life she got a letter from the screenwriter Anita Loos, who is best known for her much adapted novel *Gentlemen Prefer Blondes*.* Loos had written the screenplays for a number of films in which Crawford had starred, and her letter was a thank you to Crawford. The notepaper itself made the thank you additionally heartfelt: Loos explained that it had been a birthday present from the English writer Aldous Huxley 'a thousand years ago'. 'I've always saved it,' she explained, 'for extra special letters.'

23 March was also the birthday of the cross-dressing, Oxford-educated Prince Felix Yusupov, who was born in St Petersburg towards the end of the bitter winter of 1887. He was fabulously rich, having

* Loos also wrote a play called *Happy Birthday*, which opened in New York just after the Second World War.

fallen heir to the family fortunes after his elder brother was killed in a duel, and the family palace is one of the finest in St Petersburg. It was Felix who led the band of assassins who murdered Rasputin, the mystic healer who many at the time believed exerted undue influence over the tsar and tsarina and through them on the Russian state itself. The assassins bungled the murder, and although precisely how Rasputin died remains a mystery, he was certainly beaten and shot, and possibly first poisoned and then drowned. On a lighter note, Yusupov records in his autobiography how his father's fancies sometimes took extravagant forms, even to the extent of once giving his mother a birthday present of a mountain. Ai Petri is a rocky peak entirely without vegetation overlooking the sea on the southern coast of Crimea. Yusupov Sr organized a livestock fair there one autumn, tying blue ribbons round the necks of the sheep and pink ones round the necks of the goats. He invited the local villagers as well as his noble friends, and plied everyone with food and drink. No one really knew why they were there, but all returned the following year in a show of goodwill.

24 MARCH

Designs on his birthday

William Morris, the English Pre-Raphaelite designer and one of the founders of the Arts and Crafts movement, was born on this day in 1834. He was an ardent socialist and champion of workers' rights, so he was very touched when his own workers gave him a present on his 50th birthday. The engraved silver snuff box was decorated with his own designs of birds, acorns, oak leaves and roses. A simple inscription read: 'William Morris on his 50th birthday from his workpeople Merton Abbey and Oxford Street.'

The Godfather

Elton John was born Reginald Kenneth Dwight this day in 1947 at Pinner in northwest London, but later changed his name by deed poll in homage to saxophonist Elton Dean and singer Long John Baldry. For his 40th birthday his grateful record company, MCA, gave him a 380-horsepower Testarossa Ferrari. Rod Stewart was among the few to be taken for a spin. But Elton found it difficult to make time to enjoy his cars, and in 2001 – along with nine Bentleys, four Aston Martins, two Rolls Royces, a few Jaguars and a second Ferrari – he sold his birthday present at auction for £49,350. Birthday presents are a challenge for Sir Elton: he has no children of his own, but is godfather to ten, including Elizabeth Hurley's son Damian and the Beckhams' son Brooklyn.

Hair today, gone tomorrow

It was on this day in 1827 that Beethoven died. On the day following his death a young admirer called Ferdinand Hiller cut a lock of hair from the dead man's head – as was the custom in those days. (In fact when Beethoven's young friend Gerhard von Breuning called two days later to snip a lock for himself, all the hair had gone, and the deceased Beethoven was completely bald.) Many years later Hiller decided to give the lock to his son Paul on his 13th birthday. Paul Hiller died in 1934, and in 1943 it came into the possession of Dr Kay Flemming, a Danish doctor who helped Danish Jews escape the Nazis. The Flemming family sold the lock at Sotheby's in London in 1994 for £3600 to members of the American Beethoven Society. The words on the back of the frame in which the lock is kept record its early provenance: 'This hair was cut off Beethoven's corpse by my father, Dr Ferdinand v. Hiller, on the day after Ludwig van Beethoven's death, that is, on 27 March 1827, and was given to me as a birthday present in Cologne on 1 May 1883. Paul Hiller.' Other locks of Beethoven's hair are kept at the Library of Congress in Washington DC, at the British Library in London, and at the Beethoven-Haus in Bonn.

Sweet music to their ears

Cellist and conductor Mstislav Rostropovich was born in Baku, the oil-rich capital of Azerbaijan, on this day in 1927. When he returned to Baku on his 75th birthday, the president of Azerbaijan, Heydar Aliyev, gave him the Order of Independence. In return, Rostropovich gave Azerbaijan a $1.1 million grant from the Vaccine Fund, the charity launched by Bill and Melinda Gates, to immunize children against Hepatitis B.

Here comes Noddy

Neil (now Lord) Kinnock, the former leader of the Labour Party
and then EU transport commissioner, was born in Tredegar in
South Wales in 1942, the only child of a district nurse and a coal
miner. Shortly before his 65th birthday he got wind that his wife
Glenys was going to mark the event with a new car, which he
secretly hoped would be a sexy sports model: 'The great day came,'
Kinnock recalls. 'My wife gave me knowing looks with our first cup
of tea. There were no small exciting packets of cufflinks or ties.
Clearly something stupendous was about to happen. And it did.
When the post arrived it included a letter congratulating me on my
decision to buy a remarkably advanced vehicle and telling me that
because of a huge demand, delivery could not take place until June.
That didn't depress my delight at all. As soon as I looked at the
pictures and spec, I realised that all my life what I'd really wanted
was an all-electric, environmentally friendly, top speed of 35 mph
G-WIZ. Just a few months on, I'm a besotted
enthusiast.' His son-in-law is less impressed:
'Look out!' he says, 'here comes Noddy!' As
you might expect, Jeremy Clarkson
has been very rude about the Reva
G-WIZ, while Kinnock's ex-
employers in Brussels refuse to
classify it as a car.

Horseplay and caviar

The Conservative politician John Major was born on this day in 1943.
For his 50th birthday in 1993 Major – who had succeeded Margaret
Thatcher as prime minister three years previously – was given a fine
stallion, apparently worth £30,000, by Saparmurat Niyazov, president
of Turkmenistan. The gift was the cause of some diplomatic

embarrassment: the horse languished for several months in its stable back in Turkmenistan before eventually being brought to England, where it suffered the indignity of being turned down by the Life Guards for being 'too frisky' – and was exiled to a stud farm in Wales.

John Major shares his birthday with the late William Walton. Born in 1902, the British composer was the Oxford-educated son of a choir master from Oldham in Lancashire. In 1969 he was commissioned to write the score for the film *Battle of Britain*, but the studio was not entirely happy with the results and turned instead to Ron Goodwin (Sir Laurence Olivier, who starred in the film, was particularly angry that Walton's version had been pulled). The original manuscript went missing for a while until it was unearthed in the studio's archives. On hearing of the find, Edward Heath, the music-loving former Conservative prime minister, bought it and gave it to Walton as a birthday present.

On the composer's 80th birthday, Lady Walton arranged a small party in their suite at Claridge's, the luxurious London hotel. Russell Harty, the television talk-show host, was invited to the small party but was unsure about a suitable gift until Walton's wife suggested caviar. So Harty arranged for a large tin of hugely expensive Beluga caviar to be sent to the Waltons' suite on the basis that he would only be charged for the amount consumed, which Harty assumed would be minimal given the very few people invited to the party. What he had not counted on was the entire cast of *Aida* coming round from Covent Garden and singing in the street beneath the Waltons' window. Sir William was so delighted with the gesture that he invited them all up to join the party. The entire tin of caviar was polished off, leaving Harty with a bill for over £600.

A short and troubled life

Born on 30 March in 1853, Vincent van Gogh's life was short and troubled, his artistic career spanning little more than ten years. His first job was with an art dealer, and he spent a happy period working in the firm's London office. He then tried his hand at teaching, but his religious zeal got the better of him and he went off to work as a missionary in one of the poorest and roughest parts of Holland. It was his younger brother Theo who supported him financially and finally persuaded him to take up art seriously, by which time Vincent was already 27. The ensuing years were hugely productive but dogged by increasingly troubling mental problems. After the breakdown in his relationship with Paul Gauguin he cut off part of his left ear, wrapped it in some

newspaper and gave it to a prostitute with whom he was on friendly terms. He was subsequently admitted to a mental hospital in St Remy. He continued to paint, and for his mother's birthday sent her a self-portrait (*see opposite*), intended to reassure her that he was well and happy. A year later – aged only 37 – he shot himself. In 1998 the birthday portrait changed hands in America for $65 million.

31 MARCH

Gift options

Learning to swim or learning to ski – learning most things come to that – when you are young is so much easier than when you are grown up enough to fear failure. Even so, giving a 12-year-old a bundle of shares as a birthday present and encouraging him to play the market is, well, a bit high risk. But young John Rogers, like all those juvenile swimmers and skiers, learned fast. Born to Chicago lawyers on 31 March 1958, he spent his after-school hours in the office of a local broker, and by the time he was 16 he was selling hot dogs at Chicago White Sox games and ploughing the profits into his expanding portfolio. At 18 he had his own broker, at 22 he was a broker himself, and by the time he was 25 he had his own investment management company based on $180,000 he raised from family and friends. Today he manages billions of dollars and writes a column for *Forbes* magazine. So if you are looking for a broker, ask him or her how old they were when they started. If they were past their teens, keep looking.

1 Otto von Bismarck	**2** Camille Paglia	**3** Dr Hans Pinckernelle
8 Vasiliki Hatzis	**9** Hugh Hefner	**10** Joseph Pulitzer
15 Kim Il Sung / Henry James	**16** Sir Peter Ustinov	**17** Nikita Khrushchev
22 Jack Nicholson	**23** Shirley Temple	**24** Barbra Streisand
29 George Jamieson	**30** King Carl Gustav of Sweden	**1** Naim Attallah

4 Robert Downey Jr	5 Herbert von Karajan	6 Michael Delahaye	7 Gerhard Schröder
11 Bernardo Provenzano	12 David Letterman	13 Julius Nyerere	14 Princess Marie of Saxe-Altenburg
18 King Mswati	19 Antoinetta Crowley	20 Adolf Hitler	21 Queen Elizabeth II
25 Vladimir Zhirinovsky	26 Eleanor Elliot	27 Jay Leno	28 Saddam Hussein
2 Bianca Jagger	3 Henry Cooper	4 Audrey Hepburn	5 Karl Marx

A palace full of presents

He might have been born on 1 April but Otto von Bismarck was no fool. He it was who unified Germany, becoming its first chancellor in 1871 after Wilhelm I was proclaimed Kaiser ('emperor') of a united Germany at Versailles at the end of the Franco-Prussian War. Bismarck's 70th birthday celebrations were reported in *The Times* on 2 April 1885, the words 'By Telegraph' appearing beneath the Berlin date line. 'Well may the Prince have exclaimed that he had never beheld in his life such a moving scene, and that he would never see the like again. Every room in the palace was literally piled full of birthday offerings of every conceivable kind: illuminated addresses, honorary diplomas, telegrams and letters innumerable from all parts of the world.' The Kaiser, who had enjoyed a close and cordial relationship with his chancellor, made an emotional speech thanking Bismarck for 'the great things he had done for him and his house'. And he gave him what the paper described as 'a reduced copy' of the famous painting by Professor Anton Von Werner that shows Wilhelm himself being proclaimed Kaiser at Versailles.

You ain't heard nothing yet

On her own admission, she is a 'feminist bisexual egomaniac'. The American writer and academic Camille Paglia was born in New York State on 2 April 1947. She was a clever child, bordering on the precocious, and on her 16th birthday she was given a copy of Simone de Beauvoir's *The Second Sex* – tough going for a 16-year-old, yet she stuck with it. Having absorbed the book that heralded the modern women's movement, she grew up to become 'the feminist that other feminists love to hate', asserting, among other things, that 'Leaving sex to the feminists is like letting your dog vacation at the taxidermist.'

3 APRIL

Sweet thoughts

Dr Hans Pinckernelle was a prominent Hamburg lawyer born on this day in 1903. For his 50th birthday his wife Dora Marie commissioned a portrait. But this was no ordinary portrait. This was a portrait fashioned in marzipan and commissioned from the world's leading marzipan manufacturer, J.G. Niederegger, in neighbouring Lübeck. Dr Pinckernelle so liked the idea that for subsequent birthdays he commissioned dozens of the marzipan portraits and sent them to his favoured clients. He then commissioned a joint portrait of himself and his wife for their wedding anniversary, sending this out in advance to friends and family. Unfortunately Dr Pinckernelle died shortly before the great day, leaving recipients of the portrait uncertain whether to nibble away at the couple or put them respectfully in the fridge.

Keep your distance from the animals and hold your nose

The volatile Hollywood star Robert Downey Jr was born on this spring day in 1965 in Greenwich Village, New York, the son of a movie director. For his 40th birthday in 2005 Downey threw a party in Malibu, California. A friend who was unable to attend made amends by sending a singing 'gorilla' to serenade the actor with a birthday greeting. But Downey was not impressed. 'You know the guy's just had like nine events and he smelled like a kid had gacked on his suit,' he told reporters. 'It was awful.'

Allegro on two wheels

Music lovers who complained at times that Herbert von Karajan rushed the Berlin Philharmonic through their favourite pieces would not have been surprised to learn of the maestro's penchant for fast cars and motorbikes. He raced a BMW in private rallies in the years before the outbreak of the Second World War, and later drove a Ferrari and Porsches as well as a rather more mundane but nevertheless nifty Renault GT Turbo. Born in 1908 in Salzburg (he gave his first public performance there at the age of five), he was introduced to motorbikes by his piano teacher Bernhard Paumgartner, the man who encouraged his move from playing to conducting. Paumgartner would have been delighted that his pupil's most cherished 60th birthday present was a 250 cc Yamaha. Despite his love for cars and motorbikes you would not see Karajan with a map. This rather reckless approach to navigation spilled over into his music making, and on one occasion in 1939 he set out to conduct Hitler's favourite Wagner opera, *Die Meistersinger*, without the score. He got lost, the orchestra petered out into silence and the curtain came down. Fortunately, someone produced a score and the performance resumed on a surer footing, but when Hitler heard of the debacle, he tried to persuade Winifred Wagner – the composer's daughter-in-law – to ban the conductor from ever performing at Bayreuth. For once Hitler did not get his way, but Karajan was more careful from then on, especially with the Führer's beloved Wagner.

6 APRIL
Snows over Uluru

The television documentary producer Michael Delahaye had a palindromic nativity: he was born on the 6th of the 4th in '46. He and the BBC's former *World at One* presenter Nick Clarke were close friends and competed to find each other the tackiest birthday presents. On what sadly turned out to be Clarke's last birthday, in 2006, Delahaye came up trumps with a plastic paperweight with a miniature Ayers Rock inside, over which snow fell when you turned it upside down. The Australian Met Office say there is as much chance of snow over Ayers Rock as a dead dingo winning at Crufts.

7 APRIL
Foreign relations take centre stage

The former German chancellor Gerhard Schröder was born on this day. He is a friend of former president Vladimir Putin, once describing the autocratic Russian as 'a flawless democrat'. In return, after he left office, Putin got him a seat on the board of the company building an oil pipeline between Russia and Germany, together with membership of the Russian Academy of Sciences; he also pulled a few strings to enable Schröder and his fourth wife to adopt two Russian orphans (Schröder had always wanted a son). Schröder and Putin invite each other to their respective birthday parties, and in 2004 Putin travelled all the way to Hanover with a Cossack choir to sing 'Happy Birthday' for Schröder's 60th.

8 APRIL

Not such a dopey idea

They called her marijuana granny. Vasiliki Hatzis left Greece in 1962 with what might euphemistically be called useful farming skills, took a boat to Australia, and with her husband set about cultivating enough dope to keep the smokers of New South Wales very happy indeed. On 8 April 2004 police found 3.2 tons of the stuff on their property and a great deal more under cultivation. It was all worth about AU$45 million. She was arrested on 29 September and ended up in court on her 71st birthday. Her husband had already been charged, and the court decided her involvement in the business had been peripheral. She had already spent 94 days in custody, so the judge handed down what even Mrs Hatzis considered was something of a birthday present – rather than going to jail, she was given a five-year good behaviour bond.

9 APRIL

Three weird sisters for Hef

Hugh Hefner – who produced his first *Playboy* magazine in 1953 without a date on the cover because he had no idea when it would be ready for press and was uncertain whether there would be more than one issue – was born on this day in Chicago in 1926. After he had backed Roman Polanski's 1971 film version of *Macbeth*, which received hostile reviews and made a huge loss at the box office, the director showed his thanks by sending Hefner a short film of three naked witches singing 'Happy birthday, Hef'. The National Library for the Blind, a division of the US Library of Congress, provides a Braille edition of *Playboy*.

10 APRIL

Prize fighter

Joseph Pulitzer – whose eponymous prize is coveted by American writers, journalists and photographers – was born on 10 April 1847 in Hungary, then part of the Austrian Empire. He wanted to be a soldier but the Austrian army turned him down on health grounds, so he emigrated to America during the Civil War and joined the Union Army. Pulitzer was just 17. After the war ended he trained first to be a lawyer and then went into newspapers, first as a

reporter then as a publisher. He made a reputation for himself as a tough journalist not afraid to challenge big business or the state. And he made a lot of money. In 1877, on Washington's birthday as it happened, Congress accepted the idea for a Statue of Liberty as a gift from the people of France – a gift that recognized the friendship established between the two nations during America's

The head of the Statue of Liberty, on display in the Champs de Mars, Paris, 1878.

JAN
FEB
MAR
APR
MAY
J

DEC

revolution, and intended as a gift (albeit a belated one) to celebrate the 100th birthday of the USA, born on 4 July 1776. The statue was designed in France by the sculptor Frédéric Bartholdi with help on the structural designs from Alexandre Eiffel. But there was no money forthcoming at home for the base and a pedestal. Appalled by his country's lack of appreciation for the French gesture, Pulitzer campaigned through the pages of his *New York World* for funds. He got there in the end, but not without years of struggle. In 1885 the completed statute was shipped in sections across the Atlantic in 214 crates, and, after the sections were all successfully assembled, it was finally inaugurated by President Grover Cleveland in October of the following year.

11 APRIL

Custody cake

He had been on the run for nearly 40 years, but on 11 April 2006 the Italian police finally caught up with Mafia boss Bernardo Provenzano. The police got their first break in the hunt for the man believed to have taken over the Cosa Nostra top job in 1993, when he had treatment for a prostate problem at a hospital in Marseilles. He had registered under a false name, but DNA tests confirmed the patient was Provenzano. He was finally tracked down when detectives followed a parcel of clean laundry to a remote farmhouse within reach of his Sicilian home town of Corleone. On 31 January 2007, his first birthday behind bars at the top security prison at Terni north of Rome, the prison guards presented him with a cake as an expression of their good wishes. But the cake went untouched. The authorities decided the guards had got too friendly with the Mafia man and moved him at high speed and with helicopter escorts to a top-security prison near Turin.

12 APRIL

Strip show

The American TV chat-show host David Letterman was born on this day in 1947. On 12 April 1995 one of the guests on his *Late Show* was Drew Barrymore. When she realized that it was Letterman's 48th birthday, and that she hadn't brought him a present, she jumped onto his desk, turned her back on the audience, pulled up her sweater and bared her breasts – for his eyes only.

13 APRIL

Army housing of a rather special kind

Although he did not go to school until he was 12, Julius Nyerere made up for lost time, winning a scholarship first to a university in Uganda and then to Edinburgh, where he was awarded an MA in economics and history. Nyerere was born on 13 April 1922 in Butiama, a village on Lake Victoria in northwestern Tanganyika (now part of Tanzania). He became his country's first president in 1962, and although his form of African socialism failed to realize his country's potential, he remains one of the few African leaders to step down of his own free will. After he retired he immersed himself in his great passion – books and bookbinding. (He also translated Shakespeare into Swahili.) So large had his library become that for his 77th birthday (which turned out to be his last) the army gave him a new house in his home village, Butiama, to accommodate him and all his books.

Castles for an heir

Princess Marie of Saxe-Altenburg was born on this day in 1818. She married George V of Hanover, who in 1860 built a castle for his wife as a birthday present. The neo-gothic Schloss Marienburg was designed by the architects Conrad Hase and Edwin Oppler. The castle is still owned by the Hanover family, but Prince Ernst August was forced to auction off some 20,000 family heirlooms in 2005 to pay for restoration work. The birthday present is now open to paying visitors.

Missing zebra

North Korean leader Kim Il Sung was born on this day in 1912. After he assumed power in 1948, it became customary for other world leaders to send him presents on his birthday. Stalin and Mao both sent railway carriages; Gorbachev sent him a glass vase decorated with the Red Star; Yasser Arafat sent a model of a mosque in mother of pearl; Erich Honecker sent a revolver. Daniel Ortega and his Sandinistas sent a stuffed and grinning alligator sitting upright and holding a circular tray with six goblets. There was nothing stuffed about the zebra given to Kim by Julius Nyerere. A photograph confirms its existence, but no one seems to know where the animal ended up. Saddam Hussein sent some silver coconuts.

Also born on this day, in 1843, was the highly regarded novelist Henry James, author of *The Bostonians*, *The Portrait of a Lady*, *The Turn of the Screw*, *The Golden Bowl*, and other works. Edith Wharton was a disciple of James – she herself won a Pulitzer Prize with *The Age of Innocence* when she was nearly 60 – and rejoiced in taking James for long drives in her chauffeur-driven 1904 automobile through France in the years before the First World War. As his 70th birthday approached she set herself the target of raising $5000 as a birthday present from their circle of literary friends. But James rejected the gift, and in no uncertain terms. However, Wharton, whom James referred to as 'the great generalissima', was determined that her friend recognize the affection and esteem in which he was held, and used the money to commission a portrait from the artist John Singer Sargent. Sargent was a fellow American and also a friend, and waived the fee. When James saw the finished work (*right*) he praised

it enthusiastically as 'a living breathing likeness and a masterpiece of painting'. It now hangs in London's National Portrait Gallery.

16 APRIL

No justice

Sir Peter Ustinov, born on this day in London in 1921, was as convincing on the stage as he was on the big screen. He wrote for both, was an outstanding raconteur, and in later life became a highly valued ambassador for UNICEF. And he was mad about cars. His first was a Fiat Topolino, bought during the Second World War on his private's pay, supplemented by earnings from his first West End play. Lancias followed, and then came a Hispano-Suiza, a birthday present from his second wife Suzanne Cloutier. It was a brute of a car, with a 12-cylinder engine under a bonnet that could have swallowed a Mini. It was stolen the year the Berlin Wall came down, and a distraught Ustinov sent private detectives through post-communist Europe to find it. They traced it to the yard of a French haulage contractor, but the court decided the man had bought it in good faith, so that's where it stayed.

All the way from the Antarctic

The Soviet leader Nikita Khrushchev was born on this day in 1894 in the village of Kalinovka, in the Kursk region of Russia. He became involved in trade-union activities during the First World War, joined the Red Army after the Revolution of 1917, and became a member of the Communist Party a year later. His real rise to power followed the death of Stalin in 1953, when he became first secretary of the Party. The following year he celebrated his 60th birthday, and among the gifts he received was a whale's tooth, sent by the sailors of the Antarctic whaling fleet based on the island of Leskov. It was inscribed and decorated with a fleet of fishing boats, and mounted on a simple but beautifully carved stand. The gift was a clear manifestation of the cult of personality that surrounded Soviet leaders – a cult that two years later Khrushchev was famously to denounce, along with the heinous crimes committed under Stalin, at the 'secret speech' to the 20th Party Congress.

I'm all right, Jack

Swaziland's King Mswati was born on this day in 1968, just four months before Britain granted his country independence. He was the second of 67 sons of King Sobhuza II, who married 70 women and produced 210 children during his 83 years. Mswati, who was crowned six days after his 18th birthday, has proved outrageously profligate. In 2004 he bought top-of-the-range BMWs for each of his 11 wives, and then further indulged his love of motor cars by giving himself a birthday present a year later of eight Mercedes S350s with gold-plated number plates. His subjects had difficulty understanding why he needed eight cars and why the cars should have gold-plated number plates when the poorest amongst them – of whom there are many – don't even possess a rusty old bicycle.

JAN
FEB
MAR
APR
MAY
JUNE
JULY
AUG
SEPT
OCT
NOV
DEC

19 APRIL

An empress in a van

'The only emperor is the emperor of ice cream' – so wrote the American poet Wallace Stevens, who included 'The Emperor of Ice Cream' in his first volume of poems. He would not have heard of Antoinetta Crowley. Indeed the Harvard-educated insurance lawyer, who wrote in his spare time, had died before Mrs Crowley had reached her teens. Had it been otherwise he might have paid homage to the empress of ice cream – for that is what Antoinetta has become to the people of North Yorkshire. Mrs Crowley's birthday is on

19 April, and rather than a cuckoo heralding spring in these parts, it is the friendly chimes of Mrs Crowley's spanking new ice-cream van, given to her by her family for her 60th birthday.

20 APRIL

Treats and treaties

Adolf Hitler was born this day in 1889 at Braunau am Inn, a small town in Austria. He might not have been born at all if some historians are to be believed: his mother had apparently considered having an abortion. Hitler interpreted Realpolitik as a policy of signing treaties without any intention of carrying them out. On his birthday in 1942 Joachim von Ribbentrop, his sycophantic foreign minister, gave him a bound copy of all the treaties he had ignored. For his last birthday – celebrated in his bunker as the Red Army fought its way into Berlin – Hitler received, from an adulatory zoo keeper, one cleaned and carefully wrapped ostrich egg. For many

Unusual animal gifts

- Dinosaur eggs (2 January)
- Donkeys (7 January, 30 October)
- Pigs (2 February, 2 December)
- Pythons (22 February, 28 May)
- A sex-mad killer camel (12 March)
- A zebra (15 April)
- A jackass penguin and a pair of rare-breed sheep (17 July)
- A newborn lamb (29 September)
- A cut-glass crocodile (7 October)
- A frog with five legs (21 December)

years before this, the Führer had received an annual birthday present of 50,000 Reichsmarks from the American car maker Henry Ford, whom he had praised in *Mein Kampf*. In return, for his 75th birthday in 1938 Hitler awarded Ford the Great Cross of the German Order of the Eagle. It was, wrote Hitler, in recognition of Ford's publication of the anti-Semitic pamphlet *The International Jew: a Worldwide Problem*.

21 APRIL

In loving memory of Susan

Queen Elizabeth II was born in London on this day in 1926. Susan was an 18th birthday present from her parents. Susan was a corgi. The Queen has owned more than 30 of these dogs during her reign, many of them directly descended from Susan. Dogs are not just for birthdays, of course, and the Queen – then the Princess Elizabeth – took Susan on honeymoon with her along with Prince Philip. As she grew older Susan became aggressive, on one occasion biting a palace sentry – who nevertheless remained stoically at attention. Susan died in late middle age and is buried at Sandringham. Many years later, Her Majesty was given a pair of Bewick's swans for her birthday called Dylan and Deena. A strange gift – as the Queen already owns all of Britain's native mute swans.

Princess Elizabeth with her 18th birthday present, spring 1944.

Blood on the doorstep

Jack Nicholson was born in Neptune, New Jersey on this day in 1937. He began his Hollywood career as an office boy in the animation department at MGM and went on to win three Academy awards for best actor in *One Flew Over the Cuckoo's Nest*, *Terms of Endearment* and *As Good A It Gets*. It was not an act of endearment when he was left a very unwelcome birthday present some years ago by his Beverly Hills neighbour, the maverick journalist Hunter S. Thompson. Mr Thompson, best known for his book *Fear and Loathing in Las Vegas*, paid Mr Nicholson a birthday visit on Mulholland Drive at two in the morning, created a considerable disturbance, left on the doorstep a gift of the bleeding heart of an elk, and ran. Weird, but then Mr Nicholson is used to weird. He grew up believing his

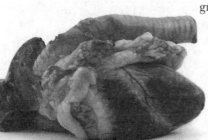

grandmother was his mother and his mother was his sister. (For his part, Mr Thompson left instructions that after his death his ashes were to be packed into firework casings and blasted from a canon in the back garden of his home.)

Diplomatic gifts

For her eighth birthday, which she celebrated on this day in 1936, the child star Shirley Temple received an astonishing 135,000 cards and gifts. She starred in 40 films in the 1930s, but later switched careers, joining the State Department and serving as US ambassador to Ghana and Czechoslovakia.

24 APRIL

Hand-in-glove with royalty

Barbra Streisand followed her hit *Funny Girl* with *Funny Lady*, shot in 1974 when she was 32. Filming was in progress on Streisand's birthday when the producer Ray Stark came onto the set with a palomino horse, a present for his star. Filming briefly came to a halt and Streisand was helped onto her new steed. The film was given a royal premiere in London the following spring, when Streisand was introduced to another lover of horses. The actress broke protocol, threw caution to the wind and asked the Queen why women had to wear gloves when greeting her. If Her Majesty managed a reply, it was not recorded.

25 APRIL

Who needs enemies with friends like this

The eccentric Russian politician Vladimir Zhirinovsky, who came third in the country's first presidential elections in 1991 and who leads the inappropriately named Liberal Democratic Party of Russia, an ultra-nationalist grouping, was born on this day in 1946. For one birthday he received a dog from Saddam Hussein, and was subsequently accused of taking bribes from the Iraqi leader. This might be because the dog was made from 6 kilos of solid gold.

26 APRIL

An island of joy

Eleanor Elliot, the American champion of women's rights, was born on 26 April, and died, appropriately enough, in Valhalla (Kentucky). Her husband Jock, an advertising man who had been chairman of Ogilvy & Mather, gave her the island of Staffa in the Hebrides for

her 60th birthday on the understanding that she hand it over to the National Trust for Scotland when the fun was over. Puffins, kittiwakes and shags make up for the total lack of humans on the small island immortalized by Felix Mendelssohn in his *Hebrides Overture*, better known as *Fingal's Cave*. Mendelssohn (who was badly seasick on his visit) was not alone in being entranced by the island's cave, with its extraordinarily regular polygonal pillars (*above*). Wordsworth, Keats, Sir Walter Scott, Turner and Strindberg were each in their way moved by the place.

27 APRIL

Star wars

Jay Leno, host of the *The Tonight Show* on NBC, got his star on Hollywood's Walk of Fame for his 50th birthday in 2000. (It appeared a day early: Leno was born on the 28th.) Leno's opposite number at CBS David Letterman does not (yet) have his star, a fact that doubtless fuels the sometimes bitter rivalry between the two.

28 APRIL

Ladies and gentlemen, we got him

Former Iraqi dictator Saddam Hussein was born in Al-Awja just outside Tikrit on this day in 1937. To honour him on his 65th birthday, 500 Iraqi couples got married in a huge mass ceremony, and a theatre in Baghdad opened with the stage version of a novel supposedly written by Saddam. Needless to say the play got rave reviews. He also had a 40-foot bronze statue of himself erected as a birthday present – the one that was unceremoniously pulled down by his detractors, with a little help from American soldiers, during the invasion of Iraq in 2003 (*below*).

Pass the parcel

George Jamieson was born on this day to Fred, a navy cook, and Ada Jamieson in Liverpool in 1935. George was born into anything but privileged surroundings. The family lived in a slum, his father was a drunk, his mother beat him, the lavatory was outside, the bath was full of coal. George waited until he was 11 for his first birthday present. He saw it on the table in the morning. He ran home excitedly from school and tore open the brown-paper parcel to find inside a pair of grey socks. But it was not so much his surroundings that George could not live with, it was himself. George was struggling with his sexuality and did so until he was 20 when, after an attempted suicide, he began to dress as a woman and to call himself April Ashley. He moved to Paris to work at a drag club and then to Morocco to become the first Briton to undergo a sex-change operation. April Ashley returned to England and embarked on a career in modelling, even gracing the pages of *Vogue*. Until, that is, the *Sunday People* newspaper, in the best tradition of prurient, cruel, tasteless tabloid journalism, decided to out her. But April survived, even thrived. She married, found herself in the company of the Rolling Stones, and ran a restaurant. A friend, Viva King, gave a birthday party for her every year. Lady Diana Cooper turned up one year in a cream trouser suit and a matching stetson with a curled brim. Hidden in the curl of the hat at the back was a tiny cream Chihuahua, which Lady Cooper, in full flow, retrieved and proceeded to tickle without the slightest pause in her conversation. April's marriage to the Honourable Arthur Corbett was annulled, and she now lives alone in the south of France.

Take the first left after the palace gates

Born on this day in 1946, King Carl Gustav of Sweden celebrated his 60th birthday with two days of present-opening accompanied by a fanfare written for him by one of his staff trumpeters, Olle Hermansen. There were the more conventional presents, such as the portrait presented to him by the prime minister on behalf of his government, and there were also one or two rather unusual presents, including some homemade strawberry jam, and – from the country's police force, who clearly did not want to have to go looking for their king – a satellite navigation receiver for his car.

1 Naim Attallah	2 Bianca Jagger	3 Henry Cooper
8 Harry S. Truman	9 Howard Carter	10 Bono
15 King Adolf Fredrik of Sweden	16 St Petersburg	17 Erik Satie
22 Sir Menzies Campbell	23 Humphrey Lyttelton	24 Queen Victoria
29 John Fitzgerald Kennedy	30 Peter the Great	31 Walt Whitman / John Prescott

4	5	6	7
Audrey Hepburn	Karl Marx	Tony Blair	Tito
11 Irving Berlin	**12** Gabriel Fauré	**13** Arthur Sullivan	**14** Sophie Anderton
18 Bertrand Russell	**19** Dame Nellie Melba	**20** Cher	**21** Andrei Sakharov
25 Sir Ian McKellen	**26** Queen Mary	**27** Henry Kissinger / Heston Blumenthal	**28** Rhianna Blackthorn
1 Gerald Scarfe	**2** Vera Howorth	**3** Rafael Nadal	**4** King George III

The colours of his socks

A blind civil servant who worked at the Ministry of Defence was frustrated by his inability to put on socks that matched. He gave up in the end, and made sure that all the socks he bought were of an identical grey. Naim Attallah, the flamboyant Palestinian-born publisher, deliberately wears socks that don't match. The one-time managing director of Asprey, the Bond Street jeweller, whose sex life has been as colourful as his socks, was born on May Day in 1931. One of his most treasured birthday presents is a 10 kg egg carved from a chunk of priceless lapis lazuli imported from Afghanistan. Funny thing is he can't remember who gave it to him. Mr Attallah was for many years the money behind the magazine *The Oldie*.

Naked in Manhattan

Bianca Perez Morena De Macias was born in the Nicaraguan capital Managua. Her life as a political and social activist was interrupted when she married Mick Jagger in 1971. She was a frequent visitor to New York's glamorous, and later infamous, *Studio 54*, where she celebrated her 30th birthday. Her present from the club's owners, Steve Rubell and Ian Schrager, was a white horse that was led into the club by an apparently naked man (on closer examination he turned out to be wearing a painted body suit). White doves were released, several of which were fried alive when they flew into the white-hot lights. Needless to say this failed to quell the enthusiasm of the partygoers, who danced on amongst the birds' charred remains.

3 MAY

Punch drunk

Former British heavyweight boxing champion and all-round good
egg Henry Cooper was born on 3 May 1934. Twenty-nine years
later, in front of a packed house at Wembley Stadium, he landed a
left hook that brought Cassius Clay to his knees. No boxer before or
since has floored the American world champion. It was such a punch
that Clay (who now calls himself Muhammad Ali) said afterwards
that his relatives in Africa felt it. The two men became and remained
friends. Another 20 years on and the BBC hosted a party for Henry's
50th birthday. The evening was in full swing when unannounced –
and as a complete surprise to the birthday boy – Ali walked in.
'The best present I ever had,' Cooper remarked.

4 MAY

Peace in our teens

The daughter of an English father and an aristocratic Dutch
mother, Audrey Hepburn, born on 4 May 1929, was raised in her
grandfather's home at Arnhem during the Nazi occupation of the
Netherlands. The star of *Gigi, Roman Holiday* and *Breakfast at Tiffany's*
began her performing career by dancing in carefully concealed vaults
to collect money for the Dutch Resistance. Her audience, she
recalled, could not have clapped even if they had wanted to for fear
of giving themselves away. Her uncle was shot in front of her for his
involvement in the Resistance. She watched trainloads of Jews being
transported to the camps, suffered from malnutrition, and narrowly
escaped being deported herself. She was the same age as Anne
Frank, and read her diary while it was still in proof. When asked
subsequently to play the part of Anne, she turned it down saying it
would bring back too many painful memories. The surrender of the
German forces in Holland came one day after her 16th birthday.
'I got the greatest present in the whole world,' she said.

The rise and fall of a city in decline

On this day was born the man whose political and economic theories had a more profound effect on mankind than any proffered before or since. Karl Marx, the son of a lawyer, was born in 1818 in Trier, the city on the banks of the Moselle that claims to be the oldest in Germany. In 1953, on the 135th anniversary of his birthday, and in the face of considerable opposition, the communist government of East Germany renamed the grimy city of Chemnitz in his honour, calling it Karl-Marx-Stadt, the name it was stuck with until the Berlin Wall was torn down and with it the ideology that Marx had espoused. Chemnitz itself seems doomed, it has the lowest birth rate in the world.

Cheap wine and cheap jibes

Former British prime minister Tony Blair was born on this day in Edinburgh in 1953. For his 50th birthday, French president Jacques Chirac sent him six bottles of Château Mouton-Rothschild 1989 and a crystal decanter to go with it. According to London wine merchant Berry Brothers and Rudd, the 1989 was good but not that good. It retailed at £195 per bottle. The '82, according to the experts, was seriously good: it cost £650 a bottle. Blair – who as a student played in a band called Ugly Rumours – also received a new guitar from the U2 lead singer Paul Hewson, aka Bono. Less welcome offerings were suggested when the BBC asked politicians and others what they might give. The former Conservative Party leader William Hague suggested a lie detector, and Blair's own former Northern Ireland secretary, Mo Mowlam, suggested a hearing aid. Gordon Brown kept his mouth shut.

7 MAY

Relaying birthday wishes

Josip Broz was born on this day in Kumrovec, in what is now Croatia, in 1892. Josip became a member of the Communist Party of Yugoslavia, although it was banned soon after he joined. In 1934 he became a member of the Political Bureau of the Central Committee of the Communist Party, then located in Vienna, and during the Second World War organized the anti-Nazi resistance in Yugoslavia, adopting the code name 'Tito'. In March 1945 he became head of the new Yugoslav government. For Marshal Tito's 53rd birthday, the Central Committee of the Communist League of Yugoslavia, through its Department of Physical Training and Sport, organized a relay of young athletes to bring a baton to Tito with messages of birthday greetings in specially created compartments. The relay became an annual birthday event starting in Kumrovec. (Tito chose 25 May for his official birthday to mark the occasion of the unsuccessful attempt on his life by the Nazis in 1944. The Nazis had found forged documents stating 25 May was his birthday, and had decided it would be a fitting day to assassinate him.)

8 MAY

Secrets of the West Wing

It seemed an odd idea. The president did not like ten-pin bowling, he preferred a game of poker or a brisk walk. But on the suggestion of a First World War buddy called Harry Vaughan, a group of Kansas City businessmen clubbed together to provide Harry S. Truman with a two-lane bowling alley at the White House for his birthday in 1947.

The alley was built under the West Wing, in what is now the situation room, and later moved to the adjoining Executive Office Building, where one of its regulars was President Lyndon B. Johnson's wife Lady Bird. President Nixon was also a keen user of the facility during his one-and-a-half presidencies. But bowling stopped after the 9/11 attacks because the Secret Service considered access to the Executive Building would have to be limited.

9 MAY

King Tut, I presume

Howard Carter was the British archaeologist who found the mummified remains of the man who has become one of antiquity's most celebrated royals. In November 1922, digging his way through Egypt, he came across the tomb of a young pharaoh whom we have come to know as Tutankhamun. Carter was born in Swaffham in Norfolk on 9 May 1873, and joined the British archaeological survey of Egypt in 1890, when he turned 17. Having found 'King Tut' he went on to find various artefacts in an annex adjoining the tomb, including models of luxury ships, which archaeologists have speculated were birthday presents for the young pharaoh, and four games tables on which the game of senet was played. This was a popular pastime in Egypt even before the young King Tutankhamun would have played it with his friends, and boards were placed in tombs so the dead could continue to play in the after-life.

10 MAY

A Russian bear comes calling

Paul Hewson was born in Dublin to a Catholic father and Protestant mother on this day in 1960. He acquired the nickname Bono, put together a band called U2, and became one of the most prominent of those rock stars fêted by politicians as they raise money for good causes and generally try to put the world to rights. He was at home in Ireland with his wife Ali and their children entertaining friends one Sunday morning when the doorbell rang. Ali opened the door to find a huge white panda snuggling up to Mikhail Gorbachev. Gorbachev was real enough but the panda wasn't – the stuffed toy was a birthday present for Bono's son John. Ali had become involved in supporting the victims of the Chernobyl disaster, and the rock star and the former Soviet leader had met on several occasions during Bono's campaign to have Africa's debt written off. Passers-by might have wondered what the architect of *glasnost* and *perestroika* was doing in the neighbourhood clutching a huge toy panda.

1 1   M A Y

Sing, but keep it quiet

Irving Berlin was born Israel Baline on 11 May 1888, the son of a rabbi, in what is now Belarus. He died in New York at the grand old age of 101, having produced some of the 20th century's most enduring popular songs. 'White Christmas' was his, first sung by Bing Crosby in the black-and-white 1942 film *Holiday Inn*. His fervent patriotism was manifest in 'God Bless America', and in writing both the music and the lyrics for *Annie Get Your Gun* he created almost single-handedly one of the greatest musicals of all time. But it was a song he did not write that landed him in trouble. 'Happy Birthday To You', probably sung more often than all Berlin's songs put together, has a complicated and convoluted history. A school teacher and her sister published the melody in 1893 in a book called *Song Stories for the Kindergarten*. But it was not until the 1930s that the Hill sisters got round to registering the copyright to the melody, by which time children had changed the words 'Happy Greeting to All' to 'Happy Birthday to You'. Berlin used the song in his musical *As Thousands Cheer* believing it to be out of copyright. It wasn't, and the Hill sisters' publishers promptly sued. The US Congress recently added twenty more years to existing copyrights, keeping 'Happy Birthday to You' out of the public domain until 2030. But you can sing 'Happy Birthday' in private to your heart's content.

Musical gifts for musical children

The French composer Gabriel Fauré was born in the south of France on this day in 1845. He was much taken with the singer Emma Bardac (the wife of a wealthy banker) with whom he had an affair and who bore him a child. Fauré wrote his *Dolly Suite* for her daughter Dolly as a birthday present, completing the work in 1896. For Emma herself he wrote *La Bonne Chanson*. Sadly for Fauré, in

1904 Emma left him for his fellow composer Claude Debussy, whose wife at the time, Rosalie Texier, could not cope and tried to shoot herself. Emma bore Debussy's child (nicknamed Chou-Chou) – for whom he wrote his *Children's Corner* suite – and the couple eventually married in 1908.

Dolly Bardac and Chou-Chou Debussy, photographed c. 1914.

Sullivan without the S

Arthur Sullivan, destined to become the composing half of the light-opera creators Gilbert and Sullivan, began his musical career as a singer. Born on 13 May 1842, he became a chorister at the Chapel Royal and lived with other members of the choir in the Chelsea home of the Reverend and Mrs Helmore. The young Sullivan won a special place in the hearts of the Reverend and his wife, and gave Mrs Helmore a signed photograph of himself as a birthday present. Sullivan was proud of his middle name Seymour, and would sign himself Arthur S. Sullivan. But Mrs Helmore never liked the name and was not shy of letting Arthur know. So when he signed his picture for her he did so without the 'S', and afterwards gradually dropped it all together.

1 4 MAY

Don't put your daughter on the catwalk, Mrs Anderton

Sophie Anderton is the model who put her all into the Wonderbra advertising campaign, and put it all back again for La Senza's Christmas lingerie collection in 2006. Before and between those campaigns things were not so rosy. Sophie was born in Bristol on 14 May 1977. At the age of 11 she was seriously hurt in a car crash, and during the four ensuing years underwent 18 operations. By the age of 16 she was fit enough to begin a modelling career, which brought her fame and fortune and no end of trouble. By the time she was 19 she was dating Robert Hanson, a man 17 years her senior, who bought her a silver Mercedes for her 21st birthday. She drove her birthday present down the King's Road, Chelsea while under the influence of alcohol, and was fined and banned from driving for a year. She took an overdose, indulged in self-harming, chose unsuitable partners, and predictably did *Celebrity Love Island* (during which she cried a lot) and lived to regret it.

Private dining

King Adolf Fredrik of Sweden was born in Prussia on this day in 1710. For Queen Luise's birthday in 1753 he had built a Chinese 'palace' in wood in the grounds of Drottningholm ('queen's islet') on the island of Lovön in Lake Mälaren on the edge of Stockholm. Adjacent to the Chinese palace were four pavilions, one of which, the so-called Confidence, was used by the royal family as a private dining room. The dining table was lowered through the floor to the kitchen below, where it was laden with food before being hauled back up again, ensuring confidential dining in the strictest privacy.

The mysteries of self-knowledge

This is the day in 1703 that the Peter and Paul Fortress in St Petersburg was founded – hence 16 May became the city's official birthday. On the city's 300th anniversary in 2003 it received a present from a man who for nearly 50 years had lived in ignorance of who he really was. Carl Fabergé, the jeweller who produced a series of stunning and priceless Easter eggs for the imperial court at St Petersburg in the latter years of the 19th century, dispatched his son Nicolas to run the London arm of the family business. While in London Nicolas fathered an illegitimate son, Theo. Theo was brought up by an aunt and uncle on his mother's side and given the surname Woodall. It was not until 1969,when he was 47, that Theo discovered he was a Fabergé. Already an able craftsman, he decided at first not to emulate his grandfather's work, but he began receiving commissions from collectors of Carl Fabergé's work, then one thing led to another and jewelled eggs once again began to carry the Fabergé name. He was in his late seventies when he began work on an egg for the birthday of Peter I's great city. The crystal egg decorated with hand-engraved images of nine of the city's palaces was embellished with engravings of emperors and empresses and crowned with a three-headed golden eagle (*opposite*). And like all the fabled Fabergé eggs it contained a surprise. Inside was a miniature of St Petersburg's *Bronze Horseman* – the famous statue of the city's founder on horseback.

17 MAY

A handkerchief for the Gymnopédist

Hands up if you have ever stooped to giving handkerchiefs as a birthday present. Those who have can take some comfort from the fact that it was the wonderfully eccentric French composer Erik Satie who set the ball rolling. Satie was the man whose often repetitive and sometimes oddly titled piano music (including *Three Pieces in the Shape of a Pear* and his celebrated *Gymnopédies*) amused a somewhat quizzical Paris audience at the beginning of the 20th century. When asked on one occasion what he would like for his birthday (he was born in Honfleur on 17 May 1866) he apparently replied, 'I saw this beautiful handkerchief the other day …' – and was never again short of something to blow his nose on. After his death in 1935, friends and family who went to sort out his apartment in Arcueil, where he had lived alone for 27 years, found in his wardrobe 84 identical handkerchiefs. They also found dozens of unused umbrellas. When it rained Satie kept his umbrella under his coat so it did not get wet.

A workout for the young brain

Of all the people who might have claimed that 'It's the thought that counts', few would have had greater justification than Bertrand Russell. The philosopher and social reformer was born on this day in Wales in 1872. His book, *A History of Western Philosophy*, would seem an unlikely present for a 15-year-old. Yet it was this tome that the lawyer Anthony Julius got from his cousin Elizabeth for his birthday in 1971. Julius went on to gain a first-class honours degree in English Literature at Cambridge, and after doing a PhD at London University joined the law firm of Mishcon de Reya. Julius represented Princess Diana during her divorce, did the same for Heather Mills McCartney (although even the lawyer/client relationship foundered during the proceedings), and was Deborah Lipstadt's chosen lawyer in the libel action brought against her by David Irving, the man for whom the Holocaust did not exist.

Would Madam care to look at the dessert menu?

In the old days opera singers were enormous. Dame Nellie Melba was no exception. Born Helen Mitchell in Melbourne on this day in 1861, she took an abbreviation of her birthplace as her stage name. She struggled continuously with her weight, and during a stay at the Savoy in London in 1897, the hotel's chef Auguste Escoffier came up with some crisp thin curly toast for her. Melba Toast was not his only offering. For one particular birthday he created a dessert with peaches, raspberry sauce and ice cream, which he christened Peach Melba in her honour. The latter would not have done her figure much good, but it assured her a place in culinary history that would endure alongside her place in the history of opera.

Sheer cheek from an Arab sheikh

Cherilyn LaPierre was born today in 1946 in El Centro, California, the daughter of a truck driver and sometime model. She abbreviated her first name to its first four letters, teamed up with a singer called Sonny Bono, and with a song he wrote called 'I Got You Babe' spun to fame in a partnership that was to become one of popular music's most enduring – even after the break-up of their marriage in 1975. (It was in the year of the divorce that Cher began to expose her navel – clinical psychologists might wish to ponder this – and set the trend for a world-wide display of flesh around the female midriff.) Cher went on to pursue a successful solo career, but had a narrow escape on her 50th birthday at the hands of a man accused at his subsequent trial of being 'a prince amongst confidence tricksters'. Masquerading as a fabulously wealthy Arab sheikh, Sulaiman Al-Kehaimi entertained the actress at a chateau he had rented in Grasse during the Monaco Grand Prix in 1996. During the birthday party, Al-Kehaimi apparently embarrassed Cher by giving her the keys of his yellow Lamborghini, saying he loved the car but wanted her to have it. But on some pretext or other he took the keys back and she never even got to drive it. He was subsequently arrested on charges of theft and deception after a Boeing 707 he claimed to own was found stranded at a British airport with writs stuck all over it from a host of creditors. The Lamborghini turned out not to be his either. Although he was acquitted by a jury at Oxford Crown Court, not much is seen of Mr Al-Kehaimi these days. But Cher's farewell performances seem to go on and on.

Stingy gifts

- A leftover stuffed snowman (22 January)

- An inch of flat champagne (22 December)

- A plastic paperweight (6 April)

- A cheap second-hand bicycle (9 June)

- Five balloons (15 November)

- A handful of dust (19 December), albeit from the Moon

The man who spoke his mind

The Soviet nuclear physicist and human-rights activist Andrei Sakharov was born in Moscow on 21 May 1921. His father was a physics teacher, and his grandfather a lawyer in the Russia of the tsars. After the Second World War Sakharov became a member of the team that built the first Soviet atom bomb, and played a key role in the subsequent development of the Soviet hydrogen bomb. Yet it was his concerns about the radioactive hazards associated with the USSR's nuclear programme that triggered his first moves into dissent. His lobbying for a test-ban treaty, and his promotion of human rights brought him the Nobel Peace Prize in 1975. But when he denounced the Soviet Union's military intervention in Afghanistan the Kremlin banished him to Gorky. The door to his flat there was guarded round the clock, and he could see no one without police permission. There was no telephone and his radio was jammed, preventing him from listening to foreign broadcasts. But he did manage a little smuggling. His supporters in the Soviet Union put together what one of them described as 'a communal birthday present' for his 60th birthday a year into his house arrest in Gorky. It was a collection of articles written by friends and colleagues, augmented by several essays of his own, which had been spirited out of Gorky and, via Moscow, had found their way to the West. But his 60th birthday brought sadness too. From texts held by the International League for Human Rights in New York it is clear that the Kremlin made his life as difficult as it could. 'My wife and I normally cannot communicate with the west by telephone,' Sakharov wrote. 'This is especially hard for us since our children live in America. Our letters often fail to get through. (They are seized illegally by the KGB.) I did not receive a single letter of congratulations from the West on my 60th birthday, not even from our children.' He went on hunger strike in his efforts to obtain permission for his wife to travel to the West for treatment after she suffered a major coronary. In 1986, under Gorbachev's reforms, he was allowed to return to Moscow, but died of a heart attack himself three years later at the age of 68.

Red, Liberal and conservatively dressed

Sir Menzies ('Ming') Campbell, former leader of Britain's Liberal Democrats, was born (on 22 May 1941) and brought up in Glasgow – which cynics say is why he learnt to run so fast. As a sprinter he represented Britain in the 1964 Olympics, and went on to captain the British athletics team in 1965 and 1966. After studying law, he enjoyed a distinguished career as an advocate before becoming a Member of Parliament. On his 63rd birthday Sir Menzies was intrigued to find that a pair of bright red braces had arrived at his office. The accompanying note offered birthday wishes while expressing admiration for his performance on the floor of the House. There was no signature, but Sir Menzies's aides reckon the note was penned by a feminine hand.

The eye of an elephant

George and Pamela Lyttelton had four daughters and Humphrey. Humphrey was born at Eton College, where George was a master, during the summer term in 1921. His interest in music surfaced early, and when his uncle, a vicar in the East End of London, gave him a birthday present of a side drum deemed superfluous by a Boys' Brigade band, his parents secured the services of a retired Coldstream Guards bandsman called Mr Glass to teach him how to play it. Humphrey took to military music and mastered the paradiddle – a quick succession of drumbeats – to such a high standard that Mr Glass was prompted to usher his protégé into the orchestra pit at Windsor's Theatre Royal at the end of the show one night to play the roll that signalled the national anthem. It was not until his teens that he bought his first trumpet, and not until 1948 that he formed his first jazz band. It was much later still that his wife

Jill bought him the birthday present that used to hang in his hall at home. The abstract painting is the work of a three-year-old: 'It's uncanny,' Humph said, 'and difficult to imagine it was not given any guidance.' The three-year-old is an elephant called Luuk Add, who produced the work (*right*) at a rescue centre at Lampang in northern Thailand. Apparently

while some elephants show little interest in painting, others produce work with recognizable characteristics and show a preference for working with certain colours.

24 MAY

Victoria's secret

Queen Victoria was born in London on 24 May 1819. For many years the Austrian Emperor Franz Joseph, a colonel in the Austrian army by the time he was 13, sent her an annual birthday present of Hungarian Tokaji wine – a 12-bottle case for each year of her life. The emperor remained on top of his maths, sending Victoria 972 bottles for her 81st birthday in 1900.

25 MAY

From Monica with love

British actor Sir Ian McKellen was born on this day in 1939 in Burnley in Lancashire. For his 60th birthday former White House intern Monica Lewinsky gave him a scarf she had knitted herself in navy-blue chenille and grey wool. A gift tag read: 'Made especially by me, Monica'. The two had met at an Oscars ceremony, and President Clinton's occasional White House lover was a guest at the actor's birthday party.

A present from Auntie

Queen Mary was born in Kensington Palace on this day in 1867. Married to King George V (she had been engaged originally to George's younger brother Albert but he died at an early age of influenza), Mary became a keen collector of antiques. Her husband added to the collection one birthday with a present of a Fabergé egg – the Mosaic Egg commissioned originally from Fabergé by Tsar Nicholas II and subsequently confiscated during the Russian Revolution. Like all Fabergé eggs it contained its surprise, in this case

an enamel medallion decorated with profile portraits of the imperial children Olga, Tatiana, Maria, Anastasia and Alexis. Delighted though Mary must have been with her egg, it was a present on her 80th birthday that ranks as one of the most unusual ever given to any member of any royal family. The BBC enquired of Buckingham Palace what Queen Mary might like to listen to on her birthday. Amongst the requests – and this one

came from Queen Mary herself – was something from the pen of Agatha Christie. So the BBC commissioned Christie to write a 30-minute radio play, which she called *Three Blind Mice*. It was broadcast on the Light Programme at 8.00 p.m. on 30 May 1947. What neither Queen Mary nor Christie herself could have foreseen was that her birthday present was to make theatrical history. Soon after the broadcast, someone suggested to Christie that she turn it into a short story, which in turn gave Christie the idea of expanding the 30-minute radio play into a full-length stage play. Queen Mary's *Three Blind Mice* became *The Mousetrap*, which opened in London's West End in November 1952 and is still running today.

27 MAY

A dove on the wing

Henry Kissinger, who was Richard Nixon's national security adviser and then secretary of state, was born on 27 May 1923 in Bavaria to Jewish parents whose family took their name from the town of Bad Kissingen. In 1974 he was shuttling his diplomatic skills between Syria and Israel at the time of his birthday – a period that brought despair and hope in equal measure. Things were not going well in the Syrian capital on 26 May and his mood was not helped by the news that the Soviet foreign minister, Andrei Gromyko, was to visit Damascus the next day. 'I could have wished myself a better present,' Kissinger wrote in his memoir. When his birthday arrived he was greeted with an enormous cake organized by the embassy staff, and set off to bid farewell to President Assad, believing he had failed to reconcile the differences between the Syrians and the Israelis. Assad was walking Kissinger to the door when he suddenly stopped in his tracks. The Syrian leader was playing brinkmanship for all it was worth, and, invoking the personal relationship with the American, gave him one small offering to take back to the Israelis to keep the talks alive. 'I had received the best birthday present of my life; if not peace in the Middle East, then at least the absence of war for long enough to give diplomacy a chance.' Nearly 40 years on and diplomacy is still having to take its chances in that divided and unhappy part of the world.

Also born on 27 May (in 1966) was Heston Blumenthal, the molecular gastronomist who brought snail porridge and bacon-and-egg ice cream to the tables of his Michelin-starred Fat Duck restaurant in the Berkshire village of Bray. Voted the world's best restaurant in 2005, the Fat Duck opened its doors in August 1995 and gained its third Michelin star in less than ten years. Blumenthal's fascination with food began on a family holiday to France when he was still a teenager, but it was a book from his parents on his 19th birthday that set the style for his very particular culinary inventions: *On Food and Cooking: The Science and Lore of the Kitchen* by Harold McGee, the American writer on culinary science, inspired the aspiring young chef to embark on a chemistry-led quest for new ways of tickling our taste buds. Another birthday present twenty years later – a CD of sound effects from a television producer – led to one of the Fat Duck's more recent innovations: a complex fish dish accompanied by an MP3 player playing sounds of the sea. The senses, Blumenthal maintains, work together, and the sounds of the sea enhance the taste of the fish.

28 MAY

It should not happen to a snake

Rhianna Blackthorn runs an Australian wildlife rescue service. On a Sunday morning in 2005 she received a phone call from a man worried about a snake. He had apparently been given the snake, a coastal carpet python, as a birthday present the previous day, 28 May, but had became concerned for its welfare and called the rescue service. Rhianna collected the snake and named it 'Happy Birthday'.

About to return it to its native Queensland, Rhianna found a nasty lump near the animal's vent, so she took it to the vet who decided the lump was calcified faeces and gave the animal an enema. A week later another lump appeared, which turned out to be a rock-hard lump of rabbit fur. Enema number two. Happy Birthday remained in care for a further week until all signs of constipation had gone.

The wrong kind of time on his hands

John Fitzgerald Kennedy was born on this day in Brookline, Massachusetts in 1917. His least cherished birthday present was probably the gold Rolex watch given to him on his 45th birthday by Marilyn Monroe. She had inscribed it 'Jack, with love as always from Marilyn. May 29th 1962', and around it had wrapped a love poem entitled 'A Heartfelt Plea on Your Birthday'. Monroe apparently handed it to Kennedy's aide Kenneth O'Donnell, asking him to hand it over when the moment was right. When he tried to do so, Kennedy told O'Donnell to get rid of it. Unaware of the slight, Monroe went on to sing 'Happy Birthday, Mr President' at the birthday bash in Madison Square Garden. A much more treasured birthday present, from a more innocent age, was the sail boat his parents gave him for his 15th birthday: 26 ft long and made entirely of wood, the *Victura* was a life-long love. He taught his wife Jackie to sail in it, and it was the subject of countless Oval Office doodles, not least during times of crisis. A small sailing boat was amongst the doodles Kennedy drew on a piece of hotel notepaper the night before he was shot in Dallas.

Arms and the man

Tsar Peter I of Russia, popularly known as Peter the Great, was born on 30 May 1672. As a boy he liked to invent and play rather complicated war games with his friends, who were persuaded to form mock regiments. In a clear case of misguided parental indulgence, Peter was given some real guns for his 11th birthday with the result, according to some accounts of his life, that in one of his mock battles 24 young men died. The deaths were glossed over, and Peter continued to behave irresponsibly given half the chance. On his travels through Europe at the end of the 17th century, primarily to glean as much knowledge as he could about new technologies, especially in respect of shipbuilding and navigation, Peter stayed in Deptford at a house that belonged to the writer and diarist John Evelyn. Peter and his friends apparently trashed the house, and ruined Evelyn's prized holly hedge by staging races that involved pushing people in wheelbarrows through it. The king's surveyor Sir Christopher Wren was asked to report on the damage and recommended that £350 be paid to Evelyn in compensation.

Dead poet's society

American poet Walt Whitman was born on this day in 1819. He was surprised and delighted when £10 arrived unexpectedly on his 68th birthday from two admirers in the north of England. John Johnston, a doctor, and J.W. Wallace, a 33-year-old architect's assistant, had formed a Whitman Appreciation Society in the Lancashire mill town of Bolton. With their £10 was a note that read: 'We, two friends chiefly united by our common love of you, wish to congratulate you on your birthday and express to you personally our very best wishes and love.'

On this same day, John Prescott, the croquet-playing deputy prime minister to Tony Blair, was born in 1938, the son of a railway signalman. He was for a time secretary of state for the environment, and in this role had been involved in negotiations to create the Kyoto treaty on cutting greenhouse-gas emissions. On his birthday in 2002 he got an early-morning telephone call. He was told the Japanese foreign minister wanted to talk to him. Ms Kawaguchi began by wishing Mr Prescott a happy birthday and went on to say she had a birthday present for him. It was a real surprise, not just for the birthday boy but for the world at large. Japan, she said, had decided to ratify the treaty. Australia followed at the end of 2007. The United States has yet to do so.

APR

MAY

JUNE

1 Gerald Scarfe	2 Vera Howarth	3 Rafael Nadal
8 Paul Burrell	9 Eric Hobsbawm	10 Prince Philip / Judy Garland
15 Belinda Lee	16 Enoch Powell	17 John Ross
22 Billy Wilder	23 Napoleon Bonaparte	24 Sir John Ross
29 Bernhard of Lippe-Biesterfeld / Anne-Sophie Mutter	30 Allegra Versace	1 Diana, Princess of Wales

4 King George III	**5** Grand Duchess Anastasia	**6** Walter Handforth / Frau Rommel / Henry Allingham	**7** Jessica Tandy
11 Julia Margaret Pattle	**12** Anne Frank	**13** W. B. Yeats	**14** Donald Trump
18 Thabo Mbeki / Sir Paul McCartney	**19** Boris Johnson	**20** Errol Flynn / Nicole Kidman	**21** Prince William
25 George Orwell	**26** Mikhail Khodorkovsky	**27** Ruth Parasol	**28** A.A. Gill
2 Jerry Hall	**3** Leoš Janáček	**4** King Taufa'ahau Tupou IV of Tonga	**5** Sir Paul Smith

Good intentions

Gerald Scarfe, the cartoonist as well known to fans of the band Pink Floyd as he is to readers of the *Sunday Times*, was born in Hampstead on 1 June 1936. On the other side of London lived the caricaturist Ronald Searle, and Scarfe, by the time he had reached his teens, decided that he too wanted to be a cartoonist. So he would get on his bike and cycle across London with the intention of asking Searle how to get started. He thought carefully about what he was going to say, but by the time he arrived his courage failed him and he stood at the door unable to ring the bell. He would then ride around in circles before going home. When he met Searle many years later he recounted the story, and some time after this Scarfe's wife, the actress and cake-maker Jane Asher, arranged a surprise birthday lunch to which she invited the Searles – who brought a parcel for Scarfe containing a door bell mounted on a block of marble. With it was a note that read 'Please Ring Me Any Time'.

Let them eat cake

Vera Howarth was born on 2 June 1908. For her 98th birthday the family gave her a cake. Well, they did not exactly give her the cake, they put it in front of her and then took it away again. The seven-tier fruitcake had been made by her mother for her wedding to her father in 1895. They did not eat it all and kept what remained in a tin. It kept pretty well, and Vera's parents apparently ate a slice on their golden wedding anniversary at the end of the Second World War. But since then it has not been touched – except on birthdays, and then only for show. Probably would not have done Vera's teeth much good.

JAN
FEB
MAR
APR
MAY
JUNE
JULY
AUG
SEPT
OCT
NOV
DEC

3 JUNE

Game, set and a birthday present

It was a gift for the sports writers. Rafael Nadal beat Roger Federer in
the semi-final of the French Open on his 19th birthday in 2005, and
the hacks could not resist hailing it a 'birthday present'. Nadal went on
to beat Mariano Puerta in the final. Federer and Nadal met in the final
at Wimbledon in 2006, 2007 and 2008, leaving sports writers
searching for superlatives to describe the quality of the tennis.

4 JUNE

Guarding against morning madness

King George III of England was born on this day
in 1738. For his 66th birthday he received an
ingenious present from his five youngest daughters.
The silver-gilt egg-boiler was just the thing for an
excitable man in search of an effortless breakfast
but incapable of boiling an egg. The boiler was
placed on the table with the water already at
boiling point, and the king would then
open the double lid and place the
egg inside. The water was kept on
the boil by a lamp below, and the
timer on the lid ensured the perfect
cooking time. The result? Sanity
prevailed – during breakfast at least.

Boy wanted, preferably a ball boy

Anastasia, the youngest of Tsar Nicholas II's four daughters, was a disappointment – not because of her looks or her character, but because she was not a boy. She was born on 5 June 1901 at Peterhof, and her parents had to wait two more years for a son and heir. Anastasia was a bright and lively child with a charm that could be turned on and off. When it was turned off she could be quite unpleasant. She was also competitive, and tried very hard to beat her siblings at any and every opportunity. According to the diaries of her sister Maria, Anastasia was given a table tennis set for her birthday: 'Shvybz [Anastasia's nickname] got a ping-pong as a present for her birthday – that is a table-tennis [sic]. And we played it with her. It was very tiresome as we had to lie on the floor all the time to look for and pick up the balls.' There are still those who believe that Anastasia somehow escaped when the family was murdered by the Bolsheviks in 1918. But there is scant evidence to support these claims. Anastasia was just 17 when she was shot.

Life vest

D-Day, the day when Allied forces stormed the Normandy beaches, took place on 6 June 1944. The day was to produce many remarkable stories, of which two in particular are remarkable for very different reasons. The first involves Walter Handforth, a Royal Navy reservist who was in command of one of the landing craft. He was on the bridge while his ship was disgorging its men and machines. Too busy directing the landing operation, he failed to notice snipers in the Arromanches lighthouse. With commendable skill one of the snipers managed to hit Handforth in the chest. He went down, pulled himself back up and was shot again. And as he fell back the second time another bullet caught him in the chest. Yet he suffered only bruises and shock. His mother, with foresight that can only be described as divine, had given him a bullet-proof vest for his 21st birthday. His ship's heavy machine-guns destroyed the lighthouse before the German snipers could do any real damage.

In charge of German troops in northern France at the time was Field Marshal Rommel, and it seems no less remarkable that on this day of all days he managed to remember his wife's birthday. Not only did he remember it, but he had somehow got her a pair of handmade grey suede shoes – one of the more curious footnotes to the history of D-Day.

6 June is also the birthday of Henry Allingham, who celebrated his 110th birthday in 2006 to become the oldest surviving veteran of the First World War. Gordon Brown, who was chancellor of the exchequer at the time, went to see him with a message from the Queen and a bottle of House of Commons whisky: Allingham likes to attribute his longevity to 'cigarettes, whisky and wild, wild women'. On 6 June 2008 Allingham, Europe's oldest living man, celebrated his 112th birthday; the RAF's Battle of Britain Memorial Flight performed a fly-past in his honour.

7 JUNE

PPE

American actress Jessica Tandy, best known for her title role in the movie *Driving Miss Daisy*, was born on this day in 1909. Her 80th birthday fell while she was making the film on location in Atlanta, and to celebrate the event the cast of the movie clubbed together and gave her a pair of Paloma Picasso earrings.

The rock's box

A certain Paul Burrell was born on this day in 1958. As a humble butler, Burrell became Princess Diana's 'rock'. One of her birthday presents to him was an oval ceramic pill-box on which was inscribed a 'D' with a coronet above it. Burrell added it to items being auctioned at a charity ball at the Regent Beverly Wilshire hotel on Rodeo Drive in Los Angeles in March 1998. In a splendidly royal gesture, the woman who bought it immediately returned it to Burrell.

Berlin bicycle

Eric Hobsbawn, the Marxist historian and writer, was born on this day in Alexandria in 1917, and was brought up in Vienna and Berlin. By the age of 14 he was an orphan. His mother's last birthday present to him was what he describes as 'a very cheap second-hand bike', which was apparently a cause of considerable shame as he rode it across Berlin to school each day. Despite his later political beliefs, as a teenager Hobsbawm was clearly as status-conscious and materialistic as any boy his age.

Royal gods

His Royal Highness Prince Philip, Duke of Edinburgh was born on the Greek island of Corfu in 1921. Why Corfu? Because his grandfather was King George I of Greece and his parents happened to be on their summer holidays in Corfu at the time. The people of Corfu, represented by the mayor and the chairman of the city council, along with Queen Olga, are his godparents. No, he does not get birthday presents from each and every islander. He does, however, get presents from islanders on the other side of the world. The villagers of Yaohnanen on Tanna, one of the many islands that make up the South Pacific state of Vanuatu, worship Prince Philip as a god, believing him to be the son of an ancient spirit. It is unclear how the prince's cult-like status arose. 'You must tell King Philip that I'm getting old and I want him to come and visit me before I die,' the village chief told a reporter in 2007. The chief will know that the prince is no spring chicken either, and will probably have to make do with another framed portrait of his god.

Frances Ethel Gumm was also born on this day in 1922, but far away from Corfu – in Grand Rapids, Minnesota. One can never be sure about these things but if she had not changed her name to Judy Garland, things might just have turned out a little differently. Ms Gumm was given a first edition of L. Frank Baum's *The Wonderful Wizard of Oz* for her 16th birthday in 1938, and with it a contract to play Dorothy Gale in the film version of the book. Ms Garland made the song 'Over The Rainbow' her own, and went on to a glittering film and recording career. But she spoiled Hollywood's liking for happy endings – or rather Hollywood spoiled it for her. In company with a number of other teenage stars she was given drugs to help her keep up with the hectic schedules of film making. She became addicted and died in London of an apparent overdose of sleeping pills at the age of 47.

Portraits in a chicken coop

Julia Margaret Pattle was born in British India in 1815. Her father was a civil servant in Bengal and her mother a French aristocrat. At the age of 23 she married Charles Cameron, a man twenty years her senior, and when he retired they returned to England. They had five children of their own and adopted a sixth. It was on her 48th

birthday that her eldest daughter Julia and son-in-law Charles gave her a camera. At home on the Isle of Wight, she converted the coal hole into a darkroom and the glass-enclosed chicken house into a studio, and produced some of the most enduring portraits of the Victorian era. In a letter to her friend Sir John Herschel she wrote: 'My aspirations are to ennoble photography and to secure for it the character and uses of High Art by combining the real and ideal, sacrificing nothing of Truth by all possible devotion to Poetry and beauty.' She was true to her word, and we have a lot to thank her for.

The 16-year-old Ellen Terry in a photograph probably taken with Julia Margaret Cameron's 48th birthday present.

Prison record

Anne Frank was born on this day in 1929. For her 13th birthday her parents gave her a diary. Anne and her family spent just over two years during the Nazi occupation of Holland hiding in an annexe of her father's Amsterdam office. It was during this period that Anne filled the pages of her birthday present. In 1944 the hiding place was discovered and with her elder sister Margot she was taken first to Auschwitz and then to Bergen-Belsen. The two sisters died there of typhus. But their father Otto survived the camps and returned to Amsterdam to find Anne's diary strewn across the office floor. The diary was first published in 1947 and has since sold more than 6 million copies. Not published were five pages torn out by Otto Frank: they apparently contain passages critical of Anne's mother.

1 3 J U N E

The Kelmscott *Chaucer*

The Irish poet William Butler (W.B.) Yeats was born in Sandymount, County Dublin on this summer's day in 1865. Yeats had a number of patrons, among them Lady Augusta Gregory, who collaborated with him on a number of his plays, and in setting up the Irish Literary Theatre (the precursor of Dublin's Abbey Theatre). She it was who organized a collection for a surprise birthday present for Yeats – a copy of the richly illustrated Kelmscott *Chaucer*. It was one of the greatest achievements of William Morris's Kelmscott Press, and Yeats thought it the most beautiful book in the world.

'You're fired!'

Donald Trump owns a lot of Manhattan – something approaching 20 million square feet of it. Some of the very best of New York's prime real estate is under his belt. In addition he owns casinos, golf courses (he controversially plans a couple for the northeast of Scotland) and a share in the three biggest beauty pageants in America. He also produced and starred in *The Apprentice*, the wildly successful American reality television show that earned him a star on Hollywood's Walk of Fame. (The show has been copied in Britain with Sir Alan Sugar, who owns a lot of property in London's West End, in the hot seat, delivering the catchphrase 'You're fired' with as much audience-grabbing heartless finality as his American counterpart.) Donald Trump was born on this day in New York in 1946, and went to work in his father's real-estate business after studying economics and finance at Wharton Business School. His father and Wharton failed somewhere along the line because by the early 1990s Trump Jr was facing bankruptcy. But their fight-back strategies seemed to work, and the consummate deal-maker clawed his way to the top again. One of Trump's employees, John Perry, could be forgiven for thinking that the boss was back in his television role when he fired him during his 61st birthday party in Atlantic City. But this was reality without the TV.

Perry was forced to step down and his number two, Mark Juliano, given his job. Warning! If you work for Trump, watch your back when his birthday comes around.

15 JUNE

Papal intervention

Belinda Lee was born in Budleigh Salterton, a Flanders and Swann kind of town on the south coast of Devon. Her father was a former army captain, her mother a florist, and she went to a very proper *gals'* school. So how on earth did she end up mixing it with the blonde bimbos of the silver screen? It was her curve-hugging dresses rather than her acting skills that found her curtsying with difficulty in royal line-ups alongside Marilyn Monroe, Jayne Mansfield, Diana Dors and all the other red-carpet cleavage to whom she was often compared. She married Cornel Lucas, the Rank Organization's stills photographer, but within four years met an Italian prince, Filippo Orsini, who was married with two sons and worked at the Vatican. They began a liaison, the gossip became deafening and the Pope was moved to condemn the affair and finally ordered Prince Orsini to stay away from the starlet. Distraught, Belinda and the prince made a suicide pact, both taking sleeping pills, but this seems to have been no more than a dramatic gesture. The couple recovered both health and spirits, and Belinda appeared at Cannes with Orsini in tow, turning up in a very smart car. This, it turned out, had been given to her by her husband as a birthday present. Two days later Lucas started divorce proceedings. Ms Lee died in a car accident in 1961.

16 JUNE

A gentleman and a scholar

Enoch Powell was the son of schoolteachers. He was born in Birmingham on 16 June 1912, and after graduating from Cambridge University, at the age of just 25 gained a professorship in Greek at the

Gifts of musical compositions

- John Adams's *Lollapalooza* (19 January)
- Michel Legrand's 'Rachel' (24 February)
- Rossini's annual birthday piece for his dog (29 February)
- A polonaise written by an 11-year-old Chopin (1 March)
- Fauré's *Dolly Suite* (12 May)
- Janáček's wind sextet *Youth* (3 July)
- Percy Grainger's 'Country Gardens' (8 July)
- Berg's violin concerto (31 August)
- Schumann's symphony in D minor (13 September)
- Shostakovich's 2nd violin concerto (30 September)
- A specially adapted version of 'The Lady is a Tramp', sung by Sinatra (12 December)
- Wagner's *Siegfried Idyll* (25 December)

University of Sydney. The strength of his intellect was to leave others in the shade. After a distinguished war record – he was the youngest man to hold the rank of brigadier – he entered politics and became the Conservative Member of Parliament for a new constituency in Wolverhampton. The defining moment in his career came on a Saturday in April 1968 when he made a speech in Birmingham about immigration and Labour's proposed anti-discrimination laws. Powell, a fine orator and a classics scholar, quoted Virgil's prediction of war, saying that he seemed to see 'the River Tiber foaming with much blood'. The 'rivers of blood' speech was to prove Powell's undoing. Edward Heath sacked him from his job as shadow defence spokesman, and he was never given a senior post again. He left the Conservatives because they were about to take Britain into the Common Market, and joined the Ulster Unionists instead, serving the constituents of South Down from 1974 until 1987. The silver salver he was given as an 80th birthday present described his character with just four words: 'Scholar, Poet, Soldier, Statesman'.

1 7 J U N E

Shoot to thrill

John Ross was born on this day in 1957. He lives in Missouri. He had what he describes as a life-changing experience on his 14th birthday when his uncle gave him a .44 Magnum Smith & Wesson revolver. The teenager already owned a .22 Smith & Wesson. Mr Ross has grown up. Or maybe he hasn't. Articles on his website include: '30 years of loading the .44 Magnum' and 'Defensive Firearms Advice for Newbies'. He offers private machine-gun shoots. The list of weaponry available to punters includes Thompson, Sterling and Lanchester sub-machine-guns; AK47 and M2 Carbine battle rifles; Glock machine pistols; and, under the heading 'Other Fun Stuff', Krupp 50 mm Mountain Cannons. Have a nice day, Mr Ross.

Will you still need me?

Thabo Mbeki, who inherited the presidency of South Africa from Nelson Mandela, and ex-Beatle Sir Paul McCartney were born within hours of each other on this day in 1942 – Mbeki in South Africa's Eastern Cape and McCartney in Liverpool. Sir Paul wrote 'When I'm Sixty-Four' for the Beatles' *Sergeant Pepper's Lonely Hearts Club Band* album, which the group recorded at London's Abbey Road studios in 1967.

When I get older losing my hair
many years from now

It was almost 40 years later, when Sir Paul himself was approaching his 64th birthday and still had plenty of hair, that the same studios were the venue for a second and secret recording of the song. Sir Paul had just parted from his second wife Heather Mills, and his three children from his marriage to Linda Eastman – Mary, Stella and James – reckoned their father needed cheering up. So they slipped unnoticed into the studios, and with the lyrics of 'When I'm Sixty-Four' re-written for them by Giles Martin, the son of the Beatles' producer Sir George Martin, the family made their own recording of the song. When they gathered at Sir Paul's home in Sussex on the birthday itself (*'birthday greeting, bottle of wine …'*), the special present was slipped into the tape deck – and Sir Paul had his answer to the question he had posed all those years ago.

Stuff

Alexander Boris de Pfeffel Johnson was born on 19 June 1964 in New York, which did nothing to get in the way of his becoming the quintessential Eton- and Oxford-educated eccentric Englishman. With his mop of untidy blond hair and upper-class airs, he seemed

eminently suited to represent the blazers and twin-sets of Henley-upon-Thames in Parliament, but less obviously qualified to be London's mayor. He has a habit of having his bicycles stolen, and as one wag put it, 'If he can't look after his bicycles how on earth is he going to look after London?' That aside, Johnson, with typical eloquence, recalls his most treasured birthday present: 'a large can of John Bull homebrew lager stuff'. It seems he first gave it to his brother Leo 20 years ago, who retaliated by giving it back the following year. Apparently the two Johnson boys have been sending the can back and forth on birthdays ever since, the receiver forgetting it is coming and the sender watching in anticipation as the wrapping paper is torn away. It seems that neither has been brave enough to sample the can's contents – not even to celebrate Boris's mayoral victory over Ken Livingstone.

20 JUNE

My friend the Baron

Not a lot of people know this: Hollywood has a cricket club. Founded just over 75 years ago by the actor and cricketer Charles Aubrey Smith, who played for Sussex and England, it still flourishes, with former test players not infrequently taking the field. Douglas Fairbanks Jr, P.G. Wodehouse and Boris Karloff were all members, and every English newcomer was eagerly recruited whether or not they could hold a bat. On his arrival in Hollywood, Laurence Olivier found a cryptic note from Aubrey Smith waiting for him on his arrival in Hollywood: 'There will be nets tomorrow at 9.00 a.m. I trust I shall see you there.' Errol Flynn – the swashbuckling, hard-drinking, womanizing Australian actor born on 20 June 1909 in Hobart, Tasmania – was also a member. The club did not gain much from Flynn's membership, but the studios that employed him had much to thank him for. Jack Warner, the head of Warner Brothers, marked one of Flynn's birthdays with a gift of a sterling-silver cigarette case with the inscription: 'My Friend the Baron – May we always share an open bottle and a good smoke. Happy Birthday, Jack.' The case was sold at auction in 1999 and fetched $1912. There is no evidence of anyone wanting to buy Flynn's cricket bat. Or, indeed, his box – that essential piece of armour that protects the batsman's vital parts.

This is also the birthday of Tom Cruise's wife of ten years, Nicole Kidman, born on this day in 1967. The couple divorced in 2001, and five years later, on her 39th birthday, Cruise somewhat perversely sent her a framed portrait of his baby daughter Suri, born to his new fiancée Katie Holmes. But she got a bunch of flowers from the media pack that had besieged her Sydney home – which proves, if proof were needed, that journalists are the good guys.

21 JUNE

For art's sake

Prince William was born on this day in 1982. For his 24th birthday his father, Prince Charles, gave him a range finder for the rifle he gave him when he celebrated his 21st birthday. Boys will be boys. More interestingly (at least if one is to believe the tabloids), his on-off girlfriend Kate Middleton, who like William had studied the History of Art, painted a picture of them in a nude embrace for his birthday.

Hot seat

As I was sitting in my chair,
I knew the bottom wasn't there,
Nor legs nor back, but I just sat.
Ignoring little things like that.

That little ditty by the American poet Hughes Mearns would have brought a smile to the lips of the brothers Eames. Charles and Ray Eames dedicated their lives to producing chairs with the most comfortable bottoms, the most elegant legs and the most ergonomically satisfying backs. Their first lounge chair and ottoman, produced in 1956, was a birthday present for their friend, the film director Billy Wilder, born on 22 June 1906. Wilder's 1959 comedy *Some Like it Hot*, which starred a very pregnant and forgetful Marilyn Monroe (Wilder had to stick prompt boards at strategic points all over the set), won the American Film Institute's accolade of funniest American film of all time. The Eames chair was already a star in its own right with a place in New York's Museum of Modern Art.

Not tonight or any night

Joséphine de Beauharnais was born on 23 June 1763 on the island of Martinique, and was already widowed when she met Napoleon Bonaparte in 1795. (Her husband the Vicomte de Beauharnais had been guillotined in the Place de la Concorde during the Reign of Terror.) There is no evidence whatsoever that Napoleon ever said 'Not tonight, Joséphine.' On the contrary, there is plenty of evidence to suggest Napoleon had sex on his mind rather a lot, and found body odours part of the erotic pleasure: 'I will return in five days. Stop washing,' he wrote to her on one occasion. (The celebrated and oft-quoted rebuff has nothing to do with the fact that his penis was for many years in the possession of a professor at Columbia University: it was not in the professor's hands until long after Napoleon had died.) Joséphine for her part had been a consummate lover: 'Your image and the memory of last night's intoxicating pleasures has left no rest to my senses,' Napoleon wrote to her soon after they met. But she was probably never in love with Napoleon in the way he was with her, and within two years of their marriage rumours of an affair all but destroyed his love for her. But nonetheless she did give him a birthday present that he always had with him in battle. *The Book of Fate* was a translated and bound edition of an oracle discovered in the royal tombs near Mount Libycus in Upper Egypt. There was a list of 32 questions to choose from, which Napoleon would turn to at times of crisis. It was not, however, a crisis that led to his penis parting company with his body. The emperor's member was, it seems, removed by the priest who performed the last rites. It found its way into the collection of military memorabilia assembled by John Lattimer, who taught at Columbia University and who also claimed to have Hermann Goering's suicide capsule. Other parts of Napoleon – namely pieces of his intestines – were once in the possession of the Royal College of Surgeons in London, but were lost in an air raid during the Second World War.

Did anyone check the sell-by date?

This is a strange tale about a can of beef – a widely travelled can of beef. According to museum records it began the first of many journeys in 1812, crossing the Atlantic to Bermuda. It somehow remained unopened and came back again. Six years later this same can was acquired by the explorer Sir John Ross. He took it with him on his first Arctic expedition – and brought it back again. Off it went again on his next expedition and back it came, still unopened, in 1833. By now it had clearly taken on some kind of talismanic importance, and Ross, born on 24 June in 1777, presented it to his local lairds, the Stair family of Lochinch Castle on White Loch in the far southwest of Scotland. Again it remained untouched until 1869 and the 21st birthday of the young Earl of Stair. A party was thrown to celebrate the coming of age and the tin ceremoniously opened. Each guest had a forkful of the contents and all survived to tell the tale.

Sir John Ross's can of beef was taken on three voyages of discovery – including two expeditions to the North Pole – between 1812 and 1833, before finally being consumed at a birthday party in 1869.

25 JUNE

Rats and a farm

Eric Arthur Blair was born on what was a sweltering summer's day in the part of India known now as Bihar. His father was in the civil service. It was 25 June 1903. A year later his mother brought young Eric back to England. He went first to a primary school in Henley-on-Thames, and then to Eton on a scholarship. In time the family moved to Suffolk, renting a house near the lighthouse in Southwold. Here Eric spent six months at a crammer working for the exams that would give him entry to the Indian Imperial Police Service. It was during this time that Eric, angry about the local population of rodents, sent a dead rat to the borough surveyor as a birthday present. The surveyor's reaction was never recorded, but the angry young man passed his exams and spent five years serving in Burma, an experience that inspired his first novel, *Burmese Days*. A period of poverty followed until he was commissioned to write about the mass unemployment in Yorkshire and Lancashire, and under his pen name George Orwell wrote *The Road to Wigan Pier*. *Animal Farm* followed in 1945, and then *Nineteen Eighty-Four* in 1949.

26 JUNE

It's his birthday, so go kill someone

Mikhail Khordorkovsky was born on this day in 1963. The head of Yukos, the Russian petroleum company, he was Russia's richest man until he was arrested in October 2003 on charges of tax evasion and sentenced to nine years imprisonment on 31 May 2005. Allegations of murder and attempted murder as well as tax evasion were levelled at Yukos shareholders and staff. Yukos and Khordorkovsky robustly denied all the charges. However, the murder of the mayor of Nefteyugansk, a town in an oil-producing region of Siberia, continues to raise eyebrows. The mayor had opposed Yukos's plans for expansion and was shot dead on Khodorkovsky's birthday. The killing in 1998 prompted the oligarch's critics to talk of the assassination as a birthday gift from one of his zealous supporters. It would seem that assassinations have become quite fashionable as birthday presents in Russia. When Anna Politkovskaya, the campaigning Russian journalist, was shot dead in 2006, commentators were quick to point out that the day of her murder, 7 October, was Vladimir Putin's birthday. A member of Putin's secret service, the FSB, was among those charged with her murder. Numerous conspiracy theories surrounded the murder of Alexander Litvinenko, the former Soviet spy poisoned in London with radioactive polonium-210. No one has so far tied the killing to anyone's birthday, but British police want the Russians to extradite Andrei Lugovoi, who they believe was responsible.

27 JUNE

Talking of sex ...

27 June 2005 was the day PartyGaming announced its offer price prior to launching on the London Stock Exchange. The company – then valued at around £5 billion – deals in online gaming, making most of its very substantial profits from online poker. PartyGaming was created by two people: Californian lawyer Ruth Parasol, who had already made a fortune from 'adult' websites; and an Indian software wizard called Anurag Dikshit. (And before anyone suggests that Dikshit and a a woman who used to be involved in the adult-entertainment industry are natural partners it should be pointed out that his name is pronounced 'Dixit'.) Ms Parasol, the eldest of three sisters, is the daughter of an eccentric Holocaust survivor who apparently likes to adorn his several boats with topless women. Legend has it that he started his daughter off in the adult-entertainment business by making her a birthday present of two of his phone-sex chat lines while she was still a teenager.

I can't eat THAT !

The British journalist, restaurant critic and TV reviewer A.A. Gill – known for his acerbic and even brutal wit – was born on this day in 1954. When the reformed addict (he used to be addicted to most things, he says) celebrated his 52nd birthday in 2006, his partner Nicola Formby came up with just the present for a sharp-tongued restaurant critic: a pile of crap. But this was no ordinary common-or-garden turd. This was a coprolite (*left*) – the fossilized faeces of a long-extinct turtle.

Worlds apart

They were both Germans, born on the same day in different eras and destined to lead very different lives. Bernhard of Lippe-Biesterfeld was born in Jena on the River Saale on 29 June 1911; Anne-Sophie Mutter was born in Rheinfelden in 1963. The German nobleman married into the Dutch royal family and as Prince Bernhard became consort to Queen Juliana, while Rheinfelden's prodigal daughter played the violin with the world's greatest orchestras. Bernhard brought shame on his queen and country by accepting bribes from the Lockheed Aircraft Company, which was selling fighter aircraft to the Dutch air force. Mutter charmed audiences from New York to Sydney. The musician had asked her parents for violin lessons as a present for her fifth birthday; they initially insisted she start with the piano but soon relented. Bernhard, who had been a Ferrari fan for most of his life, ordered a new one for his 88th birthday, although he was too old and too infirm to drive it. But the roar of its engine would still have been music to his ears.

30 JUNE

Working model

Gianni Versace and his sister Donatella were responsible for building up the enduring and hugely successful eponymous fashion brand. Gianni had a soft spot for Donatella's daughter Allegra, and left her half the Versace empire in his will. She came into possession of her inheritance on 30 June 2004, her 18th birthday – seven years after Gianni's tragic murder. Gianni added to the posthumous birthday present by giving her his villa on Lake Como and his townhouse in Manhattan. Allegra's father, Paul Beck, was formerly a male model. With her kind of money, he would not have to be a working model.

1 Diana, Princess of Wales	2 Jerry Hall	3 Leoš Janáček
8 Percy Grainger	9 Tai Shan	10 Julia Robinson
15 The Sultan of Brunei	16 H.H. Asquith	17 Angela Merkel / Camilla, Duchess of Cornwall
22 Bob Dole	23 Michael Foot	24 Jennifer Lopez
29 Jo Grimond / Benito Mussolini / Dan Hammarskjold / Jehangir Tata / Fernando Alonso	30 Arnold Schwarzenegger	31 J.K. Rowling

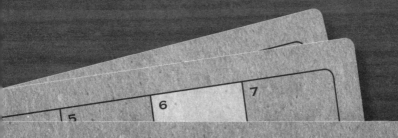

4 King Taufa'ahau Tupou IV of Tonga	5 Sir Paul Smith	6 George W. Bush	William Murray, 8th Earl of Mansfield and Mansfield
11 Giorgio Armani	12 Kirsten Flagstad	13 Hartmut Rausch	14 Jane Carlyle
18 Nelson Mandela	19 Veronica Berlusconi	20 Sir Edmund Hillary	21 Ernest Hemingway
25 Adnan Khashoggi	26 George Bernard Shaw	27 David Hughes	28 Karl Popper
1 Yves St Laurent	2 Paul Bedworth	3 Stanley Baldwin	4 Queen Elizabeth the Queen Mother

Egg on his face

Of all the fabulous presents Diana, Princess of Wales received during her lifetime, there is one birthday present that poses something of a mystery. According to her former butler and porous 'rock' Paul Burrell, there was a Fabergé egg box amongst her possessions in a dressing room, with a note attached to the effect that it had been a present from the Queen for her 20th birthday – which fell on this day in 1981, four weeks before she married Prince Charles. No doubt the Queen was at this stage still delighted with her future daughter-in-law, but the likelihood of her parting with one of her three Fabergé eggs was remote, to say the least. A Fabergé box, on the other hand, would have been entirely probable. One has to bear in mind that the coroner at the inquest into Diana's death, Lord Justice Scott Baker, did suggest in the strongest terms that Mr Burrell was not a reliable witness.

A very proper function

Jerry Hall was born a Texas girl in 1956 and married Mick Jagger in 1990 during a holiday on Bali. But the marriage turned out to have no legal basis. After the couple separated in 1999 Mick continued to give Jerry birthday presents. One year it was a rather nice and very sensible Peugeot 206 cabriolet with classy leather seats just a shade darker than her own skin. Ms Hall is now a global ambassador for an erectile dysfunction treatment produced by Bayer HealthCare. 'I'm working with Bayer HealthCare to encourage men to confront erectile dysfunction and take action,' she said. Let's get this clear. A pharmaceutical company wants to sell lots of pills to men who have a hard time (so to speak) getting an erection – so it thrusts the erotic charms of Jerry Hall in front of them and still expects them to need pills?

Cold comfort

The majority of the Czech composer Leoš Janáček's better known operas were written when he was well past 50, and he waited till he was 70 before writing a morale-boosting musical birthday present for himself: a wind sextet that he called *Youth*. Janáček was born in Hukvaldy, in what is now the Czech Republic, on 3 July 1854. He began his life in music as a choir boy, becoming a conductor by his late teens and then creating his own music school at Brno where, at the age of 27, he married Zdenka Schulzová, one of his piano pupils, who was only 15. The marriage was not a success and Zdenka even attempted suicide. Janáček was in his sixties when he produced the three operas, including *The Cunning Little Vixen*, for which he became famous. Some say the prodigious output of these later years can be put down to his love for a married woman 38 years his junior. He found time to write to her on an almost daily basis, but the long-distance and apparently platonic affair ended in a tragedy of operatic proportions. The object of his love, Kamila Stösslová, came to stay, bringing her husband and their 11-year-old son. The young lad went off exploring on his own and got lost. Janáček, now well into his seventies, joined the search party combing the woods. But the temperature had dropped sharply and in the rush to find the boy the composer failed to wrap up properly. The cold got to him, and he developed pneumonia and died. In so doing Janáček joined the brief but melancholy roll-call of celebrities who – despite not being mountaineers or polar explorers – have died of a chill. On 9 April 1626 the philosopher, statesman and essayist Francis Bacon died after contracting a chill while carrying out an experiment involving stuffing a dead chicken with snow to see whether it would delay putrefaction.

A king under canvas

King Taufa'ahau Tupou IV of Tonga – who stood 6 ft 5 in tall and weighed in at an impressive 31 stone 6 pounds – was born on this day in 1918 as the First World War was drawing to a close. He succeeded his mother in 1965, and was crowned on his birthday two years later. The king enjoyed the outdoor life, and in his later years took a fancy to Indian ceremonial tents – *shamianas*. The Indian high commissioner in Tonga, T.P. Sreenivasan, got to hear of the king's interest in tents and put his diplomatic skills to good use by securing the finest *shamiana* from Delhi. He then presented it to the king as a birthday present. His Majesty apparently lost little time in erecting it in the palace gardens and then threw a party to show it off.

The sweet smell of success

'Large, very fragrant, growth vigorous, bordering on carmine, flowers continuously.' That's how they describe Sir Paul Smith – or rather the new rose that bears his name, developed at the request of Lady Smith as a birthday present for her husband, the famous fashion designer, who was born on 5 July 1946. The rose was unveiled at the Chelsea Flower Show in 2006.

Intoxicating music

George W. Bush, America's 43rd president, was born on this day in New Haven, Connecticut in 1946. He was two when his parents moved to Texas, and 54 when he moved into the White House. Tony Blair gave him a Burberry sweater for his 60th birthday. 'Awfully thoughtful of you,' Bush told Blair. Nintendo, the computer games firm, cheekily gave the president a DS Lite and a copy of the popular Brain Age game designed to keep the brain active and fight mental fatigue. According to the *New York Times*, his two daughters gave him an MP3 player for his birthday in 2005. Dubbed 'iPod One', it contains a lot of country music, some Van Morrison and songs by the country singer and recovering alcoholic George Jones. Bush has admitted to 'drinking too much' in the past, but gave up alcohol altogether when he turned 40.

7 JULY

The earl and the orchid

William David Mungo James Murray, 8th Earl of Mansfield and Mansfield, born on 7 July in 1930, followed the typical career path of Britain's upper classes (whatever their academic or military aptitudes): Eton, Oxford (Christ Church) and a Guards regiment – in his case the Scots Guards. It was for his birthday in 1971, when he was still just plain Lord Scone, that his parents gave him an orchid, whereupon the earl proceeded to build the largest collection of orchids in Britain at Scone Palace, his seat in Perthshire, and to win medals at the World Orchid Conference in Glasgow.

8 JULY

Mummy's boy

The Australian composer Percy Grainger was born in a suburb of Melbourne on this day in 1882. His family took him to Germany where he studied music in Frankfurt before moving to the United States at the outbreak of the First World War. There he joined a US army band, and it was in his barracks that he composed 'Country Gardens' as a birthday present for his mother Rose, with whom he was to live in White Plains, New York. (His father, a drunken architect who contracted syphilis – and passed it on to Percy's mother – left them during a trip to London.) Rose was the centre of Percy's life, and there were even rumours of an incestuous relationship, although these were never substantiated. As a child he had written that he thought his mother was God. But their relationship was to end suddenly and tragically when Rose committed suicide by jumping from the building in which Percy's manager had her office. The composer became an American citizen and went on to write 'Early One Morning' and 'The Jolly Sailor' amongst a host of gentle folk songs – not perhaps the sort of repertoire you would expect from a sadomasochist with racist leanings. Although a friend and admirer of both the African-American Duke Ellington and the Jewish George Gershwin, Grainger was a believer in the superiority of the blond and blue-eyed northern European, and rejected conventional Italian musical directions, such as *crescendo* (which he replaced with 'louden'), on the grounds that they were non-Anglo-Saxon. As regards his bedroom activities, he photographically documented his flagellatory sessions with considerable care, and when he endowed a museum at the University of Melbourne dedicated to himself, he not only donated all his manuscripts and instruments, but also his photographic collection. Not to mention 83 whips.

9 JULY

Eats shoots and leaves

Tai Shan (*above right*) was born on this day in 2005, weighing just four ounces. The panda's parents, on loan from China to the zoo in Washington DC, had delighted her keepers by producing an heir. Pandas eat shoots and leaves, so on Tai Shan's first birthday the zoo produced a present in the form of a grand frozen cake consisting of a very healthy mix of bamboo shoots, leaves, carrots, peas, beets and

apples. So popular had Tai Shan become with his American fans that shortly before his second birthday the Chinese ambassador in Washington, Zhou Wenzhong, announced, with slightly less formality than is customary in Chinese diplomats, that the panda loan agreement had been extended and that Tai Shan was free to remain with his American friends until the summer of 2009.

1 O JULY

Full-bodied

Jancis Robinson is one of Britain's most respected wine writers. Her first daughter Julia was born on this day in 1982, 'just', Mrs Robinson recalls, 'as the grapes in the vineyards of Château Margaux were swelling'. Mum clearly kept one eye on the harvest while the other doted on the bundle in her arms. And much good it did the bundle too. On Julia's first birthday her mother bought a case of the '82 Bordeaux for £295, in the certain knowledge that it would mature in both flavour and value. It did. Julia, however – penniless in her last year at university – was solely interested in its value. So Mrs Robinson sold the wine for a handsome profit and sent her daughter a birthday cheque for £3000.

For the love of Giorgio

Unlike most of his contemporaries who thought fashion was only of interest to women, Giorgio Armani began by designing clothes for men. He was born in Piacenza on this day in 1934 and began his student life studying medicine. But he rejected medicine in favour of photography, although he had to give up the latter when he was called up to do his national service. Back in civvie street he got a job as a window dresser and became hooked on fashion. He did a stint designing for Nino Cerruti and then went freelance, eventually creating his own label. He now heads a retailing empire second only in size to that of Ralph Lauren. He runs it from his 16th-century palace in Milan's Via Borgonuova. (He also has a nice little sideline in sushi, which he dispenses from his trendy Nobu bar.) When he turned 60, six of the world's leading fashion buyers, not usually known for their generosity, clubbed together to buy him a birthday present – a very fine silvered bronze table crafted by the French art deco furniture designer Jacques-Émile Ruhlmann. The table's legs were some of the very few legs in Milan that year not squeezed into Armani jeans.

On a shy note

Her mother was a pianist, her father a conductor, so no surprises that Kirsten Flagstad made music her life. And having been given the score of Richard Wagner's opera *Lohengrin* for her tenth birthday, it was even less of a surprise that she chose opera in particular. Born in Hanmar, Norway on this day in 1895, Flagstad spent the first 18 years of her professional career in Scandinavia, and then created a sensation on her first trip abroad in 1935, singing Wagner at New York's Metropolitan Opera. But success never rid her of a desperate shyness, and she would regularly leave critics, friends and well-wishers disappointed by barring the door to her dressing room, and slipping away through a side door at the end of a performance.

Pictures at an exhibition

13 July 2007 saw the opening of a very unusual exhibition in Frankfurt. The Portikus Gallery, located in a fine old building on an island in the River Main, presented for the first time publicly the extraordinary collection of Hartmut and Helga Rausch. Herr Rausch and his wife Helga are joint caretakers at Frankfurt's Städelschule, one of Germany's leading art schools. When Hartmut reached 50, two of the school's artists, Thilo Heinzmann and Hans Petri, each gave him one of their paintings as a birthday present. The gesture caught on and for the past 15 years students – and teachers – have been giving their caretakers examples of their work on their birthdays. The couple's apartment has become a repository of unique and highly contrasting works of art from more than 200 students, graduates and lecturers, all of whom have come to regard Herr and Frau Rausch as caretakers not only of their school, but of their emotional and spiritual wellbeing as well. Hartmut says he has no intention of selling any of the works and so has no idea what they might be worth.

Better late than never

The marriage between Jane Welsh and Thomas Carlyle was not a particularly happy one. Jane, born in Haddington, East Lothian on 14 July 1801, married the great writer in 1826, and letters between them suggest that while there was affection there were also frequent quarrels. And the marriage was childless. It was not until the death of Jane's mother – who had always sent birthday presents to her daughter – that Thomas was prompted to start giving presents to his wife. His first, for her 41st birthday, was a rather fine marble washstand for their house in Chelsea. Robert Browning, Tennyson, Dickens, Ruskin and George Eliot were all regular visitors to the house, and would have scrubbed up in Jane's birthday present before lunch.

The sky's the limit

The Sultan of Brunei, one of the world's richest men and ruler of one of its smallest states, was born in 1946 and crowned in 1968. He is not only the oil-rich country's head of state but also its prime minister and finance minister. He does not want for much. His possessions tend to be in multiples. Aeroplanes, cars, homes, palaces, hotels, yachts and wives are all in the plural. Yet for all his self-indulgences he has moments of generosity. On his birthday on 15 July 1998 he gave his people – 80 per cent of the nation's working population are employed by his government – a massive 14 per cent pay rise. But his gift to his subjects pales into insignificance against the birthday present he gave his daughter when she turned 18. The A340 Airbus was painted in her favourite colours. The 'flyaway' price tag for a basic A340 is £161 million. Of the 386 A340s sold by Airbus Industries up until October of 2006, seven were sold privately, but Airbus declined to say how many of these were earmarked as birthday presents.

The poet physician

On 16 July 1913 Britain's prime minister, H.H. Asquith, did rather a strange thing, even for a Liberal politician: he appointed a doctor to the post of Poet Laureate. Robert Bridges, the only medical graduate to have held the post, was born in Kent on 23 October 1844. He went to Eton and Oxford and then to St Bartholomew's Hospital Medical School. He did practise as a physician for some years, but retired early to devote his time to writing – although he never really established himself as a poet and certainly never became well known.

The National Portrait Gallery has a photograph of him, taken by Lady Ottoline Morrell, sitting at a clavichord given to him for his 80th birthday. No one seems to know exactly who gave it to him or whether he could play it. George V was on the throne at the time, but there is little evidence that Bridges wrote much poetry for him or indeed for the state.

17 JULY

We don't want a jackass in the Chancellery

Germany's first female chancellor was born in Hamburg on this day in 1954. Her father, a Lutheran pastor, was given a church in the German Democratic Republic, so she grew up under Erich Honecker and the communists about 50 miles north of Berlin. For her birthday in 2002 Angela Merkel was given a jackass penguin by Christian Wulff, minister-president of Lower Saxony. Dr Merkel christened her gift Helmut – she had been a protégé of Helmut Kohl, German chancellor from 1982 to 1998 – and the baby penguin hatched after 38 days in an incubator. Having visited her birthday present in Hanover's zoo, Chancellor Merkel wisely left him in the care of his keepers.

Today is also the birthday of Camilla, Duchess of Cornwall. Her 60th birthday present from Prince Charles had eight woolly legs and an awful lot of wool. The ram and ewe belong to a rare breed of sheep, one that is kept under the watchful eye of the Rare Breeds Survival Trust, of which the prince is patron. The prince is also the founder the Mutton Renaissance Club. There may be a conflict of interest here.

BIG BOYS' (AND GIRLS') TOYS AS GIFTS

☆ A FAIRGROUND ROUNDABOUT (12 JANUARY)

☆ A FERRARI (25 MARCH, 29 JUNE, 8 NOVEMBER)

☆ AN ICE-CREAM VAN (19 APRIL)

☆ AN EVENING WITH MUHAMMAD ALI (3 MAY)

☆ A BOWLING ALLEY (6 MAY)

☆ A LIFE-SIZE MODEL OF BROOKE SHIELDS (29 AUGUST)

☆ A STEAM LOCOMOTIVE (24 SEPTEMBER)

☆ AN AIRBUS A-319 (1 NOVEMBER)

1 8 J U L Y

The man who made things easier

Nelson Mandela was born on this day in 1918. On his 85th birthday 85 children led by singer Yvonne Chaka Chaka sang 'Happy Birthday', and 17,842 well-wishers posted greetings on a birthday website. The message from Ruad Hendricks read: 'Happy Birthday, Sir. You made everything so much easier for us. Thank you. I love you.'

1 9 J U L Y

Viva Italia

Veronica Lario was born on this day in 1956. She was 35 when she married a man 20 years her senior, a billionaire who ran an Italian media empire as well as running the country. Silvio Berlusconi, re-elected for a third term as Italy's prime minister in April 2008, enjoys a bit of fun. For his wife's 50th birthday in 2006 Mr Berlusconi, then in opposition, arranged a surprise treat in Marrakesh, a secret so well kept that Mrs B believed her private jet was flying her to Spain. When the plane landed she was escorted, bemused, to the city's main square, the Djama el Fna, and up to the terrace of the Café de France. According to the Moroccan daily *Aujourd'hui Le Maroc*, she was enjoying her mint tea when the group of veiled Arab women at the next table began to get increasingly interested in her, to a degree that caused her some irritation. When she was about to get up and leave, the women removed their veils to reveal themselves as seven of Mrs Berlusconi's closest friends. Mrs Berlusconi was still in a state of endearing gullibility the following day – the day of her actual birthday. At dinner one member of a dance troupe – his head and face covered by a swirl of blue silk, took a particular interest in the birthday girl and invited her to dance. She refused, whereupon the music stopped. The rejected dancer fumbled beneath his robes and, with a flourish, produced a diamond necklace. The Berber dancer was, of course, Silvio Berlusconi himself, who had just flown in from Rome after a tense parliamentary debate on Afghanistan.

A climbing rose

Before Tenzing Norgay left the summit of Mount Everest on that May morning in 1953, the Sherpa left chocolates in the snow as an offering for the gods. Edmund Hillary left a cross given to him by the expedition leader John Hunt. Tenzing and Hillary, a New Zealander born on 20 July 1919, were the first to conquer Everest. James (now Jan) Morris was covering the climb for *The Times*, and timed the filing of his report – carefully coded to avoid others spoiling his scoop – so that it would appear in the newspaper on the very morning of Queen Elizabeth II's coronation. There are very few New Zealanders whose names are so indelibly etched in the chronicles of human endeavour, and yet it has taken 50 years for a New Zealand rose grower to name a new variety after Sir Edmund, who died early in 2008. It's a white rose with a touch of yellow at its centre. (Hillary Clinton also once claimed she was named after the heroic climber, but was forced into an embarrassing climb-down when it was pointed out that she was born six years before the Everest ascent.) The New Zealand rose nursery that produced the 'Sir Edmund Hillary' also offers a variety called 'The Birthday Present'. A Sir Edmund Hillary grafted onto a Birthday Present might be interesting.

Great stories, disastrous ending

Ernest Hemingway was born on this day in 1899 in Oak Park, Illinois. He was in his fifties when his fourth wife Mary, a correspondent with *Time* magazine, chose a rather nice sweater as a birthday present, which she had designed especially by Christian Dior. It was hand-knitted in a combination of wool and suede, and had a turtle neck. (Dior did not let her off lightly: the bill, when it came, cost her a month's housekeeping.) When the Canadian photographer Karsh came to photograph Hemingway at their home on Cuba, it was the sweater the photographer chose for his portrait (*below*). 'A true portrait,' Karsh said afterwards. 'The face of a giant cruelly battered by life, but invincible.' Perhaps 'invincible' was not quite right, as it was not long afterwards that Hemingway put the barrels of his Abercrombie and Fitch 12-bore in his mouth and pulled both triggers.

According to his wife, it was a wind-up

Republican politician Bob Dole is the man his fellow Kansans returned to the Senate time after time, and who led the Republicans on Capitol Hill from 1985 until 1996 – yet he failed on three occasions to win national office. Dole was born on 22 July 1923 in Russell, Kansas, where his father managed a creamery. During the Second World War, at the age of 19, he enlisted in the Reserve, and in 1945 found himself with the 10th Mountain Division in Italy, fighting the Nazis. He was hit by machine-gun fire, and the medics wrote an M (for morgue) on his forehead with his own blood. He survived, but with a useless right arm and with only two working fingers on his left hand. The injuries did not prevent him from teaching himself to drive, and he bought an automatic Chevrolet Celebrity. But the car had its challenges: Dole says that one of his most treasured birthday presents were the electric windows his wife Elizabeth had specially made and fitted to his much-loved Chevy.

Sporting chance

Michael Foot, leader of Britain's Labour Party from November 1980 to October 1983, was born on this day in 1913. He has been a life-long supporter of Plymouth Argyle Football Club and a director of the club for many years. The club left it a bit late, but for his 90th birthday they registered him as a player. His birthday present was a club shirt with the number 90 on the back.

Miss Jyotsana does her best

The pop singer and actress Jennifer Lopez was born on this day in 1969 in the Bronx. In Hollywood it can be difficult to separate truth from fiction – and not just on the screen. There are stories that Ms Lopez was paid more than a million dollars for a 40-minute gig at the birthday party in England of a Russian banker. There are also stories that her then boyfriend, the actor Ben Affleck, gave her a blue Bentley convertible for her 32nd birthday and then a Rolls Royce Phantom for her 33rd. For her birthday the following year, she got a lavatory seat. Not any old lavatory seat. It was made of plastic, but encased within the clear plastic – so protecting one of the most highly valued bottoms in the business – is an array of rubies, sapphires, pearls and a diamond. When inquiries were made at the Sulabh International Museum of Toilets in Delhi as to the truth or otherwise of this story, a very helpful Miss Jyotsana said she had a cutting about the precious toilet seat from the *Hindustan Times*. She said she also had a cutting about the gift in the *Daily Star* of London. 'But I am afraid I have no way of confirming the report,' she said. 'The *Daily Star* is a tabloid newspaper,' she added. Whatever the truth about the toilet seat, Affleck and Lopez split up shortly afterwards, blaming excessive media attention.

An arms dealer in the cosmos

Born in Mecca in 1935, Adnan Khashoggi is the son of a Turkish doctor who tended the Saudi royal family. Determined to start life at a pace, he was doing business deals while still at university in California. He went on to seek and attain the company of beautiful women, threw wildly extravagant parties, and became a regular at the world's top nightclubs, all on the back of the huge fortune he made from arms deals, mostly between American defence contractors and Arab governments, especially Saudi Arabia. His personalized McDonnell Douglas DC-8 aircraft is so brashly appointed as to make the Las Vegas Strip look positively understated. It is equipped with three bedrooms, chamois and silk banquettes, cut-glass goblets, and a dinner service with the initials 'A.K.' embossed in gold, while its cabin crew include a valet, a barber, a masseur and a chiropractor. There is also a map of the cosmos built into the ceiling of the aircraft's cabin, a present for his 50th birthday. It is all electric, with twinkling stars and glowing outlines of the constellations. Khashoggi is a Leo, and as the constellation Leo brightens, an outline of his image appears in the vault of heaven, flashing on and off.

Avoiding a calamity

George Bernard Shaw was born on this day in 1856. He loathed the idea of birthday presents. A note written by a member of his staff when he lived at Ayot St Lawrence reads: 'Mr Bernard implores his friends and readers not to celebrate his birthdays nor even mention them to him. It is easy to write one letter or send one birthday cake, but the arrival of hundreds of them together is a calamity that is not the less dreaded because it occurs only once a year.'

27 JULY

Marzipan men

David Hughes, born on this day in 1930, read English at Oxford, where he edited *Isis*, before going on to become first a journalist and then a novelist. In 1958 he married the Swedish actress Mai Zetterling, and for 17 years collaborated with her on films and plays, wrote travel books and taught himself photography. But living abroad did not agree with him so he returned to England, divorced Ms Zetterling and began to write novels – his best known and most successful work being *The Pork Butcher*, which appeared in 1985. In his early seventies he wrote a witty and thoughtful book called *The Hack's Tale*, about what he considered to be the failings of modern journalism. A cruise in the Mediterranean – a birthday present from his second wife Elizabeth – prompted him to search out Boccaccio, whom, with Chaucer and Froissart, he considered to be the sources of the modern media. (More importantly – at least to those with a sweet tooth – Boccaccio includes a passage in *The Decameron* where Ferondo refers to his wife as 'sweet as the sweetest honey, much more sugary than marzipan'.) Marzipan in the Middle Ages. Fantastic.

28 JULY

Shelf life

The distinguished philosopher Karl Popper, celebrated for his influential account of the scientific method, was born on this day in Vienna in 1902. Popper came to England via New Zealand, settling in Croydon on the southern outskirts of London. Still sprightly as he entered his tenth decade, Popper celebrated his 90th birthday on a summer's day in 1992. Friends and colleagues marked the occasion with an eclectic array of gifts – some scholarly, one edible. Eugene Yue-Ching Ho of Hong Kong's Institute of Economic Science presented him with a bound *festschrift*, put together with his colleague Pui-Chong Lund, comprising 12 essays, each written by a leading Chinese academic, on topics central to Popper's work. The philosopher's publisher sent a cake. The art historian Sir Ernst Gombrich and his wife came with the seven volumes of Mozart's letters, and there was an embroidered cushion from a Polish nurse. Last but not least, his secretary gave him a ladder to allow him access to the higher shelves of his very considerable library. A ladder? For a 90-year-old?

All about Fernando

A British Liberal, an Italian dictator, a Swedish mediator, an Indian industrialist and a Spanish racing driver were all born on 29 July. Jo Grimond was leader of Britain's Liberal Party from 1956 till 1967 (and briefly in a caretaker role in 1976); Benito Mussolini, who said once that 'The history of saints is mainly the history of insane people', was one of the founders of fascism and held power from 1922 until 1945 when he was captured and executed by communist partisans and then hung upside down at an Esso petrol station in Milan. Dag Hammarskjöld was the Swedish diplomat who, as secretary general of the United Nations during the Suez Crisis, dispatched a peace-keeping force (the model for all subsequent UN peacekeeping forces); and Jehangir Ratanji Dadabhoy Tata became the fourth chairman of the Indian industrial conglomerate which, in a nice reversal of colonial fortunes, now owns the British steel maker Corus as well as Tetley Tea, Rover and Jaguar. The Spanish racing driver is Fernando Alonso, who was born in Oviedo on 29 July 1981 and became the youngest driver to win the Formula One world championship. His team-mates when he was at Renault put together a video for his birthday. It is on You Tube, and it's brilliant.

Californian tractor

The man they call 'The Guvernator' – former Terminator 1 and 2 and the present governor of California Arnold Schwarzenegger – was born near Graz in Austria on this day in 1947. The Austrian postal service marked his 57th birthday by issuing a 1-euro stamp featuring his portrait

with the American and Austrian flags as background. Before that, in 2002, he was given a Hummer H2 for his birthday by General Motors. The Hummer H2 is a Chelsea tractor and some, averaging between 8 and 10 miles to the gallon. The governor already owned five Hummers. Schwarzenegger is keen to promote measures to reduce carbon emissions and combat global warming.

Harry who?

J.K. Rowling and Harry Potter were born on this day – Rowling in 1965, Potter on the same day some years later. Rowling was born in Chipping Sodbury, Potter was born somewhere else. For his 13th birthday he got a broomstick servicing kit from his thoughtful friend Hermione Granger. From the Weasleys' owl he got an equally useful pocket sneakoscope. And his creator got very rich and wrote lots more words and got even richer.

JAN FEB ... NE JULY AUG SEPT OCT NOV DEC

1 Yves St Laurent	**2** Paul Bedworth	**3** Stanley Baldwin
8 Ronnie Biggs	**9** Melanie Griffith	**10** Antonio Banderas
15 Ben Affleck	**16** Madonna	**17** Mae West
22 Leni Riefenstahl	**23** Natascha Kampusch	**24** Yasser Arafat
29 Michael Jackson	**30** Alexander Litvinenko	**31** Alma Schindler

4 Queen Elizabeth the Queen Mother	**5** Neil Armstrong	**6** Andy Warhol	**7** Charlize Theron
11 General Pervez Musharraf	**12** Queen Sirikit of Thailand	**13** Fidel Castro	**14** Peter Costello
18 Emily Carter	**19** Bill Clinton	**20** Slobodan Milošević	**21** Christopher Robin / Liam Howlett
25 Leonard Bernstein / Erich Honecker	**26** Prince Albert	**27** John Hay Whitney	**28** Sir John Betjeman
1 Lily Tomlin	**2** Jimmy Connors	**3** Fearne Cotton	**4** Beyoncé Knowles

Yves et Dior

Yves St Laurent, a man whose name has appeared on birthday presents received by wives, lovers, girlfriends, aunts, mothers, daughters, sisters and long-suffering secretaries without number, was born on this day in 1936 in Oran, Algeria. He was not yet 20 when he joined the fashion house of Christian Dior, and two years later contributed no fewer than 35 outfits to the 1957 Dior autumn collection. When all the fittings for the collection were finished, Dior took himself off for a rest cure in the spa resort of Montecatini in northern Italy, where he died of a heart attack after choking on a fish bone (another theory attributes his fatal coronary to his exertions with two young men). St Laurent kept the house of Dior together, triumphed with his first show in charge and was hailed as a national hero by the Paris fashionistas. Dragged off to do his national service during the Algerian War of Independence, St Laurent suffered a nervous breakdown and was institutionalized. He recovered, left the House of Dior to its own devices and set up his own label, establishing his eponymous *haute couture* fashion house as one of France's most respected and most enduring. He died in Paris in 2008.

The boy who hacked it

A royal commission in the United Kingdom into computer hacking and other misuses gave birth to the Computer Misuse Act, which became law at the beginning of August 1990. One of the first hackers to fall foul of the new legislation was schoolboy Paul Bedworth, from Ilkley in Yorkshire, who had been given a computer by his mum for his 14th birthday. Over the next few years he used his birthday present to hack into supposedly secure systems, including those at the White House, the *Financial Times*, and the European Organization for the Research and Treatment of Cancer. He was arrested in 1992 and charged with causing damage worth

£120,000, but his defence team pleaded a lack of criminal intent, and computer addiction. The jury at Southwark Crown Court decided it was a reasonable defence and acquitted him, giving rise to outraged accusations that the court had established a hacker's charter. Mr Bedworth went on to study artificial intelligence at Edinburgh University, where horrified researchers showed real intelligence by hiding their computers under their kilts and running for the hills.

3 AUGUST

Stumbling over the truth

Three men whose surnames begin with the letter B and whose lives could not be more different were born on 3 August: the singer Tony Bennett, who left his heart in San Francisco, was born in 1926; the poet Rupert Brooke, for whom a corner of a foreign field was forever England, was born in 1887; and Stanley Baldwin, the Conservative politician and three times prime minister, was born in 1867. Although Baldwin gave Winston Churchill the job of chancellor of the exchequer in his 1925 cabinet, the two men never really got on, and Churchill was forever tossing barbed comments towards the man he described as 'a countrified businessman who seemed to have reached the cabinet by accident'. Baldwin, Churchill said, 'occasionally stumbled over the truth, but hastily picked himself up and hurried on as if nothing had happened'; he was, Churchill said on another occasion, 'no better than an epileptic corpse'. Hardly surprising then that when it was suggested that Churchill mark Baldwin's 80th birthday in 1947, he said there would be no present nor even birthday greetings. Churchill believed Baldwin had taken too conciliatory a stance toward Adolf Hitler, and pulled no punches. 'I wish Stanley Baldwin no ill,' Churchill explained through an intermediary, 'but it would have been much better had he never lived.' Harsh words from a man normally as magnanimous towards his foes as he was towards his friends.

Matching ice cream

Queen Elizabeth the Queen Mother was born on this day in 1900, her 101 birthdays tallying neatly with the 100 years of the 20th century and first year of the 21st. For her 80th birthday the Royal Household clubbed together to give her an array of gifts that included the latest hi-fi sound system, a video recorder, and a painting of her racehorse Inch Action. Nineteen years later, on her 99th birthday, 10-year-old Debbie Caldicott reached forward during a royal walkabout to hand her a '99' ice cream – the cornet with a chocolate flake in it. Her Majesty was apparently much amused. The origin of the term '99' is shrouded in mystery. One popular theory involves an Italian king who employed 99 of his very best men to act as his bodyguards, which led to anything first class being dubbed '99'. It is a theory hotly contested by a Scottish ice cream maker in Edinburgh, who claims her grandfather invented it in 1922, naming it after the address of the family shop at 99 High Street in the Portobello district of the city.

One small step for man

Astronaut Neil Armstrong was born on this day in 1930 in Wapakoneta, Ohio. He got his student pilot's licence on his 16th birthday – one small step for a young man on his way to making one giant leap for mankind. It was 23 years later that Armstrong stepped out of the Eagle lunar module and on to the surface of the Moon.

JAN
FEB
MAR
APR
MAY
JUNE
JULY

6 AUGUST

The money's rubbish

On this day in 1928 in Pittsburg, Andrew Warhola was born to working-class immigrants from Slovakia. His father worked down the mines. Having dropped the final 'a' from his family name, and eschewing a life underground, Mr Warhol became an icon of 20th-century art, blending fame with notoriety. Warhol's work decorated the dance club run by Steve Rubell, the man who in partnership with Ian Schrager created and ran New York's *Studio 54*, a nightclub that also managed, in its short life, to blend fame and notoriety. In August 1978, for Warhol's 50th birthday, Rubell gave him a silver garbage can filled with new one-dollar bills – 1000 of them. A little over a year later, the *54* was raided by the Internal Revenue Service, who found dollar bills – and bills of a somewhat higher denomination – in similar garbage cans hidden behind insulating boards. Rubell and Schrager both received prison sentences for tax evasion. Rubell died of AIDS-related complications; Schrager owns and runs trendy boutique hotels in London, New York, Miami and San Francisco.

7 AUGUST

The sexiest woman alive

Today is the birthday of Charlize Theron, the South African-born American actress. She seems remarkably well balanced given she was in the house when her mother shot and killed her father (he was an alcoholic and she shot him in self-defence). Born in 1975, the cigarette-smoking, back-packing satin blond whose first language is Afrikaans and whose mother now runs a construction company, was already 32 when *Esquire* magazine named her the sexiest girl alive. It was the year that her boyfriend, the British actor Stuart Townsend, threw her on a plane to Belize as her birthday present. 'He came home at six and said "Start packing, we are leaving at midnight."' What else might you give a woman named the sexiest girl alive? Some cosmetic surgery vouchers for when the curves hit the straight? A copy of Einstein's *General Theory of Relativity* to show you know that sex is as much to do with the mind as it is to do with the body? A pair of very heavy (designer) boots to keep her feet on the ground?

8 AUGUST

What a way to spend a birthday

In the early hours of the morning of 8 August 1963 the overnight mail train from Glasgow to London came to an unscheduled stop at a red light on Sears Crossing in Buckinghamshire. The train was carrying a large amount of cash amongst the mail. The driver's mate walked to the phone box to call the signalman, but found the phone lines cut. When he returned to the train he was assaulted and pushed down the bank. What was then the biggest and most daring robbery in British history was underway. A glove had been stuck over the green light and a battery used to power the red one. A gang of 15 robbers was now in place. But the diesel engine was not the type with which the robbers had made themselves familiar, so, with a quick change of plan and a little persuasion from one of the gang members, a certain Ronnie Biggs, the driver was kept on board and instructed to take the train half a mile down the track to a bridge where the getaway vehicles were waiting. It was Ronnie Biggs's birthday. At a deserted farmhouse the gang divided the £2 million in used notes (today worth more than £40 million). Biggs took his share, smiling wryly to himself at the size of his birthday present. But the smiles did not last long. All but two of the gang, Biggs included, were arrested, charged and imprisoned. But Biggs escaped from Wandsworth prison after just 15 months and ran first to Australia and then to Brazil where, protected from the British authorities by the absence of any extradition treaty, he lived the high life on his ill-gotten gains. He finally returned to Britain in 2001, saying what he wanted most was to go to a pub in Margate and order a pint of bitter. But he was arrested and returned to prison.

9 AUGUST

Horror story

The master of horror could not help himself. Actress Melanie Griffith was born on this day in 1957, and as a present for her sixth birthday, Alfred Hitchcock gave her a doll dressed as the character her mother 'Tippi' Hedren played in his horror masterpiece *The Birds*. So far so good – but the six-year-old's doll was packed in a miniature pine coffin. In a coffin? What was Hitchcock thinking of?

1 0 AUGUST

A legend in its own lifetime

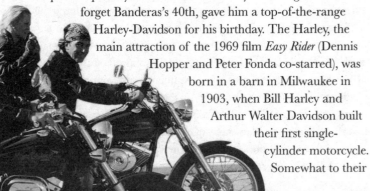

The son of a policeman from Malaga, movie star Antonio Banderas was born on this day in 1960. Banderas has a lot of *vroom* appeal, clearly understood by his partner Melanie Griffith, who in 1980, not so preoccupied by her own 43rd birthday on 9 August as to forget Banderas's 40th, gave him a top-of-the-range Harley-Davidson for his birthday. The Harley, the main attraction of the 1969 film *Easy Rider* (Dennis Hopper and Peter Fonda co-starred), was born in a barn in Milwaukee in 1903, when Bill Harley and Arthur Walter Davidson built their first single-cylinder motorcycle. Somewhat to their

JAN FEB MAR APR MAY JUNE JULY AUG SEPT OCT NOV DEC

surprise, it sold. By 1908 they were selling 154 bikes a year. Ten years later, theirs was the biggest motorcycle factory in the world. Harleys are used by the LAPD and dozens of America's other police forces. Malcolm Forbes, who created *Forbes* magazine, liked them so much he had 50 of them.

11 AUGUST

Birthday cruise

Pakistan's former leader General Pervez Musharraf was born on this day in 1943 in Delhi. After independence and partition in 1947, Musharraf's family, all Muslims, moved northwest across the new border to settle in Lahore. The general took power in Pakistan after a military coup in 1999, and six years later, on his 62nd birthday, Pakistan test-fired its first cruise missile capable of carrying both conventional and nuclear warheads. Announcing the test, Pakistan's information minister Rashid Ahmed said the successful firing was a birthday present for the president from the nation's scientists. (In 2004 one of those scientists, Abdul Qadeer Khan, had passed atomic secrets to the governments of Libya, Iran and North Korea.)

12 AUGUST

A queen's lesson in recycling

There can be few monarchs more admired and loved by their subjects than the king and queen of Thailand. Curious then, at first sight, that the queen should be given some dilapidated rail freight trucks for her 71st birthday in 2003. One hundred of them. And there was no suggestion that she was fed up with her pale primrose Cadillac. The trucks were the gift of the state railway company, which had shunted the old and disused rolling stock into retirement. Did the railway company wrap each truck in a huge bow using the national flag? Well, no. But it did know Queen Sirikit had a use for them. A keen conservationist, Her Majesty had pledged her support for the efforts to restore coastal life to the southern provinces of Pattani and Narathiwat, and the trucks were to be used to form artificial reefs where the coral had been destroyed.

13 AUGUST

Tea with Simón Bolívar

The world's longest-serving leader (until his formal retirement early in 2008) was born on a sugar plantation on this day in 1926. Resorting to cash as a birthday present is a common fallback for those whose imagination goes blank. Fidel Castro, who took over in Cuba in 1959, received regular birthday gifts of cash – but not because the givers had run out of ideas. At one birthday party a Cuban government official, who later defected, saw Castro's interior minister José Abrahantes hand over a suitcase containing $10 million. In 2006, shortly before Fidel handed over power to his brother Raoul while he recovered from stomach surgery, *Forbes* magazine, surveying the wealth of world leaders, estimated his worth at around $900 million, based on his control of Cuba's state-owned companies. (The magazine qualified its estimates of the world's leaders' wealth by saying their estimates were 'more art than science'.) One of the Cuban's most ardent fans, President Hugo Chávez of Venezuela, has not resorted to cash gifts. For Castro's 75th Chávez gave him a treasured rifle he had kept since he was a boy, and for the Cuban leader's 80th Chávez was again generous, presenting him with a dagger and a porcelain cup-and-saucer set that had belonged to Simón Bolívar, the 19th-century hero of the South American struggle for independence.

No love lost

Today is the birthday of former Australian treasurer (i.e. finance minister) Peter Costello. He was 50 in 2007, an event that on its own might not have warranted inclusion in this book, but which highlighted similarities in his relationship with his prime minister John Howard, and the relationship between Gordon Brown, when he was UK chancellor, and his prime minister Tony Blair. Costello and Howard struck a deal about the leadership just as Brown and Blair had supposedly done. Howard held on to the top job just as Blair did. And in both cases, the relationships between premier and finance minister became very strained. In fact a recent biography of Howard revealed that not once in the 11 years that he and Costello had been running the country together had the Howards invited the Costellos to dinner. No surprises then that there was no 50th birthday present for the treasurer from his boss. Asked on a radio show what he would like as a present, Mr Costello rather limply said he would like a day off. He soon got more than a day off when both men lost their jobs, kicked out of office by the Australian electorate.

Fair play

Hollywood poker player, political activist, screenwriter and actor Ben Affleck was born in Berkeley, California on this day in 1972. An ardent baseball fan and supporter of the Boston Red Sox, he once reached from the crowd for a foul ball at Fenway Park, only to have it snatched from his grasp by Los Angeles Angels star Howie Kendrick, who claimed the out. Kendrick subsequently signed the ball and sent it to Affleck as a birthday present.

Megastar comes down to earth – with a bump

Madonna came screaming into the world on this day in 1958 in Bay City, Michigan. As a child she went to ballet classes and eventually won a dance scholarship to university. She found her voice after moving to New York, where a DJ-cum-record-producer put some of her demo tapes in front of Sire Records, an off-shoot of Warner Bros. Records. And the rest, as they say, is history – a history of song, sex and celebrity. In addition to her two husbands she had relationships with her bodyguard, her fitness trainer, a bisexual porn star, Warren Beatty and a rapper called Vanilla Ice. It was her present husband, the film director Guy Ritchie, who gave her a horse for her 47th birthday. Not the most experienced of riders, she came off within minutes of mounting it in the grounds of their estate near Salisbury in the west of England. She was airlifted to hospital, where she was found to have a cracked collar bone, three cracked ribs and a damaged hand. She should be more careful on her birthdays: she married Sean Penn on her 27th birthday and was divorced within four years.

Is that a gun in your pocket?

Her fans seem to be as keen to celebrate her birthday after her death as they were when she was alive. On Mae Day in 1993, the 100th anniversary of the day Mae West was born in Flatbush, Brooklyn, coach tours carried fans around her New York haunts. Highlights of the tour included the site of Daly's Theatre, where she made her first Broadway appearance in 1926 in *Sex*, a play she wrote and directed and in which she took the lead. The show landed her in jail on obscenity charges and paved the way for a career in which the moralists and censors were forever lurking in

Gifts for the man or woman who has everything

- The highest mountain in Africa (27 January)
- A painting by Turner (8 February) or Manet (27 August) or Miró (9 November), or Magritte's easel (21 November)
- A gold Monopoly set (15 March)
- Silver coconuts (15 April)

- The isle of Staffa, with Fingal's Cave included (26 April)
- A city (5 May) or a new breed of rose (5 July) or a star (12 November) named in one's honour
- A jewel-encrusted toilet seat (24 July)
- A postage stamp with one's portrait on it (30 July)

- An offer of oral sex (19 August)
- A solid gold mousetrap (5 October)
- A dose of colonic irrigation (7 December)

the wings. (Daly's Theatre had been built by the Bible Students' Association for religious lectures and biblical films.) On the anniversary of her birth in 2005, a New York artist created a portrait of her using a water melon. He put a light inside so she glowed. Where or when she uttered the immortal words 'Is that a gun in your pocket or are you just pleased to see me' remains unclear. One version of the story has her saying the words to a policeman who had drawn the lucky straw and been dispatched to escort her home from the railroad station in Los Angeles.

18 AUGUST

The best way to remember your wife's birthday is to forget it once

Emily Rosalynn Smith was born in Plains, Georgia on this day in 1927. She was just 19 when she married Jimmy Carter, and 50 when she became first lady. President Carter was a stickler for punctuality, and regularly refused to see people who turned up late for meetings. His wife did not get an easy time either, being chided whenever she kept him waiting. But things changed the year Carter forgot his wife's birthday. Appalled and ashamed, Carter wrote her a note in lieu of a present, promising never again to make a fuss if she was late. Carter has a habit of making up for things. He was an unpopular president, but by common consent has proved one of the most effective past presidents America has ever had.

Washington man counters potential blow to his resolve

Bill Clinton was born on this day in 1946. According to Kenneth Starr's report to the US Congress, Monica Lewinsky came to the White House a few days before his birthday in 1997. She gave him birthday presents which she set up in his back office, kissed him, touched his genitals through his trousers and 'moved to perform oral sex'. But on this occasion the president apparently rebuffed her. According to Starr's report, Lewinsky recalled the president saying, 'I'm trying not to do this and I'm trying to be good.' Seems a shame really, on his birthday and all.

Presents for a butcher

Slobodan Milošević and Horatio Hornblower met in prison. The former Yugoslav leader read widely while incarcerated, but kept on returning to E.M. Forster and the Hornblower books. The man the tabloid press had taken to calling 'the Butcher of the Balkans' was born on 20 August 1941 at Požarevac in central Serbia. He studied law, joined the Communist Party and became the president of Serbia in 1989. He was arrested by Serbian police on 1 April 2001 on charges of corruption and abuse of power during his time as president of Yugoslavia, and was subsequently put on trial by the United Nations for war crimes committed during the Balkan conflict. He spent his 60th birthday at the Scheveningen detention centre in The Hague with his wife Mira, their daughter-in-law and their grandson. The family had brought presents, but they were not allowed to give Milošević the birthday cake they had brought with them. However, they had eaten cake at the last meal the family had together in Belgrade. They were visiting Milošević in the city's prison, where the governor recorded in his diary that on 28 June, three months after his arrest and immediately prior to his transfer to The Hague, Milošević ate cake and cheese, deep-fried courgettes, potato salad, watermelon, peaches, pears and one sardine.

21 AUGUST

Teddy bears and transports of delight

A.A. Milne's son Christopher Robin was born on this summer's day in 1920. For his first birthday he was given a teddy bear (*right*), which the family called Winnie-the-Pooh. More soft toys followed: Eeyore was a Christmas present and Piglet a gift from a neighbour. Christopher Robin and his menagerie of stuffed animals were to become the subjects of the Pooh stories, Milne's best-known works. Winnie probably got its name from a black bear cub of that name entrusted to the London Zoo by a Canadian soldier who had named it after his home town of Winnipeg. The animal was one of Christopher Robin's favourites at the zoo.

Today is also the birthday of Liam Howlett, who fronts the band Prodigy. Mr Howlett got the surprise of his life when he received a double-decker London bus for his birthday. Born in Braintree in 1971 and brought up on the classical piano, Howlett was treated to the retired Routemaster by his wife Natalie Appleton, the former All Saints star. He was in good company – Andrew Lloyd Webber had already given one to his friend, the impresario Cameron Mackintosh.

A huge talent put to bad use

Hitler's film-maker and propagandist Leni Riefenstahl was born in Berlin on 22 August 1902. She began her career as a dancer, turning to acting after injuring her foot. But it was for the making of films that she became famous, or, in the eyes of her many detractors, infamous. While *Triumph of the Will*, her film of the 1934 Nazi rally at Nuremberg, established her credentials as a director, it also exposed her infatuation for the Führer, who appeared in the film like a demigod, emerging from the clouds to the music of Wagner's *Die Meistersinger von Nürnberg*. As Jonathan Petropoulos, director of the Centre for the Study of the Holocaust, puts it: 'Her talent cannot be disregarded even though she put it at the service of a genocidal dictatorship.'

After the war Ms Riefenstahl turned her talents to stills photography, recording the Nuba tribe of Sudan, and then, having taught herself to scuba dive at the age of 70, returned to film with an exploration of the exotic life beneath the waves. She celebrated her 100th birthday in style with a party to which many of Berlin's A-list celebrities were invited. But the event was spoiled somewhat when the Prosecutor's Office in Frankfurt announced that very morning that it would be investigating charges that she denied the Holocaust. There were no presents either from the German press: 'Happy 100th Birthday,' wrote Franz Josef Wagner in *Bild*. 'One day you are going to be celebrating your birthday either in heaven or in hell. In hell you'll see Hitler and Goebbels again, and in heaven Van Gogh, Einstein, Da Vinci. Birthday girl, something went wrong with your genetic makeup. Maybe that's the reason not all Germans hit out at you, our greatest living artist. But happy birthday to you all the same, you lady of two masks.'

JAN
FEB
MAR
APR
MAY
JUNE JULY
AUG
SEPT
OCT
NOV
DEC

Life below stairs

Natascha Kampusch is the girl who vanished on her way to school
in the Donaustadt district of Vienna when she was just ten years old.
And 23 August was the day she re-appeared eight-and-a-half years
later. She had spent her youth held captive in a windowless room
9 ft by 6 ft underneath a garage. Within hours of her escape her
kidnapper Wolfgang Priklopil had thrown himself under a train.
Natascha was apparently not harshly treated, and Priklopil even gave
her birthday presents, on one occasion rising to an electric toothbrush.
After her release, her parents threw a party on her 19th birthday – in
a windowless wine cellar of all places – and her sister brought along a
present of a bedside lamp. Within two years of her ordeal Natascha
was signed up by the Austrian TV company PULS 4 to host her own
chat show. Other TV chat-show hosts chosen for their celebrity, rather
than any presentational skills, include the Duchess of York, who
hosted a short-lived show in 1998, and Heather Mills, the expensively
divorced ex-partner of Sir Paul McCartney, who once stood in for
Larry King on his late-night show.

Flower power

If you were born on 24 August you share your birthday with the
English novelist A.S. Byatt, with the bible-thumping, guitar-strumming
2008 Republican presidential hopeful Mike Huckabee, and with the
man who for five decades dedicated his life to the cause of Palestinian
self-determination. Mohammed Abdel Rahman Abdel Raouf Arafat
al-Qudwa al-Husseini, more commonly known as Yasser Arafat, was
born in Cairo in 1929, the son of a textile merchant and one of seven
children. His war with Israel began while he was an engineering
student, when he smuggled weapons into Palestine. He became
chairman of the Palestine Liberation Organization (PLO) in 1969,
and in 1996 became the first president of the Palestinian National

Authority. His headquarters were in Ramallah on the West Bank where, at the end of his life he became, to all intents and purposes, a prisoner, beset by ill health and besieged by Israeli tanks. So who was the least likely recipient of flowers from Arafat on their birthday? Exactly. Yet Israel's hawkish prime minister Benjamin Netanyahu received a very nice bunch from Arafat for his 49th birthday in 1998. The two leaders were meeting in Maryland, not far from Washington DC, with President Clinton and Secretary of State Madeleine Albright. 21 October was Netanyahu's birthday, and having had an early morning birthday call from Albright he was even more surprised to find a bunch of flowers outside his room from Arafat. Forty-eight hours later, in front of the world's media, the Israeli prime minister called Arafat his 'partner', and the two men signed an agreement to continue their search for peace.

Something for the weekend, sir?

Leonard Bernstein was born on this day in 1918 in Lawrence, Massachusetts. He made his conducting debut while still at Harvard, and then had a lucky break when in November 1943 he stood in for Bruno Walter, conductor of the New York Philharmonic, who was ill. Lauren Salamone had met one of his children during a graduate programme in Oxford and became a family friend. For his 72nd birthday she rather cheekily gave him a Chitlin fur-lined jockstrap that she found on a trip to Alaska. One can imagine what a comfort this could be for an Alaskan, and winters are cold in Bernstein's native New England. But in August?

Today was also the birthday of a man who did little to entertain his fellow men but much to make them despise him. The son of a politically militant miner, Erich Honecker was the man in charge of building the Berlin Wall. Born on this day in 1912, Honecker went on to lead the German Democratic Republic from 1971 until his Wall came down in 1989. For his 60th birthday he was given a rather nasty desk set (*left*) by Lieutenant Colonel Kurkotkin, the commander of Soviet armed forces in Germany. The set consisted of a calendar, a clock with a tank on top, a thermometer and four ballpoint pens made to look like missiles. It was doubtless intended to convey to the first secretary that the might of the Soviet Union was behind him.

Sex in the bathroom

Queen Victoria's consort Prince Albert was born in Germany on this day in 1819. Victoria, considerably less 'Victorian' than one would imagine, was bold in her choice of birthday presents for Albert. She gave him an erotically charged fresco for his bathroom at Osborne House on the Isle of Wight. It shows François Boucher's naked Hercules with Omphale, queen of Lydia, amorously draped across his knees (*right*). Less erotic was the paperweight she gave him made of Balmoral granite and deer's teeth. But decidedly risqué was her present for his 33rd birthday, when she bought him the bust of a Sudanese man from Darfur entitled *Said Abdullah*. The work had caused a scandal when the French

sculptor Charles Cordier, out of step with society at that time with his strong beliefs in racial equality, first put it on show in 1848. And if a fur-lined jockstrap was wasted on Leonard Bernstein (*see 25 August*) it would have been just the thing for Victoria's kilted ghillie John Brown. But she had probably thought of other ways of warming his nether regions.

27 AUGUST
Damage control

John Hay Whitney, born on this day in 1904, was the man President Eisenhower sent to the Court of King James in 1957 to help restore Anglo-American relations after the Suez Crisis. Whitney was something of a Renaissance man – an oarsman, polo player, financier, publisher (he owned the *New York Herald Tribune* for five years in the 1960s), diplomat and horse breeder. It was his love of horses that prompted Mrs Whitney to buy him Edouard Manet's *Racecourse at the Bois de Boulogne* for his birthday.

28 AUGUST
'Silver and ermine and red faces full of port wine'

The former poet laureate Sir John Betjeman was born on 28 August 1906. Lady Elizabeth Cavendish, a childhood friend of Queen Elizabeth II and lady-in-waiting to Princess Margaret, became a close friend of the writer, and for his 70th birthday she commissioned the Yorkshire-born silversmith Keith Tyssen to fashion a personalized silver mug. (Tyssen, who had an almost gushing respect and fondness for the 'noble' metal he worked with, subsequently had the privilege of dining with Betjeman, an occasion on which they both drank from his silver mug.) Taught briefly by T.S. Eliot at Highgate Junior School, Betjeman went on to Marlborough, a public school in

Wiltshire, and thence (in company with Archibald Ormsby-Gore, his teddy bear) to Magdalen College, Oxford. Academically, as an undergraduate Betjeman was not a success – his tutor was C.S. Lewis, for whom he had little regard – but many years later, in 1974, Betjeman received an honorary doctorate from the university. 'I don't think I am any good,' he once said. 'If I thought I was any good I wouldn't be.' Betjeman died in 1984.

29 AUGUST

Confusion at Radio City

Michael Jackson, the enigmatic African-American 'King of Pop', was born in Gary, Indiana on this day in 1958. His album *Thriller* became the best-selling album in pop music history, selling more than 59 million copies. Having narrowly missed getting a life-size model of Brooke Shields for his birthday (the two dated in the 1980s and Ms Shields only gave up on the idea when she learnt she would have to spend three weeks sitting in front of the modellers), Jackson faced another birthday disappointment, this time from Britney Spears. On his 44th birthday, Jackson was invited to the 2002 MTV Video Music Awards at New York's Radio City Music Hall. Spears gave him a silver treble clef as a birthday present, telling him he was 'the artist of the millennium'. Jackson thought the silver gift was an MTV special millennium award and made a thank you speech to that effect, leaving the Radio City audience, the management of MTV and a dejected Ms Spears in a state of embarrassed confusion.

30 AUGUST

Death of a strange present

Alexander Litvinenko was a birthday present. He was born in Voronezh on 30 August 1962 and died a horrible death from polonium-210 poisoning in London on 23 November 2006. Litvinenko had been a KGB agent and then worked for its successor organization in the Russian Federation, the FSB, where he had responsibility for protecting the billionaire Boris Berezovsky. When his charge was the subject of a failed assassination attempt Litvinenko publicly accused his superiors of attempting the assassination, was arrested, released and fled to Britain through Ukraine and Turkey. British police accused another former Russian spy, Andrei Lugovoi, of his murder and asked the Russian government to extradite him – a request that was flatly turned down. In a statement dictated to a friend three days before he died, Litvinenko thanked his wife Marina for standing by him. 'My love for her and our son knows no bounds,' he said. He had met Marina when two of her friends brought him to her 31st birthday party. She told them at the time she thought a KGB officer was a strange birthday present. The alleged killer of the strange birthday present, Andrei Lugovoi, remains at liberty in Russia.

31 AUGUST

Joy in a time of sorrow

Alma Schindler was a woman of beauty and intelligence, a *femme fatale* who enriched and destroyed men in equal measure. She was born in Vienna in 1879, the daughter of an artist. She married the composer Gustav Mahler, but after the death of their daughter she began an affair with the architect Walter Gropius. After Mahler died (he was 20 years her senior) she did not at first go back to Gropius but had a passionate and torrid affair with the young artist Oskar Kokoschka. But she walked away from the affair, leaving Oskar in a state of despair and embracing a substitute for Alma in the form of a life-size look-alike doll. Returning to Gropius, she married him in 1915 and had a daughter called Manon. Gropius was away much of the time on military service, and Alma was to become unfaithful again, this time falling in love with the poet Franz Werfel. They had an affair and Gropius eventually agreed to a divorce, and Alma and Franz were married. But illness was to strike again, this time in the form of polio, and Manon died when she was 19.

Alma's friend the composer Alban Berg, who was clearly very fond of the family, was writing a violin concerto at the time and adapted it to reflect his sorrow and compassion, and dedicated it to 'the memory of an angel' – by whom he meant Manon. When a perceptive critique of the concerto appeared in a Vienna newspaper on Alma's birthday, she wrote immediately to Berg by telegram: 'With this enormous deed of love you have made me the only birthday present that could give me joy.' Alma and Werfel eventually made their way to America to escape the Nazis, and after Alma's death in 1964, the satirist Tom Lehrer was moved to compose a poem in her memory. The penultimate stanza ends with the lines:

The body that reached the embalma'
Was one that had known how to live.

1 Lily Tomlin	2 Jimmy Connors	3 Fearne Cotton
8 Margaret Hodge	9 Siegfried Sassoon	10 Arnold Palmer
15 John Julius Norwich	16 Jean Arp	17 Anne Bancroft
22 Mike Matheny	23 Augustus Caesar / Kublai Khan / Cherie Booth / Robert Bosch	24 Joan MacLean
29 Colin Dexter	30 David Oistrakh	1 Jimmy Carter

4	5	6	7
Beyoncé Knowles	Russell Harty	Tim Henman / Greg Rusedski / Caroline Dale	Georgi Markov
11 D.H. Lawrence	**12** Adam Nicolson	**13** Clara Wieck	**14** Terence Donovan
18 Lance Armstrong	**19** Ferdinand (Ferry) Porsche	**20** Reuben Singh / Charles Bluhdorn	**21** Liam Gallagher
25 Christopher Reeve	**26** T.S. Eliot / Manmohan Singh	**27** King Louis XIII / Alvin Stardust	**28** Confucius / Brigitte Bardot / Gwyneth Paltrow
2 Sting	**3** Gore Vidal	**4** Anne Widdecombe	**5** Ray Kroc

A mad monk's wishes for eternal life

Lily Tomlin was born at the outbreak of the Second World War in Detroit, where her father worked in a car factory. The actress/comedienne started off performing stand-up gigs at nightclubs in Detroit and New York before joining the TV show *Laugh-In* in 1969. The online Lily Tomlin guestbook is a repository of messages from a devoted worldwide audience who become especially attentive around her birthday. 'A very early happy birthday from the Mad Monk of Lexington!' wrote Brother Damien Simmons from Lexington in Kentucky. 'I just found out today that you and I were born on the same day which goes to show what a bizarre sense of humour God has (and what good taste She has as well) … Oh, my dear, you really must live for ever, and do drop in if you're ever in the neighbourhood.'

Bad boy comes good

Some would say it was the most remarkable game of tennis ever played. Certainly the crowds at Flushing Meadows for the 1991 US Open had little doubt about what they had witnessed. For 4 hours and 42 minutes they watched a 39-year-old, the one-time bad boy of tennis, fight his way to a breathtaking victory over a mere lad of 24. Jimmy Connors was celebrating his birthday and faced Aaron Krickstein in the fourth round of the grand slam tournament. The crowd sang 'Happy Birthday' as Connors walked onto the court, and their unflagging roaring support was the best birthday present they could have given him. The fact that Connors was there at all was remarkable. His age was one thing, but he had also had surgery on his wrist the year before and suffered back problems, which had forced him out of the French Open. And he was ranked 174th in the world at the start of the tournament. Sure enough he lost the first set. His argumentative and sometimes vulgar behaviour was back in evidence too (his one-time fiancée Chris Evert used to tell the story about him going to confession and the priest telling him to come back the next Sunday because he wasn't finished). But he won the second set in a tiebreak. The third set went all Krickstein's way and he took it 6–1. Connors got his breath back and won the fourth set. Two sets all. His fans should by now have been hoarse, but their exultations only rose to new levels. It was the final set, and after seven games, Connors was trailing 2–5, by which time any sane fans would have been searching for their handkerchiefs and telling each other it had been a fine way for their hero to bow out. But there were not many sane fans in the crowd that day. They would not let their man lie down, and from somewhere deep down inside, Connors found the will and the energy to fight on and produce some extraordinary and sublime tennis to take the set to four games all.

By now most of America had stopped to watch or listen. In the commentary box every superlative had been used and re-used. The fifth game went neck and neck and into a tiebreak. The points that went Connors's way brought screams now from the crowd. He went ahead by six points to four, and then, as if there had never been any doubt about the outcome, took the next point and the match was his. Two women had produced the man of the moment – both his mother and grandmother had coached him. And John McEnroe went off to the locker room to offer his congratulations, saying he had to touch the man to 'see if he bleeds'.

The show must go on

Fearne Cotton presents things. Other people do things, she presents them. Just as there are celebrity models and celebrity chefs and celebrity wheelbarrow pushers, Fearne is a celebrity presenter. She was born on 3 September 1981 and for her 24th birthday her mum gave her a pair of silk knickers with diamanté buttons up the back. She was presenting *Top of the Pops* at the time and told her mum she would wear them for the show. Just before she was about to go on, she bent down and the buttons popped off. So she had to chance her luck and present the show with no knickers on at all. Mums are never around when you need them.

4 SEPTEMBER

A roller from a rapper

Beyoncé Knowles, the singer, songwriter, actress and all-round A-list celebrity, was born in Houston, Texas on 4 September 1981. She first hit the headlines as the lead singer in the all-girl rhythm and blues group Destiny's Child, which, having made its first public performance in the hair salon run by Mrs Knowles, became one of the most successful girl groups of all time. The group split up, as groups do, and Beyoncé went solo. Her 25th birthday was a big day. She released *B'Day*, her second solo album (which sold more than 500,000 copies in the first week in the US alone), and her boyfriend, the rapper Jay-Z, the controversial headline act at the 2008 Glastonbury muddy music festival, indulged her with a vintage 1959 Rolls Royce convertible worth about $1 million. The car might not have created quite the sensation he had hoped. His girlfriend was not new to the delights of a Roller – she had taken delivery of a Phantom three years earlier. Still, a real celebrity can never have too much of anything.

5 SEPTEMBER

Escort duty

Russell Harty, the northern-accented, Oxford-educated gay television presenter, gained fame with a celebrity chat show in the 1980s. Born on 5 September 1934, he was once sent a male escort as a birthday present. The escort was a young man called Oscar Moore, who later became a writer and critic, whose *Guardian* columns chronicling his fight against AIDS were turned into a one-man play by Malcolm Sutherland.

Not a day for champions

For summer after summer one man carried the hopes of a nation onto the tennis courts of Wimbledon. England expected so much. The nation became glued to its televisions, suffering the agony and the ecstasy, willing him to make the English summer glorious. Yet summer after summer those hopes were crushed – like so many platefuls of strawberries. They even named a hill after him, and on court his fans screamed their encouragement until their nerves were frayed and their throats ran dry. Yet Tim Henman could never quite deliver. Perhaps 6 September was not a day for the birth of champions: Greg Rusedski was also born on 6 September, in 1973, one year earlier than Tim, and he too never once reached the finals. Yet far away from Wimbledon, fortune shone more brightly on Caroline Dale, also born on 6 September, who enjoyed a distinguished career as a foreign correspondent in Japan, where a friend marked her birthday one year with a *moo cut torutoru*. What is it? It is a battery-operated rotating blade contained in a compact surgical-pink plastic housing looking like a cross between a lady shaver and some kind of sex toy. What's it for? It slices off the bobbles that inevitably form on woolly jumpers after a few washes.

No hiding place

He had parked his car in its regular spot in the shadows of Waterloo Bridge on the south side of the river. From there it was an easy walk over the bridge to his office at the BBC World Service in Bush House. It was a mild late summer's morning and the 49-year-old had a spring in his step as he walked across the Thames. His fellow commuters would not have known the significance of 7 September, but Georgi Markov and his fellow Bulgarians knew only too well that the day marked the birthday of their country's detested hard-line communist leader, Todor Zhivkov. It may have been on Markov's mind when he felt a sudden sharp pain in the back of his leg. On turning round he noticed a man bending down to pick up an umbrella. Markov spent the day in considerably pain, and by evening was suffering a high fever. He was admitted to hospital and diagnosed with serious blood poisoning. He died three days later. Georgi Markov was a dissident Bulgarian writer and broadcaster who had been a thorn in the side of his country's communist regime. Zhivkov wanted him silenced. There had been two previous attempts on his life, both of which had been bungled. But this time there had been no mistake. A tiny pellet of highly toxic ricin had been injected into his leg through a specially constructed umbrella. The assassin, apparently codenamed 'Piccadilly', was never caught, but no-one doubted that he was acting for the Bulgarian secret service, which in turn had taken orders from Zhivkov. And many believed the killing was fully intended as a present for the brutal despot's 67th birthday – Zhivkov was born on 7 September in 1911. During the summer of 2008, 30 years after the murder, Scotland Yard officers were back in Bulgaria – now a member of the European Union – hoping to find evidence in files, previously denied to them by the former communist regime, that might lead to the perpetrators of the still unsolved crime.

Put on hold for a harp

Margaret Hodge was born in Cairo on 8 September 1944. Currently the minister for culture, Lady Hodge has held a variety of posts in Labour governments, having entered Parliament as MP for Barking in 1994. Her husband, the High Court judge Sir Henry Hodge, clearly had the stresses of political life in mind when he gave her a harp for her 60th birthday. Nothing as soothing as the music of a harp. So determined was she to master her new instrument that government business would sometimes be put on hold. Once when her boss at the Department of Education, Charles Clarke – not a man to be trifled with – phoned on an urgent matter, she told him that she was in the middle of a lesson and would have to call him back. History does not record the reaction of the notoriously difficult Clarke.

Early beginnings

Born on 9 September 1886, the poet and novelist Siegfried Sassoon had little choice but to become a writer – for his third birthday his mother Theresa gave him a copy of Coleridge's *Lectures on Shakespeare*. His satirical anti-war verse, written during the First World War, along with his later pacifism, seem at odds with his ruthless determination and courage on the field of battle which, while serving on the Western Front, led him to take a German trench single-handed. He was awarded the Military Cross, but his distaste for war in general, and a conviction that thousands had died unnecessarily during the Great War, led him to throw the ribbon into the River Mersey. Curiously, the medal itself turned up many years later in the attic of a house on the Isle of Mull, off the west coast of Scotland.

10 SEPTEMBER

Playing politics

Arnold Palmer (*below left*), the American golfing legend, told a sports magazine that his best birthday present was a visit from Dwight D.

Eisenhower (*right*) on his 37th birthday. His wife Winnie arranged it, and the former president brought along his wife Mamie. Palmer, who could not get around a golf course without the aid of several cigarettes – and never won a major tournament after giving up smoking – played with no fewer than six presidents, including Eisenhower himself.

11 SEPTEMBER

Dirty pictures

In 1928 a book scandalized and divided British society like nothing else before it. Its author, D.H. Lawrence, was born on 11 September 1885, and *Lady Chatterley's Lover* was only the beginning of Lawrence's brush with the morals police. For his birthday in 1906 family friends had given him a present of facsimiles of watercolours, from which he was to learn and develop his own painterly techniques. He enjoyed his time at the easel, and in 1929 launched a one-man exhibition at the Warren Gallery in London. Most of the pictures involved nude men and women embracing in a variety of Arcadian landscapes. The critics hated the work – and so too did at least one member of the public, who took it upon himself to call the police, complaining that the pictures were obscene. The gallery was closed and 13 of the pictures confiscated.

Somewhere over the rainbow

It was, for those who like that sort of thing, a seductive advertisement. 'Very early lambs. Cliffs of columnar basalt. Wonderful caves. Two-roomed cottage.' The advertisement referred to the Shiant Isles, a group of three very small islands in the Outer Hebrides, off the west coast of Scotland (*below*). They were offered for sale in the *Daily Telegraph* in 1937 and caught the eye of the bisexual poet, novelist and creator of the magnificent gardens at Sissinghurst, Vita Sackville-West. She sent the details to her son Nigel Nicolson, who, still a student at Oxford, bought them with his grandmother's inheritance. Some forty years later, Nigel gave the islands to his son Adam as a 21st birthday present. Adam, himself a writer, produced *Sea Room*, a critically acclaimed book and a love letter, as he describes it, to the islands. He fully intends to keep the islands in the family and will pass them on to his son when he reaches 21.

13 SEPTEMBER

Minor gift

The accomplished pianist Clara Wieck, born in Leipzig in 1819, married Robert Schumann the day before her 21st birthday. The match was opposed by her father, himself a pianist who had taught Schumann as well as teaching his own daughter. (Such was Clara's talent that on tour together Schumann fell into her shadow, and was not infrequently referred to as Mr Clara Schumann. After one spectacular performance, a member of the audience came up to Robert and asked him if he too was musical.) Robert Schumann wrote less piano music after they were married, but was prolific in his orchestral work. During January and February 1841 he wrote his Symphony No. 1; in April he began his *Symphonette*, which he finished in May; he followed that with an A minor piano *Phantasie*, which evolved into his better-known piano concerto, and he followed that with his D minor symphony, which he finished on 9 September in time to give it to Clara as a birthday present on the 13th. As it turned out, the D minor was not a great success, getting a decidedly cool reception at its first performance in Leipzig. Schumann banned any further performances, and only after much reworking did it reappear as his Symphony No. 4 a decade later.

14 SEPTEMBER

Lie back and think of England

The photographer Terence Donovan was born in the East End of London on 14 September in 1936. Donovan and his old friend David Bailey (see 2 January) played a central role in making fashion a vital part of the Swinging Sixties. They and their models became celebrities almost overnight, and the glossy magazines fell over themselves to secure their services. 'The real skill of photography,' said Donovan once, 'is organized visual lying.' But there was nothing false about the birthday present Bailey gave him for his 60th birthday. It was a picture – a very explicit picture – of a vagina. Bailey used a penetrating dentist's light to shoot some thirty vaginas in anatomical detail, promising the owners that while he went about exposing their most private parts he would never expose who the private parts belonged to. Donovan received one of the anonymous vaginas for his last birthday. He committed suicide in 1996.

15 SEPTEMBER

A nice line in fish

Nothing like landing the big one on your birthday. Historian John Julius Norwich, the son of the womanizing diplomat Duff Cooper, was born on 15 September 1929. He was cruising the Aegean with his friends Sir Timothy and Lady Susan Sainsbury (of the supermarket family) when something took the fishing line. It turned out to be a fair-sized tuna, and because it was his birthday, John Julius was given the honour of reeling it in. 'It gave me a huge kick. It is the only present I can remember,' he said. They ate his birthday catch for supper. When ordinary folk get a taste for tuna they cruise around the corner to Sir Tim's nice family store, dither about buying the said fish in brine or oil, get confused about Omega-3, dither further about the chunks or the steaks, buy one of each, queue for ages at the checkout, get waylaid by a gossipy neighbour on the way home, struggle to open the tin, slap the tuna on some lettuce leaves and then maybe dream of the Aegean.

Arp's torso

The French sculptor and painter Jean Arp was born in Strasbourg on 16 September 1886, and Raymond Nasher was the Boston-born developer and art collector who put culture into Texan shopping. No, seriously, he did. He built a gigantic retail park in Dallas, decorated the open spaces with shrubs, fountains and ponds with turtles, and then installed pieces of sculpture from his own collection – one that included works by Matisse, Henry Moore, Picasso and Alberto Giacometti. But he kept one piece behind. Visitors to Nasher's house were greeted in the hall by Jean Arp's *Torso with Buds*. Nasher's wife Patsy gave the sculpture to him as a birthday present in 1967 – and it was this present that started their interest in modern sculpture. Arp was a founding member of the Dada movement and winner of the sculpture prize at the 1954 Venice Biennale. He got as far as New York on his travels, but knew little of the rest of America. He might have found Dallas, what shall we say, interesting?

Buying rights

Anna Italiano was born in the Bronx on 17 September 1931. It seems a perfectly nice name, so why she changed it to Anne Bancroft goodness knows. (She changed it the first time to Anne Marno, but the producers of her first film *Don't Bother to Knock* didn't like the sound of Marno, so she changed it to Bancroft.) She is probably best remembered for her role as Mrs Robinson in *The Graduate*, the 1967 Mike Nichols film in which she starred opposite Dustin Hoffman. Yet she was one of very few actors who have won Tony, Emmy, Golden Globe and BAFTA awards. And she won an Academy Award for Best Actress in *The Miracle Worker*. It was her second husband, Mel Brooks, who bought the film rights to *84 Charing Cross Road* as a birthday present for her, and then cast her in the starring role. Who said husbands are useless?

GIFTS FOR TYRANTS

- A STUFFED CROCODILE (15 APRIL)
- A BOUND VOLUME OF THE TREATIES ONE HAS
  VIOLATED (20 APRIL)
- A MASS WEDDING IN ONE'S HONOUR (28 APRIL)
- ASSASSINATIONS OF ONE'S CRITICS (26 JUNE,
  7 SEPTEMBER)
- A DESK-TOP SET FEATURING A TANK AND A CLUSTER
  OF MISSILES (25 AUGUST)
- THE CROWN OF THE TSARS (7 OCTOBER)
- 10,000 SOLDIERS SINGING BIRTHDAY SONGS
  (31 OCTOBER)
- ONE'S PORTRAIT IN SUGAR (19 DECEMBER) OR
  ON A GRAIN OF RICE (21 DECEMBER)
- A HAMMER-AND-SICKLE TELEPHONE HEAD-PIECE
  SITTING ON THE WORLD (21 DECEMBER)

18 SEPTEMBER

Wheels of fortune

The Dallas-born cyclist Lance Armstrong was given a bicycle for his seventh birthday in 1978. And from then on there was no stopping him: the Olympics, conquering cancer, seven times Tour de France winner, and a relationship with the American country and blues singer Sheryl Crow. And the only drugs he took were those to defeat his cancer, which, in the sport of competitive cycling, is saying something.

19 SEPTEMBER

Vroom, vroom

Porsche is developing a four-seat, four-door sports coupé. It will be called the Panamera, and will be available in 2009. The company has been toying with the idea of building a four-door model for some time. In 1984 a four-door version capable of 160 miles per hour was built as a 75th birthday present for Ferdinand (Ferry) Porsche, founder of the family firm. But this one-off did not at the time give rise to a four-door production model. In better years city traders and hedge-fund managers might have been glad of the extra space in a four-door Porsche: they could have taken their bonuses in cash and heaped the bundles of notes on the back seat. Nowadays they would be more likely to stuff their P45s in their pockets and hop on a bus.

Thanks, but no thanks

Reuben Singh was born on this day in Manchester in 1976. With wealthy parents, a job in his father's business would have been the easy option, but he was determined from the outset to make his own way. So when his parents gave him a £50,000 BMW for his 18th birthday he refused to accept it. In the 1998 edition of the *Guinness Book of Records* he was listed as the 'World's Youngest Self-made Millionaire', although the entry was subsequently withdrawn. He had made his fortune with a chain of shops selling young women's accessories, but was subsequently accused of grossly exaggerating the value of the business and his own personal wealth.

Also born on 20 September was another entrepreneur, Charles Bluhdorn, the man who built a run-down auto parts distributor into America's Gulf & Western Corporation, the industrial giant that owned Paramount Pictures amongst much else. He was born on this day in 1926. Sugar was one of the corporation's other interests, which brought Bluhdorn to the Dominican Republic. He fell in love with the place, and in 1976 began work on a monstrously extravagant birthday present for his daughter Dominique. Altos de Chavon is a faithfully recreated 16th-century southern Spanish village built by local masons, builders and carpenters under the direction of an Italian film-set designer who had worked for Paramount. It is now home to a large art school, galleries, restaurants and shops. The 5000-seat amphitheatre was christened by Frank Sinatra.

Beatles in an oasis

Liam, one of the two Gallagher brothers who created and fronted the rock band Oasis, was born to Irish parents in Manchester on 21 September 1972. Their father was an aggressive alcoholic, which might in part account for Liam's unpredictable and sometimes abrasive behaviour. His brother Noel gave him a necklace for his 25th birthday – not any old necklace but a necklace of beads once owned by John Lennon. But it did not seem to carry any soothing aura of peace with it.

Tigers and Cardinals

Mike Matheny is a celebrated American baseball catcher who made his debut in the major league for the Milwaukee Brewers and ended up playing for the St Louis Cardinals. (When the Detroit Tigers were in town back in the 1980s, a newspaper headline 'Tigers Maul Cardinals' would have been an alarming headline for the uninitiated and devastating news for the Pope; just as 'Queen In Brawl At Palace' above a story in the *Guardian* after Crystal Palace striker Gerry Queen had been sent off during a game at Selhurst Park would have sent innocent palace courtiers into a spin. Subs on the sports pages like their bit of fun.) Back in St Louis, Mike, who is a keen hunter, has a well-meaning wife who gave him a new hunting knife for his 30th birthday. But Mike got careless and cut his hand open just before a crucial game, with the result that the Cardinals' ace catcher ended up sitting on the sidelines, much to the annoyance of manager, coach, team mates and fans. It only goes to confirm the old superstition that it is bad luck to give someone a knife. Mrs Matheny should have stuck to a nice new pair of gloves.

Up close and personal in the kitchen

Augustus Caesar, Kublai Khan, Cherie Booth and Robert Bosch were all born on 23 September. Augustus, Rome's first emperor, was the great nephew of Julius Caesar. Born in 63 BC, he presided over a period of relative peace across the empire, a state of affairs we have come to know as the *pax Romana*. Kublai Khan was the grandson of Genghis. He was born in 1215 and was to found China's Yuan Dynasty and to unite the country, which thereafter enjoyed a period of considerable economic prosperity under his rule. Cherie Booth was born in 1954 at Bury in Lancashire, the daughter of actor Tony Booth. She studied law, and while training to be a barrister met another lawyer called Tony Blair. The two were married on 29 March 1980. Mrs Blair continues to practise law, and is a county court recorder. Robert Bosch was born on 23 September 1861 near Ulm on the River Danube in southern Germany. We could probably manage without Mrs Blair, and the exploits of Augustus and Kublai Khan are now just history. But where would we be without Herr Bosch? He opened his first workshop in Stuttgart when he was 25, and a century later you could peer into any car engine and walk into any kitchen and likely find components and goods from spark plugs to washing machines with his name on it. Of course almost everything with a Bosch label can be bought over the internet. But shoppers in America like to get personal – very personal. Here are a few e-mails and letters sent by customers to a Bosch distributor in Nebraska:

> Recently I ordered a dough hook and cookie paddles as a birthday surprise for my wife. Over the week-end while she was preparing some new recipes I overheard her talking to herself …

> The blender did a beautiful job of creaming the broccoli. I was sooooooo happy …

You've revolutionized our kitchen. Last week my wife Kate made some cranberry pecan scones …

Domestic bliss from Milwaukee to Michigan. Touching, generous and just a little bit absurd.

24 SEPTEMBER

Letting off steam on her birthday

It would be every boy's dream, a full-size steam locomotive with its own piece of track. But this 120-ton green beauty with a red nose and a red cab that had belonged to the Canadian National Railway was a present for a middle-aged woman. The publisher Andrew MacLean gave it to his wife Joan for her 42nd birthday in 1961, having acquired it as scrap from the railway company when it gave up steam for diesel at the beginning of the 1960s. To surprise his wife, MacLean even had a temporary branch line built so the locomotive could be delivered to the family business at Muskoka, Ontario on the day.

A 120-Ton Birthday Present

VENHURST —(Spe-
ooking for a pres-
. the lady who has
ing?
. a steam locomotive.
. Andrew MacLean
. for her birthday—
est-to-goodness 120-
am engine.

ling, it's wonderful,"
led. "Just what I've
wanted."

MacLean, board
an of Southam-Mac-
ublications and pub-
of the Weekly
a News and Banner,
locomotive will be

front page

the centre of a railway museum he plans here.

Mr. and Mrs. MacLean are interested in railway folklore.

Mr. MacLean bought the engine from the CNR. He didn't say anything about it because he wanted to surprise his wife.

The engine, built in 1912 for short-run freight hauls, will be placed in the K. C. Jones Roundhouse which Mr. MacLean plans to build soon. He will buy at least one other locomotive.

"It will be quite a tourist attraction," he said.

HAPPY BIRTHDAY DEAR

night edition
Telegram

Tues 17 Oct 1961

Blind faith

Actor Christopher Reeve was born on this day in 1952. Having made four Superman films between 1978 and 1987, he was left paralysed after a riding accident in 1995. A young high-school boy from Jamestown in New York State, who had been brought up on the Superman movies, hero-worshipped the actor who played him and treasured his action-man figure of Superman, decided he would speed his hero's recovery. So every day he gently moved the arms and legs of his Superman figure in the hope it might keep Reeve's arms and legs in shape. And then, much as he loved his toy, young Jeffrey Fardink sent it to Reeve as a 50th birthday present. Reeve told a television audience that Jeffrey had given him hope. But the young man's efforts turned out to be in vain: Reeve died two years later.

Bird spotting

T.S. Eliot was born on this day in 1888 in St Louis, Missouri (where there happened to be a furniture store run by a family called Prufrock). A much treasured birthday present was one he received from his mother when he was 14. *The Handbook of Birds of Eastern North America* was inscribed 'Thomas Stearns Eliot. September 26th 1902'. Eliot added to the inscription his own words: 'A much coveted birthday present on my 14th birthday.' The Nobel prize-winning poet and dramatist enjoyed a varied career. He went first to Harvard and then crossed 'the Pond' to continue his studies at Oxford. Settling in England, he taught at Highgate School, where John Betjeman was one of his pupils. He gave up teaching and next worked for Lloyds Bank, and when he got tired of banking found a job with the publisher that was to become Faber & Faber. His second wife, Valerie, who was his secretary at Faber, was 31 and Eliot 69 when they married in London at 6.15 in the morning. Eliot persuaded everyone invited to the wedding to get out of bed early so their privacy might be preserved.

This is also the day India's Sikh prime minister Manmohan Singh was born in what is now Pakistan. It was in 1932 – or thereabouts. His mother died young and the economist-turned-politician has readily admitted to being unsure about his true date of birth, using the day he started school as his official birthday. It was his adversary, the then president of Pakistan, Pervez Musharraf, who helped to clarify things. He set his birthday detectives to work in West Punjab, where they discovered previously unseen papers relating to the birth of the young Manmohan. At a meeting of the UN General Assembly in New York in 2004 he took his Indian opposite number aside and gave him a small gift in the form of a bound copy of his little detective story. With his birthday gift under his arm, India's delighted prime minister was able to tell reporters at the UN that he was most assuredly born in 1932, and on 26 September to be precise. The find coincided with his 72nd birthday, and on the flight home from New York, the Air India stewardesses gave their shy prime minister a birthday cake, and the journalists travelling with him managed to find a red balloon on which they chalked 'Happy Birthday'. Mr Singh seemed embarrassed by all the fuss and let go of the balloon, which then hung awkwardly from the cabin roof.

Stardust in his eyes

The leaves had yet to turn on this early autumn day in 1601 when the corridors of the Château de Fontainebleau burst with excitement. The infant who would be King Louis XIII had been safely delivered. Young Louis ascended the throne rather earlier than he had expected – his father, Henry IV, was assassinated when Louis was still only eight and a half. So his mother, Marie de' Medici, was given the job of regent – supposedly until Louis came of age at 13, but she proved reluctant to give up the reins. Marie's determination to cling to power suited Louis, who used the time to woo Anne of Austria, whom he married when he was 14. He enjoyed married life for a year, but by the time he was 15 decided his mother should take a back seat and leave him to run the country. The young king had an able and forceful lieutenant in Cardinal Richelieu, and together they guided France through the first decades of the 17th century.

Alvin Stardust with the ten-and-sixpenny 12th birthday present that set him on the road to fame.

There was doubtless also excitement, precisely 341 years later, at the semi in Muswell Hill when Mrs Jewry gave birth to baby Bernard. But the affairs of state were not to trouble the young Bernard: he was more interested in pop music. When he was 12 his parents gave him a guitar costing them all of ten shillings and sixpence. Bernard was quick to master his new instrument and bluffed his way backstage at a Buddy Holly concert, persuading his idol to hear him play. Duly impressed, Holly and his Crickets signed the young hopeful's guitar and sent him on his way. Swinging Britain embraced the sixties and seventies, and as it did so Bernard Jewry made his mark on the pop scene, first as Shane Fenton and finally as Alvin Stardust. Along the way, the solo artists and groups he met and worked with on tour all signed his guitar. The names of the Beatles, Bill Haley, the Rolling Stones, Buddy Holly and Chuck Berry all decorate his ageing instrument. The singer was recently offered $2 million for it by an American collector, but Stardust says his ten-and-sixpenny birthday present is not for sale. And never will be.

28 SEPTEMBER

Private lives

This was the day, according to legend, that the Chinese philosopher Confucius was born in what is now the province of Shandong. 28 September also saw the birth (in 1934) of Brigitte Bardot who, not content with oozing sex, said once she wished she had invented it. And actress Gwyneth Paltrow (*Shakespeare in Love*, *The Talented Mr Ripley* and *Sylvia*) was born on 28 September 1972 in Los Angeles. Paltrow's father, a descendant of a Polish rabbi, was a film and television director, her mother an actress. 'If there is one 30th birthday present I'd wish for myself,' she told London's *Daily Telegraph*, 'it's that in future I can be known more for my acting and less for my private life.' Mum's the word.

A king's ransom

The writer Colin Dexter was born on 29 September 1930. He recalls wistfully that on his sixth birthday an uncle who owned a farm in Rutland promised him a newborn lamb when the lambing season came around. The uncle was true to his word, sending a particularly fine specimen off to market and handing his nephew the forty shillings and sixpence he got for it. 'To me, at the time,' Dexter said, 'it was the equivalent of a king's ransom.' It was apparently on a rainy holiday in 1972 that a 42-year-old Colin Dexter found himself sitting around with nothing to do. So the classics scholar and one-time schoolmaster penned a few lines about a nasty murder and a police inspector he called Morse. *Last Bus to Woodstock* was eventually published in 1975, to be followed by another dozen mysteries featuring the cantankerous detective whose liking for classical music, real ale and crosswords reflected Dexter's own pleasures. (He named Morse after Sir Jeremy Morse, crossword fiend and one-time chairman of Lloyds Bank, and most of his murderers were named after winners of the *Observer* crossword competition.) The books were later turned into television dramas with John Thaw taking the part of Morse, and Kevin Whately vying with a red vintage Mark 2 Jaguar for best supporting part. The series twice won Best Drama Series at the British Television Academy Awards. The Jag sold in 2005 for £100,000 and Kevin Whately went on to star in his own TV series called *Lewis*, inspired by the Dexter stories.

Music maestro, please!

The violinist David Oistrakh was born on this day in 1908 into a family of Jewish Ukrainian merchants who lived in Odessa on the Black Sea. His fellow Russian, Dmitri Shostakovich, intended to write his 2nd violin concerto as a present for Oistrakh's 60th birthday, but he got his dates muddled and produced it a year early – Oistrakh performed it in October 1967 when he was still 59. But the composer remained determined to mark the violinist's 60th birthday and wrote a sonata for him – his Opus 134 – a year later. The two men were close friends and Oistrakh made a recording of the piece in the composer's Moscow flat. The sonata, for violin and piano, was given its first public performance on 3 May 1969 at the Moscow Conservatory with Sviatoslav Richter accompanying Oistrakh on the piano.

1 Jimmy Carter	**2** Sting	**3** Gore Vidal
8 Gus Hall	**9** David Cameron	**10** Sophie Calle
15 Hermann Goering	**16** David Ben-Gurion	**17** Peter Stringfellow
22 Annette Funicello / Sarah Bernhardt	**23** Ryan Reynolds	**24** Wayne Rooney
29 Robert Hardy	**30** Heidi Heitkamp	**31** Chiang Kai-shek

4	5	6	7
Anne Widdecombe	Ray Kroc	Le Corbusier	Vladimir Putin
11 Tarek Abdel Hamid Albasti	12 Luciano Pavarotti	13 Sir Ganga Singhji Bahadur / Margaret Thatcher	14 Ralph Lauren
18 Lotte Lenya	19 Philip Pullman	20 Diana Haun	21 Geoffrey Boycott
25 Pablo Picasso	26 Hillary Clinton	27 Sylvia Plath	28 Evelyn Waugh
1 Nita Ambani	2 Queen Sofia of Spain	3 Anna Wintour	4 Laura Bush

1 OCTOBER

Hold your fire

'Jimmy Carter is the birthday present that was needed for America's nationwide Bicentennial celebration', wrote a correspondent to *Time* magazine after the 1976 US Democratic convention at Madison Square Garden in New York. But by the time the American electorate had unwrapped their new president, found him indecisive, lacking consistent policy goals and surrounded by a Georgia Mafia that failed to understand the workings of Washington, they were minded to exchange their present for a new model. The Iranian hostage fiasco only served to seal the president's fate. But Carter, born on this day in 1924 in Plains, Georgia, proved to be an effective ex-president, establishing the Carter Center, gaining the Nobel Peace Prize in 2002 for his untiring efforts to find peaceful solutions to international conflicts, and winning the Fulbright Prize for International Understanding on his 70th birthday. He put the prize money into the Carter Center which is now chaired by John Moores. Moores tried to buy Carter a custom-built rifle from a London gunsmith as a birthday present, but was dissuaded from doing so at the last minute. 'People routinely give him outrageously expensive things,' said Moores, 'but he cares absolutely not one whit about anything material.' So Moores put his $80,000 back in his pocket, and President Carter went back to his study to prepare for his next Sunday school lesson.

2 OCTOBER

A cross word?

Gordon Sumner was born on this day in 1951 in the northeast of England at Wallsend, where his father managed a dairy. It was apparently a jumper with bee-like black and yellow hoops that got him the nickname Sting. The musician-songwriter-turned-human-rights-activist is a crossword enthusiast, reportedly skipping through the versions in *The Times* and the *New York Times*. This prowess prompted his manager Kathy Schenker to commission a special birthday crossword for him from the American compiler Patrick Merrell. None of the solutions appear to have been either 'Sting' or 'the Police'. That would have been too easy.

3 OCTOBER

A model of indiscretion

He is America's high priest of letters, respected and honoured in greater measure by his supporters than he is derided by those he pillories. For six decades he had inclined to the liberal left, exploring social and political issues in novels and essays with a pen as sharp as a chiselled poker, digging away at an American Establishment he considered spineless and dangerous at the same time. Gore Vidal was born on 3 October 1925 in the hospital at the United States Military Academy at West Point where his father was an instructor. He was brought up in Washington DC and had completed his first novel by the time he was 19. Four years later *The City and the Pillar* caused a furore with its unbridled homosexuality, and the *New York Times* pointedly ignored his next five books. But Vidal's wit and incisive mind could not help but command attention. He wrote books, plays, screenplays and essays. His collection of essays written between 1952 and 1992 was considered by the *Times Literary Supplement* to be one of the great American books of the 20th century. Tribute pieces marking his 80th birthday appeared in many journals, including the Russian daily *Pravda*, a seemingly unlikely vehicle to carry unbridled praise of an American writer, until you discover that the piece turns out to be carefully selected extracts of Vidal's work that are particularly damning of the American way of life. The piece was penned from Colorado by Christine Smith, who describes herself as author, writer, singer and 'aspiring model and actress'. She might have added 'politician': Ms Smith ran as libertarian candidate for the presidency in 2008. Of all Mr Vidal's birthday presents and tributes over the years, this must rank as one of the strangest.

Tories and teddies

Ann Widdecombe has been a Conservative MP at Westminster since 1987, the year she turned 40 and Margaret Thatcher won her third general election in a row. Born in Bath, the daughter of a right-wing civil servant, Miss Widdecombe is a convert to Roman Catholicism, and also a confirmed celibate, agony aunt, novelist and animal lover. She lives in south London with her cats Pugwash and Carruthers and her mother Rita. Some years ago her mother, now in her nineties, gave her a Franklin Mint teddy-bear plate, one of those rather cheesy tea-shop collectables. She liked it so much she was given more of them each year when her birthday came round on 4 October. Her terraced house is now full of them.

Mousetrap for McDonald's Boss

Love it or loathe it, McDonald's is the bun-and-burger face of globalization, fast-feeding 54 million customers every day in 120 countries. And if you thought producing a burger in a bun lacked academic rigour, then think again. The Hamburger University at Oak Brook just outside Chicago, along with campuses in Britain, Germany, Brazil, Hong Kong, Japan and Australia, is dedicated to ensuring that you get quality burgers with quality service every time you sit down, prop up or drive through. The world's most famous restaurant chain takes its name from brothers Maurice and Richard McDonald, who opened a burger joint in San Bernardino in 1940. Fourteen years later a certain Ray Kroc, born on 5 October 1902, turned up at the restaurant with a milkshake machine, won the first franchise and went on to launch the corporation that secured a place for fast food at the very heart of American culture. Kroc, a clever and ruthless businessman, bought out the McDonald brothers in 1961, became very rich and married three times. Faced with the man-who-has-everything challenge at birthdays, his third wife Joan beat a path to the studio of San Francisco artist Sidney Mobell, who came up with a solid gold mousetrap. Joan had it engraved 'Happy Birthday, Ray. Thanks for catching me.'

6 OCTOBER

Ideal hideaway, no reception rooms, lacks kitchen, few mod cons

Charles-Édouard Jeanneret was born in the Swiss town of La Chaux-de-Fonds high in the Jura Mountains on 6 October 1887. The city has long been associated with watch making – Tag Heuer, Corum and Breitling are based here – and Charles-Édouard began his working life as a watch engraver. But his studies at the local school of art had stimulated his imagination and his interest in art and architecture. He was in his early thirties before his talents as an architect were truly appreciated, by which time he had reinvented himself as Le Corbusier, a name he conjured from that of his maternal grandfather. Le Corbusier went on to influence 20th-century architecture and urban planning across four continents, championing his functional approach and describing the ideal home as *une machine-à-habiter* ('a machine for living in)'. Le Corbusier settled in France, and he and his wife Yvonne spent time on the Côte d'Azur; it was here that he built his smallest *machine-à-habiter* as a birthday present for Yvonne. The *cabanon* has a floor area of about 144 square feet, which is about the size of a garden shed. There is no kitchen, but there is direct access to an adjoining café. There are two beds, the toilet and bidet are part of the open-plan design, and what little other furniture there is all comes from recycled materials. The windows are small and the ceiling low enough to allow for storage above. The outer walls are of pine, the interior plywood and oak. There is a chestnut front door and a small walnut table. And nothing else. The birthday girl may not have had quite so much fun living in it as her husband did creating it.

7 OCTOBER

If the cap fits

The former Russian president Vladimir Vladimirovich Putin was born in St Petersburg on this day in 1952. Putin enjoys hunting, and for his 53rd birthday the then German chancellor Gerhard Schröder gave him a new double-barrelled shotgun, a somewhat larger firearm and more difficult to conceal than those the former KGB officer kept in his shoulder holster. But it was three years earlier on his 50th birthday that Russians really indulged their leader. One man

announced he was changing his name to Putin in honour of his president; farmers grew Putin tomatoes; spirit-makers bottled Putin vodka; and Russia's Academy of Jewellery Art gave their leader a replica of the Cap of Monomakh, the ceremonial crown worn by the tsars at coronations. It was encrusted with jewels and lined with sable. The ungrateful Putin said he had no intention of wearing it. He was more appreciative of the cut-glass crocodile given to him by the president of Moldova. Cleverly floating inside the glass, presumably where the animal's intestines would otherwise have been, is the Russian coat of arms.

8 OCTOBER

Birthday tea

Gus Hall, born Arvo Gustav Halberg on 8 October 1910 in northern Minnesota, was the son of Finnish parents, both of whom were founding members of the Communist Party of the USA. He joined the party himself when he was 17, and then spent two years in his early thirties at the Lenin Institute in Moscow. Back in America he spent eight years in jail on charges of conspiring to advocate the overthrow of the US government by force and violence. The law under which he was held was later deemed unconstitutional and, on his release in 1959, he was elected chairman of the US Communist Party. He received the Order of Lenin, and as a birthday gift from the North Korean leader Kim Il Sung a pink box of Insam tea. While he was America's communist boss, the box of tea never left his desk.

9 OCTOBER

Love in a bottle

Conservative Party leader David Cameron was born on this day in London in 1966. His father, a stockbroker, sent him to Eton, from where he went on to Oxford and gained a first-class honours degree in PPE (philosophy, politics and economics). He won the parliamentary seat of Witney for the Conservatives in the 2001 election. His birthday that year coincided with the party conference, where the delegates from his Witney constituency gave him a cake, a musical card and a bottle of Ann Summers Love Oil.

Champagne, knickers and pressure cookers

French artist Sophie Calle was born on this day in Paris in 1953. Beginning in 1980 and for 13 consecutive years, she invited friends to dinner on her birthday, asking one friend to bring someone she did not know to represent the unknown future, ensuring the total number of guests always corresponded to her age. Everyone brought gifts, but instead of using the presents she made a collection of them, creating a piece of installation art she calls *The Birthday Ceremony*. The gifts include a painted gilded angel, items stolen from restaurants, champagne, books, underwear and jewellery. Her mother would bring the sensible items of domestic equipment including, one year, a pressure cooker. *The Birthday Ceremony* was exhibited at Tate Modern in London in 1998.

Flying to the wrong conclusions

Exactly one month after the 9/11 terrorist attacks in America, FBI agents arrested the owner of a restaurant called The Crazy Tomato in Evansville, Indiana. The man was an American citizen with an American wife and a two-year-old daughter. His name was Tarek Abdel Hamid Albasti. Mr Albasti is a Muslim who came originally from Egypt. His father-in-law, a local Indiana attorney, had worked for the US Foreign Service and, enjoying the thrill of flying, had given his son-in-law flying lessons for his birthday. In its state of post-9/11 paranoia, the FBI suspected everyone with a name they couldn't pronounce – especially if they had been taking flying lessons. Which is how Tarek Albasti, deemed guilty before he could be proved innocent, spent a week in a Chicago jail. He was released without charge, and in 2003 the FBI said it had all been a mistake and the Bureau's top man in Indiana issued an apology. But the apology was too late to stop the finger pointing or to restore business at The Crazy Tomato. Albasti and his family were forced to up sticks and leave town.

12 OCTOBER

Bohemian birthday

The Guinness Book of Records relates that after singing Donizetti's *L'Elisir d'amore* at the Deutsche Oper in Berlin in 1988, Luciano Pavarotti received no less than 165 curtain calls over a period of an hour and seven minutes. His mother who produced him in Modena on this day in 1935 could not have foreseen her son's future popularity, although she probably had an idea about the strength of his voice. His operatic debut came with the role of Rodolfo in *La Bohème* in 1961. He was singing *Bohème* again on his 34th birthday in San Francisco when the director of the San Francisco Opera, Kurt Adler, dressed up in a waiter's costume and went on stage during the café scene with a real bottle of birthday champagne. From the wings it was clear that Pavarotti was momentarily stunned, but no one in the audience seemed to notice that Mr Adler had given himself a walk-on part, nor that Rodolfo was swigging real champagne.

13 OCTOBER

Riches of the Raj

Sir Ganga Singhji Bahadur, the Maharajah of Bikaner, was born on 13 October 1880 with a silver spoon in his mouth. Imagine the pomp at the birth – the size of his mother's bed, the golden drapes, the silver dish for the afterbirth, the priceless swaddling clothes. Ganga Singhji grew into a good man and an able administrator – and in turn liked to spoil his children. A child-sized silver coach drawn by two silver horses was commissioned from Rajastani craftsmen and given to his two children as a joint birthday present. An exercise in privileged self-indulgence, it was the most extravagant of presents, embossed with foliate and animal motifs including lions, tigers, elephants and rhinos. Of course it did not go anywhere and was far too valuable to be in the playroom. But it was a way of showing off the children when the neighbours came round for tea.

13 October is also the birthday of Margaret Thatcher. Throughout the 1980s, Mrs (now Baroness) Thatcher not only dominated British politics, but also brought her influence to bear on the international stage. The world may not have agreed with everything Mrs Thatcher said, but it never failed to take notice. However, she was less enthusiastic about the world taking notice of her private life. She was devoted to her husband Denis, whose support and wise counsel were always available and always gratefully received. But we know less about her relationship with her two children. When asked about birthday presents her mother had received, daughter Carol could bring nothing to mind. According to her biographer Charles Moore, a former editor of the *Daily Telegraph*, when people ask Lady Thatcher now what she would like for her birthday she suggests they give £25 towards a new building at the Royal Hospital in Chelsea where Denis's ashes are kept. Her appreciation of any gift never goes unacknowledged. According to Moore, 'There can be no one alive who has written so many "bread and butter" letters in her own hand.'

14 OCTOBER

So you really want to be in pictures?

Ralph Lauren was born Ralph Lipschitz on this day in 1939 in the Bronx, the son of a house painter. His mother had expectations of young Ralph becoming a rabbi, but he designed some ties instead and went on to create one of the world's best-known clothing brands. As a 60th birthday present Woody Allen taped a tribute. 'Ralph always thought he could be an actor. We had lunch one day and he said: "Put me in a picture." I said, "Who do you see yourself as?" He said, "Steve McQueen, Gary Cooper!" I said, "Ralph, you're a short little Jew." He said, "Not when I'm dressed."'

15 OCTOBER

Ill-gotten gains

During the night of 15 October 1946 Hermann Goering swallowed a capsule of potassium cyanide, which killed him before he could be hanged. Goering, Hitler's number two and commander-in-chief of the Luftwaffe, shared a birthday with Alfred Rosenberg, not only the most infamous of the Nazis' racial ideologists but also one of the Third Reich's greatest looters. Rosenberg acquired numerous paintings for Goering, who had little artistic appreciation but enjoyed the business of collecting. (He is credited with saying 'When I hear the word culture I reach for my Browning.') The Reichsmarschall never got round to paying for the pictures, but this did not deter Rosenberg from making a 50th birthday present of another of his ill-gotten paintings, this time a 17th-century Dutch masterpiece. It was a seascape by Jacob Bellevois. Rosenberg wrote to the Reichsmarschall on 11 January 1943: 'I take the liberty of giving you, as a friend of the plastic art, a Dutch painting as a little remembrance for your

museum. Tomorrow I shall offer you my personal congratulations on your anniversary.' Had Goering not succeeded in committing suicide, he would not only have shared a birthday with Rosenberg but would have gone to the gallows on the same day too.

US soldiers rescue works of art looted by the Nazis, Austria, May 1945.

The parrot that kept quiet

David Ben-Gurion was born on 16 October 1880 in Poland. In 1906 he emigrated to Palestine where he picked oranges, then became a journalist, studied law and eventually led Israel to victory in its War of Independence, becoming the country's first prime minister in 1948. He was, compared with many of his successors, a moderate, so here's a moderately funny joke. Benjy finally found a birthday present for his mother – a parrot that spoke Yiddish. When he called to find out how she liked the present, she said it was delicious. 'Mama, you ate a parrot that speaks Yiddish?' he cried. 'So?' she answered. 'If it could talk why didn't it say something?'

Look but don't touch

Given his reputation with women, it would seem unlikely that nightclub owner Peter Stringfellow would need a copy of the *Kama Sutra*. Stringfellow, only a touch sheepishly, agrees with the sentiment but says it does not stop him appreciating a beautiful antique edition of the treatise inscribed on ancient parchment. While Vatsyayana's treatise on love is only partially about sexual love, it nonetheless contains descriptions of 64 different kinds of sexual act – which Stringfellow would know backwards (so to speak), having claimed to have slept with more than 2000 women. (He first had sex with a girl in the back of his van down a side street in Sheffield in the Swinging Sixties.) Stringfellow's *Kama Sutra* was a birthday present from Baron Joseph De Dobrynyi, a Hungarian-born playboy living in Miami, who outflanks Stringfellow in the initiation stakes, having lost his virginity in a nunnery when he was 15. The baron, Sepy to his friends, has some 20 years on Stringfellow, who was born on 17 October in 1940. Stringfellow in turn has 42 years on his partner Bella Wright, a former dancer with Royal Ballet, who is still in her twenties. On one birthday Bella gave her man some Roman marbles. But they don't play with his marbles: like the girls at Stringfellow's eponymous London club, they are to be seen but not touched.

18 OCTOBER

Singing with Satchmo

Lotte Lenya was born Karoline Wilhelmine Charlotte Blamauer on this autumn day in 1900. In the film version of *From Russia with Love* the Austrian actress and singer played Rosa Klebb, the murderous lesbian spymaster with a poisonous flick-knife in her shoe. No one could have done it better. Lotte was married to the composer Kurt Weill, who bought a house for her as a birthday present in 1931 on Berlin's Wissmanstrasse. It was Weill who, with Bertolt Brecht, wrote *Die Dreigroschenoper* or, as it is known in English, *The Threepenny Opera*. The show opened in Berlin in 1928 and included the song 'Mack the Knife', which became a popular standard. Sinatra and Bobby Darin made memorable recordings of the song, but it was Louis Armstrong, recording it in 1956, who managed to include Lotte's name in the lyric. She was in the studio during the recording, and when Armstrong caught sight of her he managed effortlessly to weave her into the list of Macheath's victims. Listen carefully next time you hear the Satchmo version.

GIFTS OF BODY PARTS, PRODUCTS AND FUNCTIONS

- Multiple orgasms (15 March)

- A lock of Beethoven's hair (26 March)

- A chunk of one's ear (30 March)

- Drew Barrymore's breasts (12 April)

- The bleeding heart of an elk (22 April)

- A fossilized turtle turd (28 June)

- A photograph of a vagina (14 September)

- A gold-plated wisdom tooth (23 October)

- A yak's skull (17 November)

The dark side of Britain's education system

Philip Pullman, the teacher-turned-novelist who has enthralled the young and not-so-young alike with his fantastical stories laced with criticism of intolerance and fanaticism, was born on this day in Norfolk in 1946. Best known for his trilogy *His Dark Materials*, Pullman is a vocal critic of Britain's education system, although self-deprecatingly says his views on education are eccentric and unimportant. His school plays, accessible to both children and adults, inspired the ex-teacher's first book for children. For his 60th birthday a former student gave him a complete set of the 12 issues of *Theatre World* published in the year of his birth. Issue number one has a picture of Nicholas Parsons on the cover. The indomitable Parsons is still hosting the BBC radio show *Just a Minute* after 40 years. That makes the show's producers guilty of repetition – big time.

Murder most foul

They killed over custody battles; they hired thugs to kill their husbands; they shot strangers for their cash cards. Diana Haun did it as a birthday present. The women on California's death row are not a pretty bunch. But when prosecutors told the jury that Haun had given her lover a birthday present by stabbing the man's wife to death, even the judge had difficulty in hiding his incredulity. Haun was found guilty and began her sentence on 20 October in 1997 at a women's prison near Chowchilla.

Winter sports

Son of a miner, the Yorkshire and England cricketer Geoffrey Boycott was born on 21 October 1940 in Pontefract, West Yorkshire. For his 11th birthday his uncle Albert persuaded several members of the family to each put two shillings and sixpence into a fund to buy young Geoff some winter coaching at an indoor cricket school. The present was apparently renewed annually. Boycott won his first England cap less than 12 months after turning professional, and went on to become one of England's most successful batsmen. These days he works in the commentary box, dishing out advice to batsmen, bowlers, captains and anybody else who might be listening.

How to stuff a bikini

Walt Disney did not do much of his own talent scouting, but he did discover Annette Funicello, who was born on 22 October 1942 in New York State to Italian-American parents. She caught Disney's eye when she was 12, dancing the role of the Swan Queen at a drama academy show in Burbank, California. Disney cast her as a 'Mouseketeer' in his *Mickey Mouse Club* television series, and by the end of the first season she was receiving 6000 fan letters a month. Hollywood only half smiled on her adult career, giving her roles in a string of not very distinguished beach movies such as *Pyjama Party* in 1964 and *How to Stuff a Wild Bikini* a year later. At the age of 37 she was back on television in a series of advertisements for peanut butter. Still, Hollywood likes its bikini stuffers, and on her birthday in 1993 it honoured Ms Funicello with a star on its Walk of Fame. It is at 6834 Hollywood Boulevard.

Not far away, at 1751 Vine Street, is the star awarded posthumously to the great French actress Sarah Bernhardt (*opposite*), born in 1844, also on 22 October. Her talent became obvious during her time at the Paris Conservatoire, and she went on to make her debut at the Comédie Française. Without stuffing herself into a bikini, she grew in stature and popularity to become the most sought-after actress on the European stage, taking the lead in many of the plays of Victor Hugo, with whom she became a close friend. At the turn of the century she put on a French production of *Hamlet* in which she daringly took the title role. Theatre audiences in London flocked to see her performances, and her many admirers included the Prince of Wales (later King Edward VII), with whom she is thought to have had an affair. But disaster was to strike during a tour of South America when she badly damaged her knee during a

performance of *La Tosca* in Rio de Janeiro. The knee never healed properly, and in time gangrene set in and her leg had to be amputated. But rather than end her career it only restricted her movement on the stage, and she even carried out a successful tour of America, along with her wooden leg. She died in 1923 shortly before her 80th birthday.

23 OCTOBER

Mind the gap

The Canadian actor Ryan Reynolds was born in Vancouver on this day in 1976. He launched his career on the small screen, starring in the Kenny Schwartz sitcom for ABC, *Two Guys and a Girl*. At the time of writing, and we are talking Hollywood here, *at the time of writing* Reynolds is dating Scarlett Johansson. (Miss Johansson, the star of *The Horse Whisperer* and *Lost in Translation*, is herself cautious about referring to boyfriends as partners. She professes not to believe in monogamy and gets tested for HIV twice a year.) Mr Reynolds clearly accepts all this and is important enough in Miss Johansson's life (at the moment) for her to have given him a most extraordinary present – even by Hollywood standards. She went to the dentist, had her wisdom teeth removed, dipped one of them in gold, attached it to a chain and gave it to him as a birthday present for his 31st in 2007. Watch this space.

24 OCTOBER

Time – and fast cars – the great healer

He could not deliver the FA Cup for Manchester United in 2007, the year the final returned to the overdue, over-budget Wembley Stadium, but Wayne Rooney – born on 24 October 1985 – nevertheless got as near to scoring as any of his team mates. From his late teens the striker was firmly established as one of the star attractions of the English game. The injury that put his 2006 World

Cup place in jeopardy attracted even more media attention than the England manager's love life. On another occasion, the love of Wayne's life, Coleen McLoughlin, having discovered that Wayne had visited a massage parlour rather than her, found it in her heart to forgive him and gave him an Aston Martin Vanquish as an early 20th birthday present. Oh, and as a little extra she gave him a Rolex wristwatch as well.

25 OCTOBER
Pictures on the wall

The best known and most influential painter of the 20th century was born on this day in 1881 in Málaga, southern Spain. Pablo Picasso spent much of his life in France, and it was in the small town of Vallauris in the hills behind Antibes that he met and married Jacqueline Roque. He also did much to restore the town's ceramics industry. So on his 70th birthday the grateful potters of Vallauris gave the artist the disused 12th-century vault in the chapel next to the town's museum. He was to decorate it as he liked, which he happily and gratefully did with his fresco *War and Peace*. And in so doing he gave tourists another reason to leave the nearby beaches of Cannes and Juan les Pins.

26 OCTOBER
Bill gives Hillary an earful

Hillary Rodham was born in Chicago (Barack Obama's town) on this day in 1947. She was 28 when she married Bill Clinton in 1975 and 46 when he led her into the White House for his first term as president in 1993. By her late fifties Hillary was making plans to return to the White House, taking

Bill with her. It was while she was planning her run for the presidency that she revealed that for her 59th birthday Bill had given her an iPod. And in a moment of unusual spontaneity, she went on to list the music she had downloaded. There were numbers from the Beatles, the Rolling Stones, Aretha Franklin, U2 and the Eagles, along with an eclectic selection of classical music. The question is: what did Democrat voters in the 2008 presidential campaign learn about Mrs Clinton from her choice of music? And did they vote accordingly?

27 OCTOBER

Reading between the lines

The American poet Sylvia Plath contributed to the genre of confessional poetry more than most. She was born on 27 October in Massachusetts in 1932, the daughter of a biologist who specialized in bees. The death of her father from complications associated with diabetes affected her deeply, and her life was plagued with periods of deep depression, including a number of suicide attempts. She left America for Britain and a new life at Cambridge University, where she met and later married the British poet Ted Hughes. But it was a troubled marriage and there were further attempts at suicide. She succeeded finally in killing herself by putting her head in the gas oven while her two children were asleep upstairs. Shortly before her death she wrote 'The Birthday Present', which includes the lines:

I do not want much of a present, anyway, this year.
After all I am alive only by accident.
I would have killed myself gladly that time any possible way.

Later in the poem Plath compares the clouds to cotton, and then, prophetically, to carbon monoxide – *'Sweetly, sweetly I breathe in …'*

28 OCTOBER

A Philistine in a flat

Evelyn Waugh, best known for his novels *Vile Bodies*, *Decline and Fall* and *Brideshead Revisited*, was born in Hampstead on this day in 1903. He received an unusual 50th birthday present from Sir John Betjeman in the form of a Victorian wash-stand by the Puginesque designer William Burgess. Waugh's son Auberon, the writer and journalist who died in 2001, eventually sold it and put the proceeds towards a flat. The man was a Philistine.

29 OCTOBER

The archer returns

Robert Hardy was born on 29 October 1925 in Cheltenham, where his father was headmaster of Cheltenham College, the public school for boys. He read English at Magdalen College, Oxford from where he embarked on an acting career that has spanned five decades. Although he has had a number of leading roles on the big screen – most recently in the Harry Potter films – it is for his television performances that he is best known. He won critical acclaim for his extraordinary portrayal of *Winston Churchill* in *The Wilderness Years*, first shown in 1981, and for his characterization of the vet Siegfried Farnon in *All Creatures Great and Small*. Less well known is his interest in and knowledge of medieval warfare, and in particular the development and role of the longbow, about which he has written books and given expert advice to film-makers and historians. This interest inspired him to design a wrought-iron archer in swashbuckling boots with a fully drawn bow, which he commissioned his local blacksmith to forge. For years it stood on the roof of his house above the weather vane. When he moved, the archer was left behind. Some 20 years on he celebrated his 80th birthday with a gathering of family and friends. His elder daughter, the portrait photographer Emma Hardy, had persuaded the then owners of the previous family home to part with her father's archer, organized its removal from the roof, set it upon a plinth and presented it to her father for his 80th birthday. Hardy was thrilled, and chuffed to bits that his daughter had gone to so much trouble.

Donkey rides on the plains of North Dakota

Heidi Heitkamp is a lawyer, an occasional talk-show host, a campaigner against big tobacco and the former attorney general in North Dakota. She was born on 30 October 1955. There is a history in her family of exchanging animals as presents – and the animals just get bigger. So when Heidi was given a donkey by her brother on her 50th birthday, she was delighted but not altogether surprised. Colleagues throughout the state were adamant that nobody ever took the attorney general for a ride.

Healthy eating

The Chinese nationalist leader Chiang Kai-shek, who was born on this day in 1887 into a family of salt merchants, did the usual things you do when you turn 76. He listened to 10,000 soldiers singing birthday songs and then joined the younger members of the clan to open his presents. Amongst the presents that year (1963) was a gift of $750,000 from a group of Chinese businessmen in Thailand, intended to fund the building of a new basketball stadium in Taipei. Having opened his presents Chiang sat down with the family and ate bowls full of longevity noodles. The noodles did their job – he lived another 12 years, dying at the ripe old age of 88.

1 Nita Ambani	2 Queen Sofia of Spain	3 Anna Wintour
8 Gordon Ramsay	9 William Horwood / Hadley Richardson	10 Mikhail Kalashnikov
15 Aleksander Kwaśniewski	16 Sir Oswald Mosley	17 Jonathan Ross / Viscount Montgomery / Martin Scorsese / the Dalai Lama
22 Sir Peter Hall	23 Richard Kind	24 Edward Stourton
29 Jacques Chirac	30 Winston Churchill	1 Woody Allen

4	5	6	7
Laura Bush	Rory MacLean	Anna Ivanovic	Dame Joan Sutherland
11 Demi Moore	**12** Nadia Comăneci	**13** Robert Louis Stevenson	**14** Jean Monet / Condoleezza Rice
18 George Gallup / Johnny Mercer / Alexander Constantine Issigonis	**19** Jeane Kirkpatrick	**20** Alistair Cooke	**21** René Magritte
25 Andrew Carnegie	**26** Tina Turner / Charles M. Schultz	**27** Caroline Kennedy	**28** Ed Harris
2 Ann Patchett	**3** Anna Freud	**4** Francisco Franco	**5** Walt Disney

Obscene riches

Nita Ambani was born on 1 November 1963. Her husband Mukesh is the richest man in India. Being rich in India is something of an obscenity. At least being worth around $50 billion is. For his wife's birthday in 2007 Mr Ambani, whose privately owned Reliance Industries Ltd is in all sorts of things from petrochemicals and telecommunications to Premier League cricket teams, wrapped up a spanking new Airbus A-319. It has specially designed cabin comprising living and working areas, bedrooms, bathrooms, a bar with mood lighting, satellite television, and so on. The last word on this little birthday present is with a Mr P. Patel from Mumbai, who posted his reaction, appropriately seared with sarcasm, on the website of the London *Times* newspaper. 'The millions of "untouchables" in India may feel very happy to hear about his news.' Indeed they may.

Smart move

Today is the birthday of Spain's Queen Sofia, a great-great-granddaughter of Queen Victoria. Most public-relations people spin with the sort of finesse you might expect from a pirouetting sumo wrestler on hot coals. But

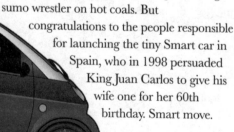

congratulations to the people responsible for launching the tiny Smart car in Spain, who in 1998 persuaded King Juan Carlos to give his wife one for her 60th birthday. Smart move.

She devil?

The editor-in-chief of American *Vogue* is arguably the most influential figure in the world of fashion. That post today is held by a British export called Anna Wintour, the daughter of a former editor of London's *Evening Standard*. Wintour was born in London on 3 November 1949. She arrived in New York in the mid-1970s, and after a spell back in London editing British *Vogue* she returned to New York and finally won the job of editing the American edition in 1988, collecting both friends and enemies on the way – and earning the nickname 'Nuclear Wintour'. One of those more persistent enemies is the animal-rights organization People for the Ethical Treatment of Animals (PETA), which objects in particular to Wintour featuring fur products in the magazine. PETA had already dropped dead and rotting raccoons on her dinner plate in New York restaurants, and then as a 54th birthday present the group's president Ingrid Newkirk sent Wintour a gift certificate worth $3600. The accompanying note said the money was for a brain scan to establish whether her brain was not fully developed and functional, 'which could explain your inability to curb violent desires that result in real harm to animal life'. Ouch. Wintour's one-time assistant Lauren Weisberger wrote what many see as a roman-à-clef based on her time as Wintour's side kick at *Vogue*. *The Devil Wears Prada*, published in 2003 and released as a film in 2006, tells the story of an arrogant, demanding and ruthless fashion magazine editor called Miranda Priestly and her new junior assistant. And although Weisberger has always denied that the character in her book was based on Wintour, there are many similarities between the two. Wintour attended the film's premiere dressed from head to foot in Prada.

They are animals in the White House

Laura Welch, the daughter of a builder, was born in Texas on this day in 1946. She was 29 when she met and married George W. Bush after a whirlwind romance lasting just three months. For her 58th birthday George gave her a second Scottish terrier, which they named Miss Beazley (*below left*) as a mate for Barney, who had been at the White House since 2000. White House photographers have

expended a considerable amount of film showing how much the two dogs enjoy playing amongst the Bushes.

Pets are not new to the White House. John Quincy Adams kept a pet alligator in a bath in the East Room, and the Calvin Coolidges kept a goose, a wallaby, a donkey, a lion cub, two cats, 12 dogs, several birds and an antelope. Andrew Johnson's daughter kept two cows on the White House lawn, to keep the family in milk and butter.

5 NOVEMBER

Island 161A

The day Guy Fawkes tried to blow up the Houses of Parliament in 1605 was also the day, more than three centuries later, that Rory MacLean was born. The best-selling Canadian travel writer (*Stalin's Nose* and *Magic Bus*) found himself, quite by surprise, in possession of an island in Georgian Bay, Ontario (part of a parcel of properties that used to belong to his father), when ownership passed to him on his 18th birthday. But what might have been a stunning birthday present turned out to be something of a disappointment. 'Island 161A, township of Georgian Bay,' turned out to be very small, uninhabited and spends much of the time totally submerged. Maclean did the decent thing and proclaimed the island an independent state, naming it the Republic of Bumpalump.

6 NOVEMBER

An investment that played well

Tennis players have a habit of getting fired up on their birthdays. Anna Ivanovic, the Serbian number one, beat the world number two Svetlana Kuznetsova in Madrid on her 20th birthday. Anna was born on 6 November in Belgrade in 1987. Her dad gave her a tennis racket for her sixth birthday and by the time she was 16 she had turned professional. Good investment. Anna reached the final of junior Wimbledon in 2004. Can she win the big one? Being knocked out in the third round in 2008 was a bit of a set-back. But there's always 2009. A new racket for her 21st might help.

Mrs Malaprop rides again

The Australian soprano Dame Joan Sutherland, born on this day in 1926 in Sydney, was given her image in bronze as an 80th birthday present by Roland Gridiger, the organizer of the 2006 Australian singing competition in which Dame Joan was heavily involved. But it was the image of her as Lucia in *Lucia di Lammermoor* at the Metropolitan Opera in New York that brought back memories for an admiring internet blogger who, hot on the heels of that matron saint of word fumbling, Mrs Malaprop, wrote of Sutherland 'darting around like a crazed moth, she was completely marvellous: voice, body, spirit, all of it … at the end of the mad scene there was a half hour of (the audience) carrying on, and remember this was 1961, pre hype, pre standing ovulations'.

The language of cooking

Gordon Ramsay, who showed an early talent for football and a later talent for good food and bad language, was born on 8 November in Glasgow in 1966. In 2006 he gave himself a birthday present of an F430 Ferrari. Now that is some ****ing car. Swearing apparently tells us a lot about the way our brains work, or so the psychologist Steven Pinker would have us believe. Ramsay's kitchen would not be a bad place for some field work.

Death by chocolate

William Horwood was born in Worthing, Sussex on 9 November 1868. After distinguished service in the Great War – he was awarded the Croix de Guerre by both France and Belgium and was made a Companion of the Bath – he joined the Metropolitan Police as an assistant commissioner with responsibilities for uniformed policing. He recruited the first women police officers, set up the forerunner of the Flying Squad, and by 1920 had the job of commissioner. But he was heavily criticized for failing to deal with corruption in the force, and was regarded as distant and even arrogant by his men. Yet it was an outsider, who knew nothing of the man personally, who tried to bump him off. On his birthday in 1922 he enjoyed a birthday lunch at Scotland Yard – roast pork with apple sauce, a glass of Guinness, and bread-and-butter pudding – and on returning to his office found a box of chocolates on his desk, which he took to be the promised birthday present from his daughter Beryl. Horwood tucked into the walnut whips, but before he had the chance to hand them round he collapsed in dreadful pain – unable to acknowledge the arrival of his daughter's gift minutes later. Arsenic in the first two chocolates was enough to take him to death's door, but luckily his life was saved by the swift intervention of police surgeons already in the building. Detectives began a massive manhunt and eventually arrested and charged a man called Walter Tatam. In court Tatam was found guilty of attempted murder but judged to be insane. It emerged that he had made previous attempts on the lives of senior police officers using poisoned éclairs. Horwood recovered and served for a further seven years.

Hadley Richardson, also born on this day but in 1891, became Ernest Hemingway's first wife in 1921. Hemingway bought her Joan Miró's painting *The Farm* as a birthday present, having paid the last instalment of the 5000 francs just in time. Taking it home in an open taxi, the wind apparently caught the large canvas and Hemingway had a struggle keeping it from blowing away. He said of the painting: 'It has in it all that you feel in Spain when you are there and all that you feel when you are away and cannot be there.' After Miró died, on Christmas Day in 1983, *Le Monde* carried a picture of the artist on the front page – the first time the paper had put a photograph on its cover.

For whom the bell tolls

If one man's name is inexorably linked with modern armed struggle – from the Cold War to global terrorism and the civil wars that plague so much of the developing world – it is that of the Russian Mikhail Kalashnikov. *Forbes* magazine ranked the rifle he invented as the seventh most important tool of all time. Kalashnikov was born on 10 November 1919. He was still only 28 when his AK-47 (A for automatic, K for Kalashnikov, and 47 for the year it went into production) won a competition amongst armourers and was selected for mass production. It may not technically be a weapon of mass destruction, but its death toll has most assuredly been massive. Nonetheless its inventor says his conscience is clear and blames politicians for failing to bring peace to the world. Kalashnikov was honoured on his 85th

Mikhail Kalashnikov indulges in a spot of grooming in the presence of his eponymous invention.

birthday when the bell-makers in the city of Voroneh produced a new 200-kilo bell for the cathedral in his home town of Izhevsk in the Ural Mountains, and inscribed it with his name. For whom does the bell toll? There are probably as many as 100 million AK-47s in circulation today. The bell tolls for every man, woman and child that has died from an AK-47 bullet.

1 1 NOVEMBER

Let's get naked

Demi Moore has not been averse to taking her clothes off for the camera. The American actress, born on 11 November 1962, started as a pin-up model and has been getting naked ever since, most recently as part of her 41st birthday present from her husband, actor and producer Ashton Kutcher. Ashton hired the photographer Mario Testino to do the shoot, expressly forbidding nude shots. But when Testino arrived the first thing he said was 'Let's get naked'. So the Kutchers relented and Demi took her clothes off again. Over a decade earlier, in 1991, while married to Bruce Willis, she appeared naked and very pregnant on the cover of *Vanity Fair*. But if you have spent as much time and money on cosmetic surgery as Ms Moore has, you would want the world to enjoy the results.

1 2 NOVEMBER

Too good to be true

Time magazine put her on the cover and added just two words: 'She's Perfect.' So perfect was she that the electronic scoreboard that had been primed for lesser mortals could not cope. A young girl from behind the Iron Curtain, barely into her teens, had become the first gymnast to be awarded perfect scores of 10. But the scoreboard at the Montreal Olympic stadium came up with 1.00 because no one had thought to programme it to record anything beyond 9.99. Nadia Comăneci, born on this day in Oneti, a city of some 52,000 inhabitants in the east of Romania, was 14 when she won no less than five gold medals. Dave Anderson, writing in the *New York Times*, described her performance on that day in 1976: 'On the uneven bars, she whirls as easily as a sparrow fluttering from limb to limb on a tree. On the balance beam, she clings to it as surely as a squirrel would. On the vault, she lands as softly as a seagull on a beach. In her floor exercises, she is part go-go dancer, part ballerina, part cheerleader.'

Some 30 years later her fans, decided she warranted a birthday present that matched her status. So they named a star after her. It shines brightly in the constellation we know as Hercules. Now living in Oklahoma and married to a former gymnast, Nadia has 'star status' in common with the Princess of Wales, Mahatma Gandhi, Elvis Presley, His Holiness Pope John Paul II and Arsenal Football Club.

13 NOVEMBER

A strange but kindly bequest

Scottish writer and traveller Robert Louis Stevenson was born in Edinburgh on this day in 1850. *Treasure Island*, *Kidnapped* and *The Strange Case of Dr Jekyll and Mr Hyde* are his best-known works. But there is something else that he wrote, which is little known but nonetheless extraordinary. Stevenson spent his last years on the island of Samoa, where he became friends with the commissioner general, Henry Ide, and his family. Annie Ide, the commissioner's daughter, complained that because she was born on Christmas Day, she lost out on presents. So Stevenson, taking pity on her, bequeathed the girl his birthday in a deed that he delivered to her in the summer of 1891. In a covering note he asks that she treat his day 'with moderation and humanity'. The deed reads in part:

In consideration that Miss Annie H. Ide, daughter of H.C. Ide in the Town of St Johnsbury, in the county of Caledonia, in the State of Vermont, United States of America, was born, out of all reason, upon Christmas Day, and is therefore out of all justice denied the consolation and profit of a proper birthday, And considering that I, the said Robert Louis Stevenson, have attained an age when we never mention it, and that I have now no further use for a birthday of any description ... Have transferred and do hereby transfer to the said Annie H. Ide all and whole my rights and privileges in the 13th day of November, formerly my birthday, now hereby, and henceforth, the birthday of the said Annie H. Ide, to have, hold, exercise and enjoy ...

First impressions

Claude Monet was born on this day in Paris in 1840. His birthday present to his son Jean on the boy's fifth birthday in 1872 was a small mechanical horse, one of the first of its kind. There appears to have been an element of self-interest in the gift,

for Monet senior proceeded to paint his son, wearing a dress and a bonnet, riding his birthday toy. In those days it was the custom in France for boys to graduate to trousers on their fifth birthday, so this would have been Jean's last day in a dress. The picture hangs in the Metropolitan Museum of Art in New York.

This is also the birthday of Condoleezza Rice, who was born in 1954 in Birmingham, Alabama, the very heart of black America. She was an only child and, while there is no suggestion that she was spoilt, her parents gave her a tiny piano for her second birthday and had her playing a real one when she was three. By the time she was 15 she was playing Mozart's piano concerto in D with the Denver Symphony Orchestra – the prize in a piano competition. George W. Bush's national security advisor and subsequently his secretary of state went on to develop her keen interest in music, and regularly plays chamber music with friends in her Watergate apartment. She has even added music to her diplomatic repertoire by playing for the British ambassador.

Diplomats left watching as the balloon goes up

Aleksander Kwaniewski is the man who defeated Lech Wałęsa in Poland's 1995 presidential election. Born on 15 November 1954, he celebrated his 50th birthday in office in 2004, and amongst a host of foreign dignitaries who went to wish him happy birthday was Canada's ambassador in Warsaw, Ralph Lysyshyn. Ambassador Lysyshyn brought with him five balloons – three red and two white. Five balloons would not have stretched Canada's foreign office budget, although having 'CANADA' printed on them would have cost a dollar or two. And it is difficult to imagine to what use the president could have put them. So was this just a lot of diplomatic hot air? On the contrary, it was the Ottawa school of diplomatic opportunism at work. Pictures of the president with his Canadian balloons appeared on the front pages in Poland the next day, and the embassy press office proudly displayed the results of their endeavours, on its self-congratulatory website.

Flirting with the enemy

Sir Oswald Mosley was born on this day in 1896 at Rolleston Hall, the family home in Staffordshire. The Mosleys were wealthy, well-connected landowners, but Oswald did not fancy running the family estates, believing he was better suited to a career in Parliament. In politics he proved to be as fickle as he was in love. He began his parliamentary career as a Conservative, fell out with them over their policy on Ireland, crossed the floor of the House to sit as an Independent, gave up his independence, joined the Labour Party, got fed up with them, founded the New Party with little success, and eventually launched the British Union of Fascists. And all the while his political flirtations were being mirrored by his flirtations with women. He first married Lord Curzon's daughter Cynthia, and went on to conduct affairs both with her younger sister and her stepmother. He also seduced Diana Mitford while she was still married to Bryan Guinness. He eventually married Diana in the drawing room of Joseph Goebbels' home in Berlin, with Adolf Hitler as the guest of honour. Goebbels and Hitler were not Mosley's only friends in Nazi Germany. A silver cigarette case has recently come to light that he gave to Hermann Goering as a birthday present in 1934 – the year the Reichstag passed a law authorizing the sterilization of the 'unfit' and the Kaiser Wilhelm Institute of Anthropology held its first course for doctors of the SS. The cigarette case has the HG monogram on the front and Mosley's signature on the back.

Keeping ahead on your birthday

Jonathan Ross, Viscount Montgomery and Martin Scorsese were all born on 17 November – Ross in 1960, Monty in 1887 and Scorsese in 1942. Mr Ross is the highest paid television presenter on British television. He suffers from rhotacism – he has difficulty pronouncing his Rs. Ross commands huge audiences for his radio and television shows, and suffers harsh criticism from detractors who think the BBC is wasting its money: a contributor to the *Daily Telegraph*'s web pages thought him 'about as funny as woodworm in a cripple's crutch'. General (later Field Marshal) Montgomery was the brilliant but arrogant wartime strategist who led the 8th Army in its decisive battles with Rommel's Africa Korps at El Alamein, and whose arrogance once prompted him to say 'As God once said, and I think rightly …' And Martin Scorsese is the Hollywood director who stunned audiences with his dark and brutal *Taxi Driver* in 1976 and went on to make a string of critically acclaimed films, including *Raging Bull, Goodfellas, The Aviator* and *The Departed* (which won Best Film and Best Director at the 2006 Academy Awards).

17 November was also the day in 1950 that Tenzin Gyatso, the 14th Dalai Lama, was enthroned as Tibet's head of state. As a rule Tibetans don't celebrate birthdays, and many don't even know the date on which they were born. They follow the lunar calendar, which makes the keeping of anniversaries difficult. Amai Cering is an exception. She was 117 in 2008 and was given a huge birthday cake by her fellow villagers in Jiarong. While Tibetans make little of celebrating their own births, they delight in making a fuss of others. Jamin Losang, an American who has lived in Tibet for six years, tells of his own birthday when Tibetan friends came loaded with presents, including a yak's skull, a goat's skull, yak-hair slings, deer antlers and blood sausages.

Mini birthday presents

George Gallup, the father of modern polling, was born on 18 November 1901, and boasted once that he could prove the existence of God statistically. The same day eight years later saw the birth of the songwriter Johnny Mercer, whose lyrics crowd the pages of the Great American Songbook – 'Moon River', 'Fools Rush In' and 'That Old Black Magic' are just three of his great hits. And this was also the birthday in 1836 of W.S. Gilbert, who contributed the words to Arthur Sullivan's music, so creating a string of very English comic operas. It was on this day too in 1906 in Smyrna (now Izmir in Turkey) that Alexander Constantine Issigonis was born. His family were Anglophiles and engineers, and Alec was soon to find himself in England and working for the British Motor Corporation (BMC). With the imposition of fuel rationing after the Suez Crisis, BMC was looking for a small, inexpensive, fuel-efficient car that, despite its size, was still able to carry four people. Issigonis came up with the Mini, which became one of the enduring icons of the 1960s and the best-selling British car ever made. Its highly competitive price even made it an attractive birthday present – and not only in its home market. A man in Michigan bought a chilli-red Mini Cooper S for his wife's birthday because she wanted a car like the ones in the movie *The Italian Job*. The parents of a Moscow student Maria Kitaeva gave their daughter one of the latest go-faster models for her 20th birthday, and a man in Arizona, coming late to small cars, bought himself a more sedate version of the Mini for his 100th birthday. But Michelle from Motherwell did not do so well. The fashion designer Sir Paul Smith had been invited to custom-design a Mini for himself, which prompted the production of a limited edition of the car incorporating distinctive elements of his designs. Michelle wanted one of the Paul Smith models for her boyfriend's birthday – his name is Paul Smith so she thought it would hit the spot. But the limited edition models have become rare and very expensive. So Paul Smith is still waiting for his Paul Smith.

Career-starting gifts

- Jacqueline du Pré got her first cello on her fifth birthday (26 January)
- Camille Paglia got The Second Sex for her 16th (2 April)
- Ruth Parasol, founder of PartyGaming, was given a portfolio of phone-sex chat lines by her father when still in her teens (27 June)

- Anne-Sophie Mutter asked for violin lessons for her fifth birthday (29 June)
- Kirsten Flagstad got the score of Lohengrin for her tenth (12 July)
- Coleridge's Lectures on Shakespeare was a surprise for Siegfried Sassoon on his third (9 September)

- Geoffrey Boycott got indoor winter cricket coaching for his 11th (21 October)
- Anna Ivanovic was given her first tennis racket when she reached the age of six (6 November)

19 NOVEMBER

Beware foreigners bearing gifts

Jeane Kirkpatrick was born on this day in Duncan, Oklahoma in 1926, and was to become the first woman to represent America at the United Nations. A neoconservative in the Reagan administration, she disliked the United Nations and endured rather than relished her four years as ambassador. While at the UN she was the subject of damaging misinformation, planted by the KGB. According to an account from the agency's former officer Oleg Gordievsky in his book *KGB: The Inside Story*, the Russians implemented a covert operation in 1982, codenamed Operation Golf, which included planting fabricated material aimed at discrediting Mrs Kirkpatrick in particular. The plan worked and a feature article exploring the relationship between Kirkpatrick and the South Africans found its way into the British political magazine the *New Statesman*. The story included a photograph of a (forged) letter to Mrs Kirkpatrick from a counsellor at the South African embassy conveying 'best regards and gratitude' from South African military intelligence. It referred to an alleged birthday present from the South Africans, which was supposedly a token of appreciation for her cooperation. Some birthday presents you can do without, even if they don't exist.

20 NOVEMBER

Letters from America

Alfred Cooke was born in Salford, Lancashire in 1908, the son of a metal worker. Alfred was a bright lad, winning first a scholarship to a local grammar school and then another to Jesus College, Cambridge. It was at the prompting of friends at Cambridge that he changed his name to Alistair. With a new name and with opportunities that arose while he was in America, Cooke began to make his name in journalism. Cooke's first *Letter from America* was broadcast on 24 March

1946, and by the time he had written his last in February of 2004 – just a month before he died – he had broadcast no fewer than 2869 of them. Most of them were crafted in his Manhattan apartment, and almost all of them were written on his portable manual typewriter, which had served him well for decades. There was a stubborn streak in Cooke, and despite attempts by his son John to give him something more up to date as a present on several birthdays, he stuck with his trusted portable.

21 NOVEMBER

The face of tragedy leads to heartbreak

René Magritte was born in Belgium on this day in 1898. His mother committed suicide when René was just 14, and he was present when the body was pulled from the River Sambre. In the water her dress was obscuring her face, and a series of his early paintings had people with their faces covered with cloth. In one of his best-known works, his self-portrait entitled *Son of Man*, an apple obscures his own face. Paul McCartney was a fan of Magritte's work, and the self-portrait inspired him to use the name Apple for the Beatles' music company. And his love of the Belgian's work inspired McCartney's first wife Linda to buy him Magritte's easel as a birthday present. It was also her way of encouraging Paul to take up painting. The Queen was one of the first visitors to his debut one-man show at the Walker Gallery in Liverpool in 2002. The show included a picture of a heart dedicated to Heather Mills, whom he was to marry later in that year. They were separated four years later. In his High Court ruling on the divorce settlement Mr Justice Bennett concluded that Ms Mills indulged in make-believe: 'The objective facts simply do not support her case,' he decided, and awarded her £24.3 million.

Good times, bad times and *Old Times*

Sir Peter Hall, born on 22 November 1930, has been the driving force behind the English theatre for over half a century. He staged his first professional production the year he left Cambridge, founded the Royal Shakespeare Company when he was 29, and became artistic director of the National Theatre in 1973. He was first married in 1956 to actress Leslie Caron, who gave him a Rolls Royce for his 30th birthday. If the Roller came with love, it was love that did not last, and in 1965 Hall divorced his wife, citing Warren Beatty as co-respondent. A 40th birthday present, the play *Old Times*, was given to him with more lasting affection and respect by its author Harold Pinter. The play was last staged by Hall at the Richmond Theatre in 2007.

False claims

The American character actor Richard Kind was born on this day in 1956. For one birthday George Clooney gave him a signed painting by himself, and Kind hung it in a prominent position at home, pointing out his new trophy to anyone who cared to drop by. Only the painting was not what it seemed. Clooney had actually found it in among the junk in someone's garage. He then signed the picture, wove a tale about going to art class, and duped his friend for more than a year. Picasso once signed a painting that was not his. It had been bought for a great deal of money by a woman who was told the artist had forgotten to sign it. When an intermediary showed the picture to Picasso, asking him to add his signature, the artist, somewhat startled, explained it was not his. But he said it was a good forgery and, to keep the duped owner happy, signed it anyway. The picture went on to be authenticated as a genuine Picasso.

Please release me

Picture if you will, and with your imagination in overdrive if necessary, Edward Stourton, the BBC Radio 4 *Today* programme presenter, sitting handcuffed to his chair in the studio while a singing policewoman stands in front of him and takes her clothes off. Too much excitement for 6.30 in the morning? Well in truth Stourton was not at the BBC and not on air but working at ITN's Washington bureau when celebrating his 30th birthday on 24 November 1987. The stripogram was, he says, not a birthday present he enjoyed, not least of all because a major story broke in the middle of the performance and the stripper refused to un-cuff him. She remained deaf to his pleading until every last item of clothing had been removed. Then, lingering in her birthday suit, she piled on the agony by making him beg for his release in a manner that Stourton says, in strangled and embarrassed tones, was decidedly undignified. The poor man still clearly shudders at the memory.

A man of steel

Andrew Carnegie was born in Dunfermline, Scotland in 1835. The family emigrated to the United States on a former whaling-ship when young Andrew was just 13. The quintessential self-made man, he became one of America's most valued Scottish imports, leading the expansion of the country's steel industry. He became immensely wealthy, but was generous with his money. His philanthropy was focused mainly on education, and he funded libraries throughout the United States, influencing their design and systems as he did so. Carnegie Hall, one of Manhattan's favourite concert venues, was also built by him.

In 1895, as a surprise for his 60th birthday, his wife Louise bought him the cottage where he was born in Scotland. But rather than living there they let it out to tenants. Carnegie himself first went back to the place in 1909 when he was 74. He wrote in the guest book: 'First visit to my birthplace, the humble home of honest poverty', a reference to his impoverished upbringing. His descendants still live in Scotland.

The US philanthropist Andrew Carnegie outside the front door of his Scottish birthplace, 1909.

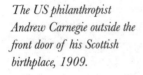

26 NOVEMBER

Over the hill

Today is the birthday of American singer-songwriter Tina Turner, born Anna Mae Bullock in 1939 in Nutbush, Tennessee to a Baptist-deacon father and factory-worker mother. She rose to stardom with husband Ike Turner, and went on to enjoy huge success as a solo artist after the marriage broke up. Gwyneth Paltrow's father Bruce, born in 1943, was also a 26 November baby, as was the Italian pornstar-turned-politician La Cicciolina, who was born Ilona Staller in Budapest in 1951. And Charles M. Schultz, the man who drew the 17,897 *Peanuts* cartoon strips over a period of almost 50 years – the first appeared in 1950 – was also born on 26 November, in 1922 in Minneapolis, into a family struggling to make ends meet. The *Peanuts* character Charlie Brown had much of Schultz in him, not least of all the cartoonist's sense of melancholy.

His remark that 'Once you are over the hill you begin to pick up speed' is a reflection of the man who told his first wife on their honeymoon that he did not think he could ever be happy. Schulz died in 2000. Had he lived a few more years he would have found a wry smile for the offering from an internet gifts catalogue that includes the Over The Hill Birthday Coffin Gift Box. Another of its offerings, the Over The Hill Birthday Condom, consists of a single condom with the words 'a year's supply' on the packet.

27 NOVEMBER

In loving memory of him and her

Caroline was the first of the Kennedys' children (apart from a baby girl who had died shortly after her birth in 1956), born in New York on 27 November 1957. She lived in the White House from 1961 until her father's assassination two years later, when she moved with her mother to New York. In 1961, while she was 'first daughter', Soviet leader Nikita Khruschchev gave her a puppy as a birthday present. Given the hard time the Russian was giving her father, it surprised many in Washington that the president did not send the puppy straight back with an appropriate note attached to its collar. But Caroline liked

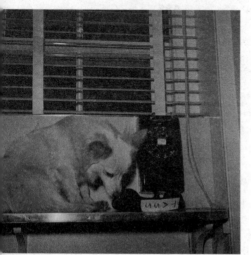

Cold War dog: Pushinka, a birthday present from Soviet leader Khruschchev to John F. Kennedy's daughter Caroline, talks on the phone to his comrades, November 1961.

the four-legged peace offering so they kept it and called it Pushinka, the Russian for 'fluffy'. Pushinka's parents had both been involved in the exploration of space – her mother spent a day on board *Sputnik 5* in the company of a grey rabbit, 42 mice and two rats, all of whom returned safely, while her father took part in land-based experiments but never got off the ground. The White House has a strange tradition of immortalizing the pets that have already left their marks on carpets, cushions and laps in the West Wing. Continuing the tradition, Pushinka now stands rigid on a small side-table in one of the corridors next to Laddie Boy, President Warren Harding's Airedale terrier. Lyndon Johnson's beagles, Him and Her, are on a mantelpiece under a painting of Johnson's wife Lady Bird; Millie, the springer spaniel that belonged to George Bush Sr, is there too, along with the blue and gold macaw that belonged to the Roosevelts. The sculptures are not very good – the sort of thing you might expect to see decorating a pets' funeral parlour in Palm Springs.

28 NOVEMBER

A long time coming

Your father works in a bookshop, so what do you get as a birthday present? Of course you do. And for actor Ed Harris it was the start of something big. His father worked in the bookshop of the Chicago Art Institute, and for his son's 36th birthday he chose a copy of *To a Violent Grave*, a biography of the artist Jackson Pollock. Harris Jr was hooked and began what turned into a 14-year project to put the artist's troubled life on film. The movie *Pollock* – directed by and starring Harris – was finally released in 2000. Harris was nominated for best actor, and Marcia Gay Harden won best supporting actress for her role as Pollock's wife, the artist Lee Krasner. Harris Sr, who started it all, failed to get a mention.

Un grand homme, moi!

Jacques Chirac was born on 29 November 1932. On his 71st birthday in 2003 Tony Blair sent the French president a very smart fountain pen, appropriately inscribed. But this wasn't just a birthday present. Relations between the two leaders had soured after an encounter at a European summit in Brussels the year before. On bumping into the prime minister in the corridor, Chirac launched into a tirade against Mr Blair in French. When Blair asked if the president would mind listening to the British position, Chirac replied that he would and walked off. The birthday present was one step in an attempt to patch things up. A further attempt was made with a flattering piece about Chirac written by Blair for the magazine *Paris Match*, in which the prime minister sycophantically referred to the French president as '*un grand homme*'.

A policeman's lot

Winston Churchill was born on this day in 1874 at Blenheim Palace, on his grandparents' Oxfordshire estate given to the first Duke of Marlborough by a grateful Queen Anne in 1704 after the duke's victory over the French. (Churchill's parents had expected their son to be born at their London home, but he arrived two months early while they were staying at Blenheim.) Churchill did well for birthday presents, especially from his Second World War comrades. His love of whiskey was recognized by Roosevelt, who sent him a crate of bourbon for his 68th birthday in 1942; and seven years later, from behind an Iron Curtain that had already descended across the continent of Europe, Stalin sent 75 bottles of brandy for the 75-year-old Churchill. His love of cigars was marked by Aristotle Onassis, who gave him a gold cigar case with a sapphire thumb piece for his 86th birthday. But a present associated with his other love, that of painting, went badly wrong. The two Houses of

Parliament commissioned a portrait of Churchill for his 80th birthday. The chosen artist, Graham Sutherland, was well respected, but Churchill hated the result and his wife Clementine liked the portrait even less. She asked Churchill's private detective, Edmund Murray, to destroy it, but being a keen painter himself the policeman could not bring himself to do it. So she had it burnt, much to Sutherland's chagrin.

Sir Winston Churchill speaking in Westminster Hall, 30 November 1954. Graham Sutherland's controversial 80th birthday portrait, later to be burnt on the orders of Churchill's wife Clementine, is in the background.

1 Woody Allen	2 Ann Patchett	3 Anna Freud
8 James Galway	9 Judi Dench	10 Sid Raymond
15 Alex Aborlleile	16 Sidney Block	17 Ludwig van Beethoven
22 Mary Archer	23 Queen Silvia of Sweden	24 Hamid Karzai
29 Madame de Pompadour / Pablo Casals / Jude Law / Andrew Johnson / William Gladstone / Alistair Darling / Charles Macintosh / Charles Goodyear / Václav Havel	30 Tiger Woods	31 Alex Salmond

4 Francisco Franco	**5** Walt Disney	**6** Andrew Flintoff	**7** Starr Porter
11 Alexander Solzhenitsyn	**12** Frank Sinatra	**13** James Murdoch	**14** Michael Owen
18 Katie Holmes	**19** Leonid Brezhnev	**20** The KGB	**21** Joseph Stalin
25 Cosima Wagner	**26** Mao Zedong	**27** Marlene Dietrich	**28** Erich Mielke
1 Clark Gable	**2** Libby Purves	**3** Norman Rockwell	**4** Charles Lindbergh

Don't knock masturbation

Born Allen Stewart Konigsberg in New York on the first day of December in 1935, this talented son of German-speaking Jewish immigrants who ran a small luncheonette in Brooklyn, was writing gags by the time he was 16 and film scripts before he was 20. Woody Allen added acting, directing and playing the clarinet to his talents. In 1977 he wrote, directed and took the male lead in *Annie Hall*, considered by many to be his finest work. It swept the boards at the Academy Awards, winning Best Picture, Best Director, Best Original Screenplay and Best Actress for Diane Keaton. In it Allen plays Alvy Singer, and there is a scene where Alvy gives his girlfriend Annie (Keaton) some sexy red-and-black underwear for her birthday. Annie responds with a telling little message for every self-interested, sex-driven male from New York to New Delhi: 'Oh,' she says, 'this is more like a present for you.' With that, she drops her present back in its box. Sex and self-interest come up again, in a manner of speaking, with Alvy's remark to a male friend: 'Hey, don't knock masturbation, it's sex with someone I love.'

Overnight success

The American novelist Ann Patchett was born in Los Angeles on this day in 1963. Her parents gave her a pig for her ninth birthday, and she has not eaten pork (or beef or lamb for that matter) since. The pig seems to have heightened her care of animals in general – she has taken to brushing her dog's teeth every morning. Ms Patchett's novel *Bel Canto* won the Orange Prize for Fiction in 2002.

3 DECEMBER

The subconscious mechanisms of defence

Anna Freud was the last of the six children of Sigmund and Martha Freud. Born in Vienna in 1895, Anna had a difficult childhood, suffered from depression, and was psychoanalysed by her father over a period of four years in her early twenties. Anna's experience confirmed her own interest in analysis, and by 1935 she was director of the Vienna Psychoanalytical Training Institute. The following year she published *The Ego and Mechanisms of Defence*, which, she explained, looked at ways and means 'by which the ego wards off unpleasure [sic] and anxiety'. As an 80th birthday present for her father she dedicated the book to him with the words: 'Writing books as a defence against danger from inside and outside.' The Anna Freud Centre in London continues to care for the emotional well-being of children, while much of her father's work has fallen out of favour with current thinking on psychoanalysis.

4 DECEMBER

The people's car

Considering that at one stage of his army career he was demoted and sent off to run the Canary Islands, Francisco Franco did well for himself. Just how well he did for Spain will be debated for a good many years to come. Born in Galicia on 4 December 1892, he joined the army when he was 18, and had been appointed its chief of staff by the time he was in his mid-40s. But when the leftist Popular Front won the 1936 election by the narrowest of margins, Franco was elbowed out of harm's way and sent to look after the Canary Islands. However, he was soon back and leading the Nationalists into a civil war, gaining support from both Hitler and Mussolini. A few months after the Republicans were defeated and Franco was installed as Spain's dictator, Hitler's advance into Poland

precipitated the Second World War. This time it was the Nazis who were looking for support from Franco, but it came only half-heartedly. Yet that did not stop Hitler sending the Generalissimo a 50th birthday present in the shape of a brand new German-made car. It may well have been one of Hitler's Volkswagens, but details of the gift have been lost. However, there are records that show that Franco wrote a thank-you letter: 'Many thanks to you and the German people,' he wrote. 'May your arms triumph in the glorious undertaking of freeing Europe from the Bolshevik Terror. With friendship and affection. Signed Francisco Franco.'

5 DECEMBER

The cheque's in the post

Farmer's son Walt Disney was born on this day in 1901, and Mickey Mouse was conceived 27 years later on a train between New York and Los Angeles. (Walt called him Mortimer to start with until his wife Lillian persuaded him that Mickey was less formal. Her advice wasn't always as sound. When Disney was planning *Snow White* she told him that nobody would pay a dime to see a dwarf picture.) Walt had a sister called Ruth whose birthday fell a day after his. This made it difficult for him to forget his sister's birthday, but like so many siblings, he never had a clue about what to buy her. So every year he sent her a cheque. A note with his present in 1952 confirmed his dilemma: 'It's time to wish you happy birthday again. I have no more notion about what I should send you than I had this time last year.' So he sent a cheque as usual. And this is the man whose imagination continues to entertain millions the world over.

6 DECEMBER

A doll called Fred

The England cricketer Andrew Flintoff was born on this winter's day in 1977. For his 27th birthday his then fiancée (and now wife) Rachael gave him a doll. The doll was based on the TV cartoon character Fred Flintstone, from whom Flintoff acquired the nickname Freddie.

7 DECEMBER

Going down the tubes

This is the day a Starr was born. But fancy being cleaned out on your birthday. The environmental and healthcare activist Starr Porter, who prefers not to divulge her age, was given a dose of colonic irrigation for her 50th birthday by her sister, the travel and beauty writer Shannon Leeman. Ms Leeman had undergone the treatment herself at a Miami clinic, and apparently found gift certificates propped up on the loo as she was going through the final stages – or rather as the final stages were going through her.

8 DECEMBER

Musical gems

The Irish flautist James Galway was once run over by a Swiss on a motorbike. He sustained a broken arm, two broken legs and a very sore head. In hospital he took to reading about the Crusades, and was struck that even God's soldiers needed a talisman – in their case a diamond. This, together with pictures of jewelled violin bows from the time of Paganini, prompted Galway to call his then instrument-maker Albert Cooper and ask him to put a diamond in the headpiece of his next flute. Cooper was happy to oblige, but was trumped some years later when Galway's Japanese flute-maker decided to mark their favoured client's 50th birthday on

8 December 1989. The Muramatsu Company of Tokyo dispatched Mr Muramatsu himself to London with a gift of a D sharp flute key inlaid with a ring of diamonds. Arriving unannounced at the birthday party, Mr Muramatsu proceeded to unscrew the existing key on Galway's flute, replacing it with the diamond version. Mr Galway would do well to keep his jewelled instrument under his pillow – on one occasion he managed to have five gold flutes stolen from the railway station in Lucerne.

9 DECEMBER

A living treasure

The actress Judi Dench rarely forgets a birthday. She told the *Telegraph* magazine that she even carries cards in her handbag for last-minute emergencies. She was born on this day in York in 1934, the daughter of a GP who brought her up as a Quaker. In a career that opened with a performance as Ophelia in Liverpool in 1957 and has yet to close (she returned to the role of M in the 2008 Bond movie, *Quantum of Solace*) she has collected enough awards to fill a manorial mantelpiece. One trophy that needs rather more space is the slinky BMW sports car she bought herself on her 70th birthday. Someone should buy her the 'M 007' number plate for her next birthday.

1 O DECEMBER

No laughing matter

10 December 2006 was the day the *New York Times* ran an obituary it probably wished it hadn't. Actor and comic Sid Raymond had died and the obituary ended thus: 'One of his last jokes involved a son sending a prostitute over to his widowed father in his nineties, still a self-proclaimed ladies' man. She tells him she is his birthday present and will give him super sex. "I'll take the soup," he says.'

11 DECEMBER

Putting Boris in his place

Alexander Solzhenitsyn's 80th birthday fell on 11 December 1998. The Russian president, Boris Yeltsin, thought the writer deserved a birthday present and announced he was to be awarded the Order of St Andrew. Thanks but no thanks said the birthday boy, whose writing had exposed life in the Soviet labour camps. He had no intention, he said, of accepting an award from the man he believed was reducing Russia to ruin.

12 DECEMBER

Chairman of the Board

He was the son of a Sicilian fireman, and they called him the Chairman of the Board. No one before or since has interpreted the American popular song quite like Frank Sinatra. He was born on this day in Hoboken, New Jersey in 1915. His jazz-inclined phrasing and timing, his sable-rich voice, and his ability to connect strongly with his audience put him in a league of his own. He made so many songs 'his songs' it is difficult to pick one as his signature tune: 'Come Fly with Me', 'My Way' and 'The Lady is a Tramp' all became Sinatra songs. And one special version of 'The Lady is a Tramp' became a birthday present. The Beatles were looking for a present for Ringo Starr's wife Maureen. Maureen was a Sinatra fan, so they asked Sammy Cahn to re-write the Lorenz Hart lyrics around Maureen, and persuaded Sinatra to sing it. A studio in Los Angeles was hired for the morning and Sinatra, with Sammy Cahn at the piano, recorded the birthday version of the song. It contains the lines:

She married Ringo and she could have had Paul,
That's why the lady is a champ.

Maureen was given a copy for her 22nd birthday in 1968, but the existence of further copies is disputed. If any do exist they would be worth a pretty penny.

In the family way

James Murdoch, son of media tycoon Rupert Murdoch, was born on this day in London in 1972. He got what he wanted for his 28th birthday – a seat on the News Corp board. Nepotism? A family business is a family business. He is still the blue-eyed boy several years down the line, having been given the job of running the whole of News Corp's European and Asian businesses. The new job puts him in charge of News International, publisher of *The Times*, the *Sunday Times*, the *Sun* and the *News of the World*, while leaving his father to harness the *Wall Street Journal* into the Murdoch stable. The grooming of the heir apparent is in its final stages.

Happy families

Newcastle United striker Michael Owen was born in a Chester hospital on 14 December 1979. His father was a footballer so the genes were in Michael's blood. And what better birthday present could a 17-year-old ask for than to be signing on as a full professional for a club like Liverpool. He enjoyed a glittering start to his career with his club and with England, spent a season with Real Madrid and then came home to sign with Newcastle United. But recurrent injuries have dogged his career of late. Still, he has kept his family on side: he bought an entire street in the North Wales town of Ewloe so his extended family could stay close to each other.

15 DECEMBER

Comings and goings

There are some birthdays best forgotten, and this is one of them. On 15 December 1950 the Port Authority Bus Terminal opened in midtown Manhattan. If ever there were a place that lent credence to that old adage about it being better to travel hopefully than to arrive, this is it. Setting off from here ain't much fun either. Why is it that bus terminals more than all other terminals are such sordid, smelly and altogether disagreeable places? This one at 8th and 42nd Street must have seemed particularly daunting to Alex Aborlleile when he arrived with his backpack, a bag of oranges and a couple of dollars. Alex had left home in Miami when he was 16 and had been on the run ever since. Now he was 18 and New York was where he was going to set his life in order. He told the *New York Times Magazine* about his life sleeping rough, the prostitution (he was gay), his scavenging for food, the drugs and his yearning to be an artist. And he recalled Gay Pride Day, which happened to fall on his 19th birthday. He had planned to march as a condom fairy but it was hot and he ended up sleeping in. He received just one birthday present – a card from his mother with a terse, loveless message. He tore it up, set it alight and threw it burning into the sink.

16 DECEMBER

Combining creativity

'The Exquisite Corpse' was an idea that sprang from the Surrealists – an idea in which a number of artists contribute separately to a work, each in their own style, none seeing the entire work until it was finished. In 2002 in Chicago 188 artists gave fresh impetus to the idea when they started work on an exquisite snake as an 80th birthday present for gallery owner Sidney Block, born on 16 December 1923. The contributors, including well-known local artists Ed Paschke, Audrey Niffenegger and Karl Wirsum, worked on paper using oils, pastels, watercolours, felt-tip markers and even ballpoint pens. It took them 14 months to complete the work, and with all the 208 individual components joined together randomly, the snake stretched nearly 250 feet. Block's partner at Chicago's Printworks Gallery secretly mounted the snake and then threw a surprise party to introduce the work to its new owner. The snake now clings to the wall at the Northwestern University at Evanston, just outside Chicago.

Notes on a remarkable journey

Exactly when Beethoven was born is something of a mystery. There is no doubting it was 1770 nor that the happy event occurred in Bonn nor that he was baptized on 17 December. But his date of birth remains a matter of dispute. His drunken father became his first music teacher (constant drunkenness may have contributed to the uncertainty about his son's birthday), but tuition was cut short after Ludwig's mother died when he was 16, and as the eldest of the Beethoven children he was left with the responsibility of bringing up his two younger brothers. His duties at home got in the way of his career, but with his very considerable talent he quickly made up for the early lost years. By the time he was in his stride one of his favoured piano-makers was the English family firm of Broadwood.

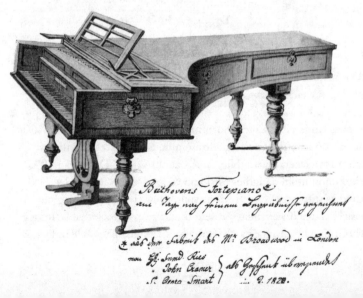

Thomas Broadwood had taken over from his father John and had met Beethoven on a sales trip to Europe. On his return to England he put his craftsmen to work on a six-octave piano made of mahogany from Spain, and with Beethoven's name inlaid in ebony above the keys. It was to be a present for the composer's 48th birthday in 1818. The completed instrument (*opposite*) was loaded in London onto a ship, which then sailed down the Thames, across the Channel, through the Bay of Biscay, down the length of the Iberian Peninsula, round the Rock of Gibraltar, into the Mediterranean and up the Adriatic to Trieste. From there it was put on a cart and hauled by mules across the mountains to Beethoven's home at Mödling, a small market town near Vienna. The journey had taken many months and the fragile instrument had not travelled well. But help was at hand. An English pianist called Cipriano Potter was in Vienna at the time and took responsibility for repairing the battered instrument (Potter was later to become the Royal Academy of Music's first professor of piano). Once repaired, the piano was delivered to Beethoven. Potter did the final tuning, and the composer, by now unwell and very deaf, put it to the test. Beethoven was delighted with his new piano and wrote to Broadwood: 'I shall immediately send you the fruits of the first moments of inspiration I spend on it.' But Broadwood never did hear from Beethoven, and the piano eventually passed into the hands of Franz Liszt. It now rests silently in a museum in Budapest.

18 DECEMBER

Cruise control

Actress Katie Holmes was born in Toledo, Ohio on this day in 1978. Actor and scientologist Tom Cruise proposed to her at the top of the Eiffel Tower and married her in the vaults of an Italian castle. Their seven-month-old daughter Suri and their A-list celebrity friends acted as witnesses. The previous year Cruise treated his pregnant fiancée to a 27th birthday present that appeared egotistical even for Mr Cruise: he gave her a DVD that contained a compendium of

Gifts of food and drink
* Breast milk from one's mother (13 March)
* A portrait in marzipan (3 April)
* Half a case of Château Mouton-Rothschild 1989 (6 May), a case of Château Margaux 1982 (10 July), or 972 bottles of Tokaji (24 May)
* The first Peach Melba (19 May)
* 111-year-old fruitcake (2 June)
* An old can of beef (24 June)
* A cake stuffed with bamboo shoots, leaves and peas (9 July)
* A 99 ice cream for one's 99th birthday (4 August)
* Bourbon and brandy to keep the black dog at bay (30 November)

every movie he had made, including those in which he has sex with his former wife Nicole Kidman. He made up for it (sort of) by taking Katie on a shopping spree to the FAO Schwarz toy store on Fifth Avenue in New York, where he bought her a pair of rocking horses, a grand piano and a miniature Audi Cabriolet with a top speed of 13 mph. The fun car was destined for their traffic-free estate, where the nervous father could keep an eye on the mother of their child-to-be. That's motoring with Cruise control.

19 DECEMBER

Health warning: nuclear warheads can seriously damage your health

One-time Soviet leader Leonid Brezhnev was born on this day in 1906. Presents came pouring into the Kremlin for his 70th birthday in 1976. Two caught his fancy. He was given a model of the LUNA-24 Moon probe with three samples of soil from the Moon in a special container with a magnifying glass in the lid. (It came from the Ministry of General Machine Building, the department he headed before becoming general secretary of the Communist Party of the USSR in 1964, having pushed aside Nikita Khrushchev.) And he was given his own portrait in sugar by Ukrainian sugar workers. Sweet gesture. On his birthday three years earlier one of his favourite gifts came from the head of design at the Soviet Air and Space Research and Industrial Centre. It was a very nice cigarette case, but it was decorated with models of very nasty nuclear warheads.

I spy with my little eye ...

This was the day in 1917, shortly after the October Revolution, that the KGB was born. At least it was the day Lenin instigated the Cheka, the All Russian Extraordinary Commission for Combating Counter-Revolution, Profiteering and Corruption, the Soviet Union's first secret police and forerunner of the KGB. First under Lenin and then under Stalin, officers of the Cheka (which in 1922 was absorbed into the NKVD) carried out unspeakable acts of terror and torture resulting in the deaths of hundreds of thousands of Soviet citizens. Later, during the Cold War, members of the KGB pitted their wits against those of the CIA and Britain's Secret Intelligence Service. The KGB murdered and tortured too, but their methods were not as sophisticated as Russia's current secret service, the FSB, who (allegedly) discovered the delights of polonium-210. It was the acute radiation from the smallest quantity of polonium-210 that in 2006 killed a one-time KGB officer called Alexander Litvinenko who was then living in London. Traces of the radioactive material led London's Metropolitan Police to another ex-KGB officer called Andrei Lugovoi. A warrant was issued for his arrest, but the Russians refused to extradite him. He is now a member of the Duma (the Russian parliament) and lives a life of Riley in Moscow. However, there are increasing signs that he doesn't feel secure. On his 41st birthday a friend gave him a heavy machine-gun mounted on wheels, and another turned up at his birthday party with an elaborate walking stick with a dagger concealed in the handle.

A frog with five legs

This day in 1878 was a dark day. It was the day Iosif Vissarionovich Dzhugashvili was born in Gori, Georgia, the son of a drunken and violent cobbler. At 14 Iosif won a scholarship to the seminary in Tblisi, where he was paid for singing in the choir and where his involvement in socialist politics began. After school he spent ten years working for

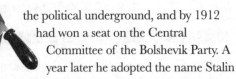

the political underground, and by 1912 had won a seat on the Central Committee of the Bolshevik Party. A year later he adopted the name Stalin – and began to collect nicknames such as the Priest, the Milkman and the Pockmarked One. The cult of personality that Stalin developed brought him grand titles too: 'Brilliant Genius of Humanity' and 'Gardener of Human Happiness' were two he particularly liked. And the cult of Stalin also brought him a constant flow of presents from fawning subjects, especially birthday presents. Two he received for his 70th birthday carried messages beyond birthday greetings: factory workers in Poland sent him a telephone with a hammer and sickle hand-piece, which sits on a globe – clearly dominating it (*above left*). And workers from a Kosyakov factory sent a collection of dolls dressed as labourers carrying a banner that read: 'Thank You Stalin For Our Happy Childhood.' On that same birthday, and on a more personal note, Nina Beria, the wife of the infamous chief of the Ministry of State Security, treated Stalin to a pot of her walnut jam. It was, she told him, a little souvenir in memory of his mother who made jam when Stalin was a boy. In a thank-you note Stalin told her that the jam would remind him of his youth.

Stalin was not the first of the Soviet leaders to be fêted with presents. The practice began with Lenin, and resulted in such a huge collection of gifts that party leaders decided to further honour Stalin's 70th by arranging an exhibition of the presents he and his predecessors had received. There were by now some 8000 objects, and staff at the Pushkin Museum of Fine Arts in Moscow were given just ten days to clear the museum of its fine-arts exhibits and replace them with the presents. These ranged from huge pieces of Trans-Siberian railway track to a portrait of Stalin etched on a grain of rice – and, preserved in a bottle of spirit, a frog with five legs.

Mary, Mary quite contrary

Mary Weedon was born on this day in 1944, and was just 22 when she married an Oxford athlete and fund raiser called Jeffrey Archer. Archer wrote bestsellers, raised money for the Conservative Party, then went off the rails and into prison. Lady Archer (her husband had been created a baron by a trusting John Major) proved a loyal wife, stayed on track and continued her career as a scientist researching solar energy at Cambridge. She stood by her husband when he sued the *Daily Star*, which had suggested he had met a prostitute (he was later convicted of perjury relating to his evidence). After she herself had taken the witness stand in that case, Mr Justice Caulfield commended her qualities of 'elegance', 'fragrance' and 'radiance' to the jury. Those qualities appeared to be absent in Lady Archer's dealings with a secretary. She employed a personal assistant called Jane Williams, whom Lady Archer sacked after Ms Williams allegedly broke a confidence about her employer's cosmetic surgery. Ms Williams appealed to an employment tribunal. During the hearings it emerged that Lady Archer had once celebrated her secretary's birthday with an inch of flat champagne.

Princely art

Queen Silvia of Sweden was born in Heidelberg in 1943, the daughter of German industrialist, Walter Sommerlath, and his Brazilian wife Alice. She met her future husband at the Summer Olympics in 1972, and the couple were married four years later after Prince Carl Gustaf had ascended the throne. The royal pair have three children, and – as any mother would be – Queen Silvia was delighted when her son created something himself for her 60th birthday. Prince Carl Philip, second in line to the throne, began studying graphic design in 2003 at the Forsbergs School of Design in Stockholm, and for his mother's birthday designed a cover for a new CD of Tchaikovsky's *Nutcracker*

Suite. The recording was released on the queen's birthday and proceeds of the sales are going to a children's charity.

24 DECEMBER
Boys' toys

Afghanistan is a country where a young man gets a Kalashnikov for his 16th birthday in the same unexceptional way a boy of the same age in England might get a cricket bat – or if he were an American, a baseball bat. Behaving more responsibly than most of their fellow countrymen, the parents of the country's President Hamid Karzai gave their son a bicycle. Karzai, familiar to television viewers in his flowing green *chapan* and Karakul hat made from the fur of lamb foetuses, was born into a leading family of the Popalzai tribe in Kandahar in 1957. Karzai recalls the bicycle birthday even now, remembering how his father put his hands over his eyes and then led him into the yard where the new bicycle was propped against the wall: 'He spent the whole day teaching me how to ride it: it is the only time I remember spending time with my father.'

25 DECEMBER
Mrs Wagner has a dream come true

Cosima Wagner was born on Christmas Day in 1837 at Bellagio on Lake Como, the illegitimate daughter of Franz Liszt and his mistress the Countess Marie d'Agoult. Cosima married first the pianist and conductor Hans von Bülow, but not long after they married she began having regular contact with the composer Richard Wagner, whom she had met through her father. The two began an affair, and eventually set up house together in a villa on Lake Lucerne provided by the king of Bavaria. Unfazed by her own illegitimacy, and with two children from her marriage to von Bülow, Cosima went on to have three children with Wagner while the two were still lovers. After Wagner's wife died and Cosima had secured a divorce, the couple (*below*) married in the summer of 1870. That Christmas was Cosima's 33rd birthday and her new husband gave her a birthday present she was to treasure above all others. He wrote a symphonic idyll for her, and on Christmas morning guided 15 musicians on tiptoe into their house and onto the stairs and landing outside his wife's bedroom. Cosima was woken by their playing: 'I could no longer imagine myself in a dream,' she told friends later. 'Music was sounding, and what music!' Wagner went into the bedroom with their five children and gave his wife the score. It was meant to be a private work, but their financial circumstances forced them to publish it. We know it today as the *Siegfried Idyll*, as Wagner also intended the piece as a thank-you to Cosima for the birth the previous year of their son Siegfried.

26 DECEMBER

Badges of allegiance

The Chinese leader Mao Zedong was born in Hunan on this day in 1893. Having led the Communists to victory over the Nationalists after 20 years of civil war, Mao proclaimed the founding of the People's Republic of China in 1949. In 1958 he embarked on the disastrous Great Leap Forward, intended to move China away from its farming base and towards an industrialized communist economy. Tens of millions of people starved to death. The Cultural Revolution, launched in 1966, was in part Mao's attempt to regain his authority, but it was also a further attempt to rid the country of the bourgeoisie, whom he believed were hindering his plans for a socialist state. During this period the wearing of Chairman Mao badges reached its zenith, and it was also during this time that Mao chose Lin Biao as his successor. Lin's wife Ye Qun was a keen collector of badges, and resolved to collect 10,000 of them to give Mao on his 73rd birthday. With a female member of her staff and two plainclothes bodyguards, she prowled the streets of Peking pouncing on anyone wearing a badge she had not seen before. The badges were made of all sorts of materials, from silver and gold to wood, bamboo, mother of pearl, porcelain and even bits of American aircraft shot down over Vietnam. She had made a good start when Mao got to hear of her plan. He signalled his disapproval, believing the cult of personality had run its course, and the badges ended up in a store room.

27 DECEMBER

Sex and a cigarette

Marlene Dietrich, the cabaret singer and actress, was born in the Schöneberg district of Berlin on 27 December 1901. Betty Grable was the first actress to insure her legs, but Dietrich followed suit shortly afterwards. My father remembered Dietrich curled up on a settee in his hotel near Elstree Film Studios carefully keeping her legs out of sight and out of danger. (Fred Astaire insured his legs for

$75,000, but that's peanuts these days: David Beckham apparently insures his for $70 million.) Dietrich was an inveterate smoker – directors had little trouble getting her to light up in most of her films. Her grandson Peter Riva, a New York literary agent and television producer, has spoken of Dietrich's smoking as an

affectation. It was, he said, a wonderful oral sexual gesture to have a cigarette held to the mouth between two fingers. Most women in Germany at that time were smoking for the same reason, and having something smart in which to carry their cigarettes was considered one of the must-have fashion accessories. It was fellow-smoker Gary Cooper who obliged Dietrich, giving her a 14-carat gold case for her birthday. Sothebys sold it at auction in 1999 for $10,925.

28 DECEMBER

Information – on a need-to-know basis

Few organizations in the former Soviet Union's sphere of influence were more reviled than the Stasi, the East German secret police. Its boss from 1957 until the Berlin Wall came down in 1989 was Erich Mielke, a Berliner himself, born there on 28 December 1907. Mielke had 85,000 full-time spies working for him, backed up by some 200,000 informers. Along the corridor from his office in Room 101 of Stasi headquarters in Berlin's Normannenstrasse, Mielke kept a trophy room that housed a number of birthday presents along with everything else. (Mielke was a George Orwell fan and contrived to work in Room 101, the name Orwell gave in *Nineteen Eighty-Four* to the torture chamber in the Ministry of Love. Mielke's office was in fact on the building's second floor, so he had the first floor designated the mezzanine allowing the second floor to become the first. Orwell, in turn, had taken the name Room 101 from a conference room at the BBC where he sat through hours of tedious meetings.) One of the birthday gifts in the trophy room was a carefully crafted and very detailed model of an electric oven given to the Stasi boss by one of the country's leading white goods manufacturers. It was meant to be a secret, but the factory's informers, following their instructions to the letter, informed on the unusual activities of their model-making colleagues and spoilt the surprise.

29 DECEMBER

Songs for freedom

29 December has seen the birth of a diverse group of men and women who have left their considerable mark on the world. Madame de Pompadour, born in 1721, was the mistress of Louis XV of France. She was a patron of the Enlightenment philosophers Voltaire and Diderot, and greatly influenced the government's (ill-fated) policy of switching from its pro-Prussian policy to one in favour of Austria. Pablo Casals was born in Catalonia in 1876, and is still regarded by many as the finest ever exponent of the cello. Some readers born on this day will rejoice in the knowledge that they share a birthday with Jude Law, a British actor born in Lewisham, south London but preferring to live in Hollywood. Others will be pleased to know that they were born on the same day as Andrew Johnson, America's 17th president, who held office from 1865 till 1869. Johnson had been President Lincoln's vice president, taking over on the latter's assassination, when he somewhat alarmingly announced

that he felt 'incompetent to perform duties ... which have been unexpectedly thrown upon me'. He might have taken comfort from Britain's four-times Liberal prime minister William Gladstone, also born on 29 December, who claimed that 'No man ever became great or good except through many and great mistakes.' (It was in Gladstone's red box that Britain's chancellor of the exchequer Alistair Darling carried his 2008 budget from Downing Street to the House of Commons.) Today is also the birthday of two inventors who share the first name. Charles Macintosh, who was born in 1766, was the Scottish chemist who invented waterproof fabrics, while Charles Goodyear, born in 1800, was the American entrepreneur who accidentally discovered how to vulcanize rubber, making it hard, strong and elastic all at the same time. 29 December was also the day in 1989 that a writer and dramatist became the tenth and last president of Czechoslovakia. Václav Havel, whose pen had challenged his country's communist regime and its Soviet masters, had been given the fresh challenge of guiding a free Czechoslovakia into a new era of political choice and free-market economics. Havel's 70th birthday in 2006 coincided with that year's gathering of the Forum 2000 Foundation, so his long-time friend Joan Baez, whose songs have so often championed the causes of human rights, travelled to Prague to sing for him at the conference opening ceremony. 'When Havel was a dissident,' she said, 'he carried my guitar and I acted as his bodyguard.' Havel reckoned his friend's songs had influenced his country's Velvet Revolution, which had peacefully toppled the communists in November and December 1989. The pen and the guitar are indeed mightier than the sword.

30 DECEMBER

Done with driving time, now for walkies

The American golfing champion Tiger Woods was born in Cypress, California on this day in 1975. He met his Swedish wife Elin

Nordegren at the 2001 British Open when she was working as an au pair. Three years later they exchanged vows at the 19th hole of the Sandy Lane Golf Resort in Barbados. The following year was Tiger's 30th birthday, which Elin marked with a present on four legs with some antisocial (although endearing) habits. The puppy was a Border collie, which they called Taz. The couple were photographed for the April 2006 edition of Men's *Vogue*. Elin went along to watch.

31 DECEMBER

First Minister Travels Second Class in Birthday U-turn

Scotland's First Minister Alex Salmond remembers his 21st birthday in 1975 with mixed feelings. He was with his sister Gail at Edinburgh's Haymarket Station waiting for the train to take them home to combined birthday and Hogmanay celebrations. With his sister expressing serious doubts about it being the right one, they clambered aboard the first train that came into the station. Her doubts proved well founded: it was not the local train to Linlithgow but the overnight sleeper to London. Salmond was not convinced of his mistake until they reached Carstairs (perhaps he'd had a birthday dram or two already). They managed to get off before the train crossed the border into England and luckily found a train back to Edinburgh. The two of them finally turned up at home ten minutes before midnight. 'I suppose you could say that my extraordinary birthday present was a trip around Scotland courtesy of British Rail.' Nice that so independent a Scot should recognize the courtesy of something British.

A birthday is just the
first day of another
365-day journey around
the sun. Enjoy the trip.

Anonymous

INDEX OF GIVERS AND RECEIVERS

Benedict XVI, Pope –
20 February
Ben-Gurion, David –
16 October
Benny, Jack – 14 February
Berg, Alban – 31 August
Beria, Nina – 21 December
Berlin, Irving – 11 May
Berlusconi, Silvio and
Veronica – 19 July
Bernhard of the Netherlands,
Prince – 29 June
Bernhardt, Sarah –
22 October
Bernstein, Leonard –
25 August
Betjeman, John – 28 August,
28 October
Biggs, Ronnie – 8 August
bin Laden, Osama – 10 March
Bismarck, Otto von – 1 April
Blair, Tony – 28 February,
6 May, 6 July, 29 November
Block, Sidney – 16 December
Bluhdorn, Charles and
Dominique – 20 September
Blumenthal, Heston – 27 May
Bonaparte, Napoléon –
23 June
Bono – 6 May
Boycott, Geoffrey –
21 October

Brandreth, Gyles and
Michele – 8 March
Braun, Eva – 6 February
Brezhnev, Leonid –
19 December
Bridges, Robert – 16 July
Broadwood, Thomas –
17 December
Brooks, Mel – 17 September
Brown, Gordon – 20 February
Brunei, Sultan of – 15 July
Burrell, Paul – 8 June
Bush, George W. – 8 January,
6 July, 4 November
Bush, Laura – 4 November
Calle, Sophie – 10 October
Cameron, David –
9 October
Cameron, Julia Margaret –
11 June
Camilla, Duchess of
Cornwall – 17 July
Campbell, Alastair –
28 February
Campbell, Sir Menzies –
22 May
Carl Gustav of Sweden,
King – 30 April
Carl Philip of Sweden,
Prince – 23 December
Carlyle, Thomas and Jane –
14 July

Carnegie, Andrew –
25 November

Caron, Leslie – 22 November

Carter, Jimmy – 18 August,
1 October

Carter, Rosalynn – 18 August

Castro, Fidel – 13 August

Cavendish, Lady Elizabeth –
28 August

Cering, Amai – 17 November

Channon, 'Chips' – 7 March

Charles, Prince – 21 June,
17 July

Chávez, Hugo – 13 August

Chekhov, Anton – 29 January

Cheney, Dick – 30 January

Cher – 20 May

Chiang Kai-shek – 31 October

Chirac, Jacques – 6 May,
29 November

Chopin, Frédéric – 1 March

Christie, Agatha – 26 May

Christopher Reeve –
25 September

Churchill, Sir Winston –
3 August, 30 November

Clarke, Nick – 6 April

Clinton, Bill – 19 August,
26 October

Clinton, Hillary – 26 October

Clooney, George – 23 November

Cloutier, Suzanne – 16 April

Comăneci, Nadia –
12 November

Connors, Jimmy –
2 September

Cooke, Alistair – 20 November

Cooper, Gary – 27 December

Cooper, Henry – 3 May

Costello, Peter – 14 August

Cotton, Fearne – 3 September

Coward, Noël – 10 February

Cradock, Fanny – 26 February

Crawford, Joan – 23 March

Crowley, Antoinetta – 19 April

Cruise, Tom – 20 June,
18 December

Dale, Caroline – 6 September

Dalí, Salvador – 9 February

Darwin, Charles – 12 February

Delahaye, Michael – 6 April

Dench, Judi – 9 December

Dexter, Colin – 29 September

Diamond, Neil – 24 January

Diana, Princess – 8 June, 1 July

Dietrich, Marlene –
27 December

Disney, Walt – 5 December

Dole, Bob – 22 July

Donovan, Terence –
14 September

Downey Jr, Robert – 4 April

du Pré, Jacqueline and Iris –
26 January

Duchovny, David –
25 February
Durrell, Gerald – 7 January
Eames, Charles and Ray –
22 June
Edison, Thomas and Mina –
11 February
Hillary, Sir Edmund – 20 July
Einstein, Albert – 14 March
Eisenstein, Sergei – 23 January
Eliot, T.S. – 26 September
Elizabeth II, Queen – 21 April,
1 July
Elizabeth the Queen Mother,
Queen – 21 April, 4 August
Elliot, Eleanor and Jock –
26 April
Escoffier, Auguste – 19 May
Fabergé, Theo – 16 May
Fardink, Jeffrey –
25 September
Farrow, Mia – 9 February
Fauré, Gabriel – 12 May
First State Ball-Bearing
Works – 3 January
Flagstad, Kirsten – 12 July
Flintoff, Andrew – 6 December
Flynn, Errol – 20 June
Foot, Michael – 23 July
Ford, Henry – 20 April
Franco, Francisco –
4 December

Frank, Anne and Otto –
12 June
Franz Joseph, Emperor –
24 May
Freud, Anna and Sigmund –
3 December
Funicello, Annette –
22 October
Gable, Clark – 1 February
Gallagher, Liam and Noel –
21 September
Galway, James – 8 December
Garland, Judy – 10 June
George III, King – 4 June
George V, King – 26 May
George V of Hanover, King –
14 April
George VI, King – 21 April
Gill, A.A. – 28 June
Gilmour, David – 6 March
Goering, Hermann –
15 October, 16 November
Gorbachev, Mikhail –
2 March, 15 April, 10 May
Gore, Al – 16 March
Grainger, Percy and Rose –
8 July
Granger, Hermione – 31 July
Green, Philip – 15 March
Greenberg, Clement –
16 January
Grenfell, Joyce – 10 February

Johansson, Scarlet –
23 October
John, Elton – 25 March
Johnson, Boris – 19 June
Johnston, John – 31 May
Joséphine, Empress – 23 June
Juan Carlos of Spain, King –
2 November
Julius, Anthony – 18 May
Kalashnikov, Mikhail –
10 November
Kampusch, Natascha –
23 August
Karajan, Herbert von –
5 April
Karzai, Hamid – 24 December
Kawaguchi, Ms – 31 May
Keaton, Diane – 5 January,
1 December (as Annie Hall)
Kendrick, Howie – 15 August
Kennedy, Caroline –
27 November
Kennedy, Jacqueline –
15 January
**Kennedy, John F., Joseph and
Rose** – 29 May
Khashoggi, Adnan – 25 July
Khordorkovsky, Mikhail –
26 June
Khrushchev, Nikita –
19 February, 9 March, 17 April,
27 November

Kidman, Nicole – 20 June
Kim Il Sung – 15 April,
8 October
Kim Jong Il – 6 January,
16 February
Kind, Richard – 23 November
Kinnock, Neil and Glenys –
28 March
Kirkpatrick, Jeane –
19 November
Kissinger, Henry – 27 May
Knowles, Beyoncé –
4 September
Koizumi, Junichiro –
8 January
Krause, Otto – 27 February
Kroc, Ray and Joan –
5 October
Küng, Hans – 19 March
**Kurkotkin, Lieutenant
Colonel** – 25 August
Kutcher, Ashton –
11 November
Kwaniewski, Aleksander –
15 November
Latifah, Queen – 18 March
Lauren, Ralph – 14 October
Lawrence, D.H. –
11 September
**Le Corbusier and his wife
Yvonne** – 6 October
Lee, Belinda – 15 June

Lee, Spike – 20 March
Leeman, Shannon –
7 December
Legrand, Michel – 24 February
Lehmann, Lotte – 27 February
Leno, Jay – 27 April
Lenya, Lotte – 18 October
Leoni, Tea – 25 February
Letterman, David – 12 April
Lewinsky, Monica –
13 January, 25 May, 19 August
Leyda, Jay – 23 January
Litvinenko, Alexander and
Marina – 30 August
Liu Chia-pei – 17 February
Lloyd Webber, Andrew –
21 August
Lombard, Carole – 1 February
Longoria, Eva – 15 March
Loos, Anita – 23 March
Lopez, Jennifer – 24 July
Losang, Jamin – 17 November
Lucas, Cornel – 15 June
Lugovoi, Andrei –
20 December
Luise of Sweden, Queen –
15 May
Lysyshyn, Ralph –
15 November
Lyttelton, Humphrey –
23 May
Ma Wan-ching – 17 February

Mackintosh, Cameron –
21 August
MacLean, Andrew and Joan –
24 September
MacLean, Rory – 5 November
Madonna – 16 August
Mahler, Alma – 31 August
Major, John – 29 March
Mandela, Nelson – 18 July
Mansfield and Mansfield,
William Murray, 8th Earl
of – 7 July
Mao Zedong – 15 April,
26 December
Marie of Saxe-Attenburg,
Princess – 14 April
Marx, Karl – 5 May
Mary, Queen (consort of
George V) – 26 May
Matheny, Mike –
22 September
McAlpine, Sir William –
12 January
McCartney, Linda –
21 November
McCartney, Paul – 18 June,
21 November
McKellen, Ian – 25 May
McLoughlin, Coleen –
24 October
Melba, Dame Nellie – 19 May
Merkel, Angela – 17 July

Middleton, Kate – 21 June
Mielke, Erich – 28 December
Milne, A.A. – 21 August
Milošević, Slobodan –
20 August
Ministry of General Machine
Building – 19 December
Molotov, Vyacheslav –
9 March
Monet, Claude and Jean –
14 November
Monroe, Marilyn – 29 May
Montgomery, John –
21 January
Moore, Demi – 11 November
Moore, Oscar – 5 September
Moore, Patrick – 4 March
Morris, William – 24 March
Mosley, Sir Oswald –
16 November
Mowlam, Mo – 6 May
Moynihan, Daniel Patrick –
16 March
Mswati of Swaziland, King –
18 April
Mugabe, Robert – 21 February
Murdoch, Rupert and
James – 13 December
Musharraf, General Pervez –
11 August, 26 September
Mutter, Anne-Sophie –
29 June

Nadal, Rafael – 3 June
Napoleon I, Emperor –
23 June
Nasher, Raymond and
Patsy – 16 September
Netanyahu, Benjamin –
24 August
Newkirk, Ingrid – 3 November
Newton, Helmut – 5 February
Nicholson, Jack – 22 April
Nicklaus, Jack – 21 January
Nicolson, Nigel, Adam
and Tom – 12 September
Nixon, Richard and Pat –
9 January
Niyazov, Saparmurat –
29 March
Nordegren, Elin –
30 December
Norwich, John Julius –
15 September
Nyerere, Julius – 13 April,
15 April
Oates, Captain Lawrence –
17 March
Oistrakh, David –
30 September
Onassis, Aristotle –
15 January, 30 November
Ortega, Daniel – 15 April
Orwell, George – 25 June
Owen, Michael – 14 December

Paglia, Camille – 2 April

Palmer, Arnold and Winnie –
10 September

Paltrow, Gwyneth –
28 September

Parasol, Richard and Ruth –
27 June

Parliament, Houses of –
30 November

Patchett, Anne – 2 December

Pavarotti, Luciano –
12 October

Peter the Great – 30 May

Petri, Manfred – 25 February

Philip, Prince – 10 June

Phillippe, Ryan – 22 March

Picasso, Pablo – 25 October

Pieck, Wilhelm – 3 January

Pinckernelle, Dr Hans –
3 April

Pinter, Harold – 22 November

Plath, Sylvia – 27 October

Plymouth Argyle FC – 23 July

Polanski, Roman – 9 April

Pollock, Jackson – 16 January

Popper, Karl – 28 July

Porsche, Ferdinand
(Ferry) – 19 September

Porter, Starr – 7 December

Potter, Harry – 31 July

Powell, Enoch – 16 June

Prescott, John – 31 May

Provenzano, Bernardo –
11 April

Pulitzer, Joseph – 10 April

Pullman, Philip – 19 October

Purves, Libby – 2 February

Putin, Vladimir – 7 April,
26 June, 7 October

Ramsay, Gordon –
8 November

Rattle, Sir Simon – 19 January

Rausch, Hartmut and
Helga – 13 July

Raymond, Sid – 10 December

Rayner, Claire – 22 January

Reeve, Christopher –
25 September

Reynolds, Ryan – 23 October

Ribbentrop, Joachim von –
20 April

Rice, Condoleezza –
14 November

Richardson, Hadley –
9 November

Riefenstahl, Leni – 22 August

Ritchie, Guy – 16 August

Robin, Christopher –
21 August

Robinson, Bethany –
13 March

Robinson, Jancis and Julia –
10 July

Robson, Bobby – 18 February

Rogers, John – 31 March

Roget, Peter – 18 January

Rommel, Erwin and Lucie –
6 June

Rooney, Wayne – 24 October

Roosevelt, Franklin D. –
8 February, 30 November

Rosenberg, Alfred –
15 October

Ross, John – 17 June

Ross, Sir John – 24 June

Rossini, Gioachino –
29 February

Rostropovich, Mstislav –
27 March

Rubell, Steve – 6 August

Ruskin, John – 8 February

St Laurent, Yves – 1 August

St Petersburg – 16 May

Sakharov, Andrei – 21 May

Salamone, Lauren –
25 August

Salmond, Alex – 31 December

Sargent, John Singer –
15 April

Sassoon, Siegfried and
Theresa – 9 September

Satie, Erik – 17 May

Scarfe, Gerald – 1 June

Schenker, Kathy – 2 October

Schrager, Ian – 6 August

Schröder, Gerhard – 7 April,
7 October

Schumann, Clara and
Robert – 13 September

Schwarzenegger, Arnold –
30 July

Schweitzer, Dr Albert –
14 January

Searle, Ronald – 1 June

Second State Clock Factory
– 3 January

Senna, Ayton – 21 March

Shah Jehan – 5 January

Shaw, George Bernard –
26 July

Shields, Brooke – 29 August

Shostakovich, Dmitri –
30 September

Silvia of Sweden, Queen –
23 December

Simmons, Brother Damien –
1 September

Simpson, Homer and
Marge – 15 February

Sinatra, Frank – 10 January,
14 February

Singh, Manmohan –
26 September

Singh, Reuben –
20 September

Sirikit of Thailand, Queen –
12 August

Smith, Alva – 17 January
Smith, Christine – 3 October
Smith, Sir Paul and Lady –
5 July
Sofia of Spain, Queen –
2 November
Solzhenitsyn, Alexander –
11 December
Soviet Air and Space
Research and Industrial
Centre – 19 December
Spears, Britney – 29 August
Stair, Earl of – 24 June
Stalin, Joseph – 15 April,
30 November, 21 December
Stardust, Alvin – 27 September
Starkey, Maureen (Mrs
Ringo Starr) – 12 December
Stevenson, Robert Louis –
13 November
Sting – 2 October
Stothard, Peter – 28 February
Stourton, Edward –
24 November
Streisand, Barbra – 24 April
Stringfellow, Peter –
17 October
Sullivan, Arthur – 13 May
Sun Myung Moon – 6 January,
16 February
Sutherland, Dame Joan –
7 November

Tai Shan (a panda) – 9 July
Tandy, Jessica – 7 June
Tatam, Walter – 9 November
Tate, Sir Henry – 11 March
Taufa'ahau Tupou IV of
Tonga, King – 4 July
Temple, Shirley – 23 April
Thatcher, Margaret –
13 October
Theron, Charlize – 7 August
Thompson, Hunter S. –
22 April
Tito, Josip Broz – 7 May
Tomlin, Lily – 1 September
Trachte Sr, Don – 3 February
Tripp, Linda – 13 January
Truman, Harry S. – 8 May
Trump, Donald – 14 June
Turner, Ted – 16 February
Ukraine – 19 February
Ustinov, Peter – 16 April
van Gogh, Vincent –
30 March
Vanderbilt, William –
17 January
Versace, Gianni and Allegra
– 30 June
Victoria, Queen – 27 January,
24 May, 26 August
Vidal, Gore – 3 October
Voloshin, Alexander –
2 March

Wagner, Richard and Cosima – 25 December

Walker, Diana – 20 January

Wallace, J.W. – 31 May

Walton, William – 29 March

Warhol, Andy – 6 August

Warner, Jack – 20 June

Waugh, Evelyn – 28 October

Weill, Kurt – 18 October

West, Mae – 17 August

Wharton, Edith – 15 April

Whitman, Walt – 31 May

Whitney, John Hay – 27 August

Widdecombe, Anne – 4 October

Wilder, Billy – 22 June

Wilhelm I, Kaiser – 1 April

Wilhelm II, Kaiser – 27 January

William, Prince – 21 June

Williams, Robbie – 13 February

Wintour, Anna – 3 November

Witherspoon, Reese – 22 March

Woods, Tiger – 30 December

Woolf, Leonard and Virginia – 25 January

Wright, Bella – 17 October

Wulff, Christian – 17 July

Ye Qun (Mrs Lin Biao) – 26 December

Yeats, W.B. – 13 June

Yeltsin, Boris – 11 December

Yusupov, Prince Felix – 23 March

Zhirinovsky, Vladimir – 25 April

Zhivkov, Todor – 7 September

Zywny, Adalbert – 1 March

PICTURE ACKNOWLEDGEMENTS

Getty Images: Tim Boyle 12, Joe Raedle 33, Justin Sullivan 45, Hulton Archive 47, 81, 89, Fox Photos 53, Popperfoto 61, 181, Twin Images 98, Anne Frank Fonds 129, Terry O'Neill 146, Sports Illustrated 193, AFP 222, Keystone 227, Imagno 284.

Deutsches Historisches Museum: 13, 185 (top).

NARA: 16.

Rex Features: 21, 68, 105, 161, 220.

PA/AP: 39, 61, 93, 106, 114, 130, 135, 151, 165, 176, 199, 228, 248, 261, 265, 286, Sutton 65, Empics Entertainment 173, 234, ABACA 244.

Bridgeman Art Library: Private Collection 72, 118, Pushkin Museum Moscow 185 (bottom), Metropolitan Museum of Art, New York, Giraudon 25.

National Portrait Gallery, London: 85.

The Royal Collection © 2008 Her Majesty Queen Elizabeth II: 123.

Stranraer Museum (courtesy of Future Museum): 139.

Corbis: Louie Psihoyos 142, Patrick Ward 200, Bettmann 233, 262, 290, Hulton-Deutsch 270.

Alamy: John James 155.

Camera Press: Karsh 159.

BBC Photo Library: 194.

Birmingham Mail: 212.

Lebrecht Collection: 276.

RIA Novosti: 281.

First published in Great Britain
in 2008 by Quercus
21 Bloomsbury Square
London
WC1A 2NS

A CIP catalogue record for this book is available from the British Library

ISBN 978-1-84724-616-5
2 4 6 8 10 9 7 5 3 1

Designed by Neal Cobourne
Printed and bound in Great Britain by Clays Ltd, St Ives, Plc